SAMUEL L. BAILY

Labor, Nationalism, and Politics in Argentina

ꞧ
Rutgers University Press
New Brunswick, New Jersey

Copyright © 1967 by Rutgers, The State University

Library of Congress Catalogue Number: 67-23508

HD6602
B3

Manufactured in the United States of America by
the Quinn & Boden Company, Inc., Rahway, N.J.

Labor, Nationalism, and Politics in Argentina

To Joan as a token of my appreciation for so many things.

Preface

The labor movement has become one of the most important political and ideological forces in twentieth-century Argentina. Many of the hundreds of thousands of migrant workers, both from Europe and from the rural areas of the country, have found at various times a political and ideological home within the labor movement. Juan D. Perón, President of Argentina from 1946 to 1955, relied heavily on labor to win and maintain power. And since the overthrow of Perón in 1955, every government has confronted the critical problem of how to deal with the 2.5 million-member Peronist-dominated labor movement.

In this book I set out to describe the political and ideological role of labor in twentieth-century Argentina, to explain why labor has played such a role, and to suggest some implications of this kind of labor activity. I have placed the history of the movement in a particular perspective—viewed it as an integral part of the process of modernization—and have therefore focused on three related effects of Argentina's transition from a traditional agricultural society to a modern industrializing one: the organization of the working class, the participation of the workers in politics, and the emergence of popular nationalism within the labor movement.

Although I begin with the establishment of the first labor federation in 1890 and end with the consolidation of the Revolución Libertadora in 1957, I am primarily concerned with the Perón period. The first two chapters are introductory in nature and the material in them will be familiar to scholars in the field. The rest of the work, covering the period from 1930 to 1957, is based on source material not previously used by others (labor newspapers, labor reports, and personal interviews), so as to provide a factual as well as an interpretive contribution to Argentine labor history. I have concluded the study in 1957 because by that time the nature of the basic issues relating to organized labor, nationalisms, and politics was clearly established and no fundamental change has occurred during the past decade.

Anyone writing about the Argentine labor movement in the twentieth century faces special problems of objectivity. The Perón period is still so close in time and its influence so widely felt today that almost all Argentines have strong emotions and opinions about it. I have assumed that Peronism—whether good or bad—is an important movement and that its adherents have a right to be heard and understood in their own terms. I have also attempted to be sympathetic with all groups and to state their positions and discuss their motivations without judging them.

Although this book deals with nationalism and politics in the Argentine labor movement, I hope that it will prove helpful for the study of labor and popular nationalism elsewhere in Latin America and possibly in other developing areas of the world. My purpose has been to point to some of the fundamental conditions and circumstances in which popular nationalisms emerge and to suggest some of the consequences of such developments for other societies.

This book has been more than five years in the making. During this time, the better part of a year of which I spent in Argentina going over the records and newspapers of the unions and interviewing labor leaders, I received generous help from many people. I am particularly grateful to Arthur P. Whitaker for his criticisms, suggestions, and encouragement. I wish to express my appreciation for the assistance of Hans Kohn, Joseph Barager, Robert J. Alexander, Otis H.

Green, José Luis Romero, Gino Germani, Sebastián Marotta, Luis Gay, Daniel Vukasovich, Alberto Belloni, Patricio Randle, and Luis Angeleri and his staff at the library of the Confederación General del Trabajo in Buenos Aires. I also want to thank my colleagues in the history department of Rutgers University for their suggestions, and to note my gratitude for financial support from The Rockefeller Foundation and the Rutgers University Research Council. Finally, I want to thank my wife Joan for her comments and criticisms, her support and encouragement, and her patience.

SAMUEL L. BAILY

New Brunswick, New Jersey
January, 1967

Contents

	Preface	vii
	Introduction	3
I	The Birth of Organized Labor in Argentina	9
II	Early Manifestations of Working-Class Nationalism	29
III	The Emergence of Liberal Nationalism	51
IV	Labor's Nationalisms and the Rise of Perón	71
V	The Triumph of the Criollo Nationalists	97
VI	Labor Opposition to Perón	121
VII	Perón Abandons the Workers' Nation	137
VIII	The Resurgence of Criollo Nationalism	163
	Conclusion	185
	Notes	193
	Bibliography	211
	Index	231

Tables

I	Real Wages of Industrial Workers, 1914–1930	31
II	Real Wages of Industrial Workers, 1929–1939	55
III	Real Wages of Industrial Workers, 1943–1951	99
IV	Real Wages of Industrial Workers, 1949–1955	142
V	Real Wages of Industrial Workers; Distribution of National Income, 1954–1959	175
VI	Strikes in the Federal Capital, 1951–1960	180

Labor, Nationalism, and Politics in Argentina

Introduction

The rapid industrialization of much of Europe during the nineteenth century profoundly affected Latin America. The industrial countries needed the raw materials and markets that Latin America could supply. As a result of this demand and the efforts of Latin American statesmen who wanted to modernize their countries, large numbers of Europeans emigrated and large amounts of European capital were invested to exploit Latin American resources. The foreigners in alliance with native partners established new mines and plantations and expanded existing ones in order to meet the growing European demand for nitrates, copper, tin, coffee, sugar, cereals, wool, and meat. In addition, they established new industries to process many of these materials and encouraged the construction of railroads, harbors, and roads to facilitate the movement of goods.

This economic activity helped bring about important social and political changes in many Latin American countries. It stimulated urbanization, immigration, and the development of the middle and lower socioeconomic groups. It led to the formation of new political parties and institutions. And it provoked the rise of new ideas and the redefinition of old ones.

In Argentina the process of modernization began during

the second half of the nineteenth century. The European demand for wool, meat, and cereals stimulated the rapid development of many sectors of the economy. Transportation facilities and ancillary industry emerged to support the major export industries. Immigrants from Europe came in large numbers to provide the labor for the expanding economy, and the growth of the cities created new demands for labor and capital. By the 1850's urban workers had begun to form protective organizations, and Argentina's first labor federation was established in 1890.

Since 1890, organized labor has played a decisive role in the transformation of Argentina from a traditional agricultural society to a modern one. This role has been political and ideological as well as economic. The workers first organized to improve their salaries and working conditions, but they also became involved in the much larger question of what kind of society they should live in and who should control it. As a consequence, organized labor has helped the lower socioeconomic groups become active in the political structure of the country and has articulated the ideology of popular nationalism to justify the social and political as well as the economic demands of these groups.

Karl Deutsch's concept of "social mobilization" is helpful in explaining why labor has played a multiple role in countries like Argentina. According to Deutsch, social mobilization is the process of change that occurs in countries developing from traditional to modern ways of life, and this process takes place in two stages. In the first stage, traditional social, economic, and psychological ties, including patterns of group affiliation and personal identity, are undermined. In this stage the consensus that binds together the traditional agricultural society is destroyed. In the second stage, the "mobilized" persons seek to develop new community patterns that will provide a sense of personal identity and a means for protecting self interest.[1]

The focus of this book is on three related effects of social mobilization in Argentina: the organization of labor, the participation of the workers in politics, and the emergence of popular nationalism within the labor movement. All three are results of the uprooting of the lower socioeconomic groups described by Deutsch in stage one, and all three are manifestations of these groups' desire for assimilation and protection suggested in stage two.

Since the term "nationalism" is vague and impossible to define in any precise, generally applicable sense, one is compelled to assume that although there are similarities among nationalisms and nationalist movements in different parts of the world and at different times, the precise meaning of the word is to be found only in a specific historic context.[2] In the pages that follow I shall try to provide an extended definition of the nationalisms of the Argentine labor movement in the twentieth century.

Popular nationalism, as it is used in this work, refers to the force generated by the "mobilized" workers seeking to establish a new identity and to protect their interests. It is a manifestation of the workers' desire to form a particular kind of community in which they have influence and control over their destiny. It is the effort to create the nation, because today the nation is what Rupert Emerson refers to as the terminal community—that is, "the largest community which, when the chips are down, effectively commands men's loyalty, overriding the claims both of the lesser communities within it and those which cut across it or potentially enfold it within a still greater society."[3]

As Emerson implies, the nation represents a consensus of society on fundamental values and procedures and therefore "effectively commands men's loyalty." In Argentina, however, no broad new consensus has yet emerged to replace the destroyed consensus of the traditional agricultural society. Many groups are striving to create the nation, but there is no agreement on what values and procedures such a nation would stand for or what membership in such a nation would mean. In other words, there are few common interests or broadly based institutions that might bind together the diverse elements of twentieth-century Argentina. Thus, the popular nationalists—though numerically very important—constitute only one of a number of competing nationalist groups which assume that they speak for an emerging national consensus and that their social and economic interests are the authentic interests of the future nation.

To establish a national consensus and to help them support their claim to be the genuine representatives of the emerging nation, the labor nationalists have attempted to transform society and to gain control of the state. Their nationalism has been a political demand for revolution, for a radical change in the structure of society that will permit more equal distribution of power, prestige, and wealth. It has been a demand for modernization through rapid industrialization, because this is seen as the best way to rid the country of foreign influence and to create an egalitarian society. The traditional power groups, the elements opposing rapid industrialization, and the foreigners are linked together, and popular nationalism becomes a "rallying cry" or justification for the creation of an independent, representative industrial society.

The appeal and use of popular nationalism in Argentina have not been confined to the lower social elements. In many cases the leadership and part of the following of the popular nationalist movements have come from the middle groups. But the force behind the idea has gathered in the lower social strata, and the demands and needs of these groups have given the movement its distinctive quality.

Two basic forms of popular nationalism have emerged in the Argentine labor movement. First, a "liberal" form ap-

Introduction / 7

peared as European immigrant workers and their sons sought to be assimilated into Argentine society. Later, an anti-liberal form developed when the *criollo* migrant workers from the interior of the country came into contact with the unfamiliar city and its inhabitants, and struggled to preserve some of their traditional way of life in the urban environment.

The terms "liberal" and "criollo" have a particular meaning when applied to the Argentine labor movement. Since colonial times Argentina has been divided into two societies —one centered in Buenos Aires and the other in the interior.

During the nineteenth century, liberalism developed in the society centered in Buenos Aires primarily as an ideology of reform. It was the philosophy of those intellectuals and statesmen who came to power after the overthrow of the dictator Juan Manuel de Rosas at mid-century and who sought above all else to modernize the country along the lines of England and the United States. The Argentine liberals rejected what they considered to be the backward personalistic government and the Hispanic-criollo traditions of the Rosas period. Their goal was to develop the country by means of constitutional government, education, economic laissez-faire, European capital, and European immigration.

But the liberals viewed the masses—in Buenos Aires as well as in the interior—with suspicion, and in effect turned their backs on the developing working class. As a result, toward the end of the century a left-wing liberalism— focused primarily in the Socialist Party—appeared. The Socialists wanted to modernize Argentina by means of constitutional government, education, European immigration, and free trade, but they also demanded a political role for the European immigrant worker in Buenos Aires and certain forms of the welfare state such as the nationalization of basic industry and protective labor legislation. The

Argentine Socialists were liberal in that much of their ideology had its roots in the country's liberal tradition, but they modified this tradition to make it acceptable to the European immigrant working class.

A criollo philosophy emerged among those in the interior of the country who rejected liberalism and who looked instead to Spain and to Argentina's Hispanic-Catholic tradition as the basis for the development of society. The criollo tradition was a native tradition, but because there were few Indians in Argentina, it was a native Hispanic tradition. As happened with liberalism, a left-wing form of the criollo philosophy appeared. The left-wing criollo supported much of Argentina's Hispanic-Catholic tradition, but he demanded an egalitarian society rather than one ruled by an elite.

This book deals with the left-wing varieties of liberal and criollo nationalism. My aim has been to explain their development as a logical consequence of the process of modernization and in this way to suggest their permanence and importance within Argentine society.

1
The Birth of Organized Labor in Argentina

The liberal generation that seized control of the Argentine government after the overthrow of Juan Manuel de Rosas in 1852 brought about the rapid economic development that was perhaps the greatest stimulus to the growth and organization of the working class. Presidents Bartolomé Mitre and Domingo F. Sarmiento had initiated the process by encouraging the use of new techniques of farming and livestock raising, the construction of railroads and ports, the expansion of immigration, and the development of education, but a series of events combined to make the decade of the 1880's the first great period of development. In 1879 General Julio Roca secured vast new areas of fertile land by exterminating the remaining Indians on the pampa. A year later the government federalized the city of Buenos Aires, thus settling the question of its formal relationship to the rest of the country and bringing about a period of political stability. The development of the refrigerated ship permitted Argentina to sell her meat in the expanding European market. The resulting economic boom attracted large amounts of foreign capital and labor, and this in turn contributed to further development. The modern Argentine economy, based primarily on the raising and exportation of meat and cereals, began to emerge.

In 1890 the process was temporarily interrupted by an economic crisis, and for a decade development slowed down considerably. The issuing of unsupported paper currency, easy credit policies, a drought on the pampa, and speculation and corruption during the latter part of the 1880's had brought about the financial collapse and with it the curtailment of foreign investment and immigration. The growth potential of the country nevertheless remained high, and by the turn of the century Argentina was entering a second period of development that was to last until the First World War. The new prosperity attracted new immigrants and reactivated the flow of European capital.[1]

The most significant result of these developments for the organization of the working class was the influx of immigrants. The Argentine working-class movement, from its rudimentary beginnings in 1857 to its temporary decline following the Centennial of Independence in 1910, was to a considerable degree a reflection of the European working-class movement. Labor groups obtained their methods of organization and agitation as well as their ideologies and specific programs from Europe, and the majority of their members and practically all of their leaders were European-born. Native workers joined the organized labor movement, but never in sufficient numbers to counteract the influence and leadership of the European immigrant. The criollo worker apparently was unwilling or at least less willing than the immigrant to quarrel with the existing social and economic order, and therefore the newcomers were practically unchallenged as they organized and led the early labor movement.[2]

Between 1857 and 1914, and particularly during the boom periods of the 1880's and the early 1900's, more than two million immigrants came to settle permanently in Argentina. By 1914 three out of every ten persons living in Argentina and half of those living in the city of Buenos Aires were foreign-born.[3]

The typical immigrant was a Spanish or Italian male from fifteen to sixty-four years of age. He was a farmer or a skilled or semi-skilled laborer who worked in a small factory or shop. Most of the immigrants were concentrated in the eastern provinces of the country, primarily in the cities of Buenos Aires and Rosario.

The immigrant was an uprooted individual, a "marginal" man psychologically suspended between two worlds. Everything that was familiar to him was Spanish or Italian. At the same time his future was in Argentina; he had endured the hardships of migration because he hoped to achieve a better life in Argentina. "Without losing his emotional identification with his country of birth," Gino Germani points out, the immigrant "acquired an identification with the new country."[4]

The act of migration from the Old World to the New was an individual act that destroyed the immigrant's traditional communal ties. "Although entire communities were uprooted at the same time," says Oscar Handlin, "although the whole life of the Old World had been communal, the act of migration was individual. The very fact that the peasants were leaving was a sign of the disintegration of the old village ways."[5]

One of the most compelling needs of the immigrant worker was to form new communal bonds, and his first attempts to do this were the non-political and non-revolutionary mutual aid societies. As early as 1857, two societies were founded to provide hospitals and schools and accident, sickness, and burial insurance for Spanish immigrants. Four years later two Italian mutual aid societies opened, one in Buenos Aires and another in Rosario. By the end of the century there were seventy-nine Italian and fifty-seven Spanish mutual aid societies in Argentina.[6]

Some of these societies were organized around a particular trade instead of a nationality and extended their activities to include defense of economic interests as well as mutual aid. The first of these, the Sociedad Tipográfica Bonaerense, was established in 1857 by the printers of Buenos Aires. In 1877, after twenty-one years of limited trade-union activity, the members of the Sociedad Tipográfica Bonaerense formed the Unión Tipográfica to initiate a more aggressive policy. When its demands for higher wages and shorter hours were not completely met, the union went on strike. It lost the conflict, and a year later the parent organization dissolved the Unión Tipográfica because it was ineffective. Other societies began trade-union activity, but none of these groups was particularly effective.[7]

Developments in the European working-class movement directly affected the Argentine situation during this period. In 1864, English, German, French, Italian, Polish, and Swiss workers established the International Workingmen's Association to effect cooperation between various workers' organizations dedicated to "mutual help, progress, and the complete emancipation of the working class."[8] The International expanded to include affiliates in other countries, but the hostile attitude of most governments and the ideological struggle between the socialists and anarchists fatally crippled it. With the suppression of the French, German, Italian, and Spanish sections of the International and the defeat of the Paris Commune during the early 1870's, a number of experienced working-class leaders sought refuge in Argentina, where they established local affiliates of the European organization.

The success of the Argentine affiliates of the International

The Birth of Organized Labor in Argentina / 13

in organizing the working class was nominal. The division of the organization between socialists and anarchists reduced the effectiveness of the Argentine sections as it had those in Europe. In addition, the Argentine government was hostile to the local sections, and the dissolution of the International at its meeting in Philadelphia in 1876 left them on their own.[9]

The limited success of the trade-union-oriented mutual aid societies and the affiliates of the International Workingmen's Association did not discourage further organization, and the anarchists and socialists who came to Argentina in increasing numbers during the 1880's competed with each other for control of the embryonic working-class movement. Both groups created a number of political and trade-union organizations among the skilled and semi-skilled workers in Buenos Aires, Rosario, and a few other cities in the eastern part of the country, but to begin with the socialists were more successful than the anarchists.

The first important Argentine group to expound socialism was the Vorwärts. The Vorwärts, formed in 1882 by working-class refugees from Bismarck's Germany, was a political group similar to the German Vorwärts, from which it got its name and inspiration. The purpose of this group was to organize the workers in order to realize "the principles and goals of socialism, in accordance with the program of the Social Democrats of Germany."[10] Although the organization emphasized political goals, it helped establish trade unions as one means of organizing the working class.

The Argentine Vorwärts, apparently more mindful of the politically sophisticated proletariat of industrializing Germany than of the Italian and Spanish immigrants in Argentina it was trying to lead, urged the workers to adopt non-revolutionary parliamentary techniques to improve their economic position. It initiated a campaign to naturalize the European immigrants, to get the workers to vote, and to win political control of the state. This kind of program, though successful in Germany, was not particularly effective in Argentina.

Argentina was only beginning to industrialize and was still a predominantly agricultural country ruled by a landed oligarchy. The vast majority of workers came from Spain and Italy, countries where anarchism was strong, and they did not understand the methods of the socialists. As the worker watched the oligarchy dominate the country by fraud and by force, he could not see much hope in parliamentary solutions to his problems.

Nevertheless, a series of historical events did help the Vorwärts in its efforts to organize the labor movement. Toward the end of the 1880's the deteriorating economic situation of the country resulted in a decline in real wages, unemployment, and a series of strikes.[11] In 1887 the shoemakers won a strike for shorter hours. In 1888 the shop workers of the Southern Railway struck for the payment of their salaries in gold instead of the increasingly inflated paper peso. And in 1889 3,000 carpenters and 6,000 bricklayers won a 20 per cent wage increase because there was a shortage of workers in both trades.[12]

Stimulated by the economic crisis, by working-class militancy, and by the establishment of the Second International Workingmen's Association at Paris in July 1889, the Vorwärts assembled the working-class organizations of Buenos Aires and formed the Comité Internacional Obrero. The program of this group, like that of the German Social Democrats, stressed evolutionary political methods. It suggested petitioning the National Congress for the passage of protective labor legislation and the establishment of a labor federation to increase the economic and political effectiveness of the workers.[13]

In mid-1890, at the time of the political upheaval that led to the replacement of President Miguel Juárez Celman,

The Birth of Organized Labor in Argentina / 15

the Comité succeeded in organizing Argentina's first labor federation, the Federación de Trabajadores de la Región Argentina (FTRA).[14] The object of the FTRA, according to its constitution, was to defend the moral and material interests of the worker by means of apolitical societies. In theory, therefore, the FTRA welcomed anarchists as well as socialists, but by the time of its Second Congress in October 1892 the organization was clearly socialist in orientation. At this congress the members supported the "politicization" of the working class, the nationalization of industry, and the arbitration of labor disputes. Consequently, the revolutionary anarchist minority withdrew.[15]

The withdrawal of the anarchists weakened the FTRA, but other factors contributed to its destruction. It lacked adequate financial support, and because of the economic crisis of the late 1880's and early 1890's, unemployment was high and many of its members were forced to return to Europe.[16] Shortly after its Second Congress, the FTRA disbanded.

Within the decade the socialists organized three additional labor federations—all of which were modeled on the FTRA and used evolutionary parliamentarian techniques—but failed to provide adequate leadership for the workers. Because of their failure to establish an effective labor organization and because their first interest was to win political control of society, the socialists began to concentrate on the formation of a political party.

Juan B. Justo was the motivating force behind the Socialist Party.[17] Justo spent most of his childhood on his father's *estancia* in the southern part of the province of Buenos Aires. He was educated at the Colegio Nacional and the University of Buenos Aires. While studying for a medical degree at the university, he worked as a reporter for the newspaper *La Prensa*. In 1888, at the age of twenty-three, he received his M.D. and spent the next two years traveling and studying in Europe.

In 1890, when Justo returned from Europe, he was concerned about the Argentine political situation. He became a member of the Executive Committee of the Unión Cívica, a recently established organization that sought to end corruption in politics, to provide free and honest elections, and to end the domination of the country by the landed oligarchy. Justo, however, became disillusioned with the Unión Cívica because he favored a popular revolution rather than a military coup as the best means by which to overthrow the oligarchy, and because he believed that the organization concentrated on political issues to the exclusion of social and economic ones.

Justo withdrew from the Unión Cívica and resumed his practice as a doctor, but he was unable to stay away from politics and soon became attracted to socialism. By 1894 he had founded the newspaper *La Vanguardia*, united several socialist groups to form the International Socialist Workers' Party, and had become one of the leading socialists in the country. The following year, 1895, the party changed its name to the Argentine Socialist Workers' Party, and in 1896 it became the Argentine Socialist Party. From 1896 until his death early in 1928, Justo was its undisputed leader.

Justo was a socialist, but he was also a liberal and a nationalist and managed to reconcile all three positions. Like Domingo F. Sarmiento and Bartolomé Mitre, he wanted to Europeanize the country and transform it into a prosperous and progressive nation. He believed in constitutionalism, a modified form of economic laissez-faire, universal public education, the encouragement of unrestricted immigration, universal suffrage, and a strong central government to implement these reforms. He rejected what he considered to be the politically conservative and anti-popular liberalism of Julio Roca and his successors, but at no time did he reject the ideals of the earlier form of liberalism.

At the same time Justo sought to use the Socialist Party and the labor movement to forge a new nation. "Our national unity," he pointed out, "is older than that of Germany, but owing to the incapacity of the governing oligarchy, we are still unable to speak of a true national unity."[18] The Socialist Party, he believed, would succeed where the oligarchy had failed; it would achieve national unity, free the country of economic imperialism, raise the standard of living of the workers, and help the "Argentine spirit" dominate all sectors of society. In order to accomplish these goals, he felt, socialists must "look for our model in the forms recently adopted by the working-class movement in this country."[19]

Justo's nationalism consisted primarily of anti-imperialism and a concern to assimilate the immigrant worker into the political structure of the country. In an article in *La Nación* in 1896, Justo attacked imperialism. "English capital," he argued, "has done what the country's armies could not do. Today our country is a tributary of England."[20] This attack, however, was not a wholesale denunciation of foreign capital. Justo the liberal recognized the benefits for Argentina of the British-owned railroad, gas, streetcar, telephone, and telegraph companies, and he opposed tariff restrictions on the free exchange of goods. His anti-imperialism was directed against the outflow of gold to other countries, absentee capital, and the political influence of foreign capitalists in Argentina.[21] Thus, to free the country of economic imperialism meant to free it of political interference by foreign capitalists.

The second goal of his nationalism, the assimilation of the immigrant worker, occupied most of Justo's attention. Although he sought to appeal to both native and foreign-born workers, Justo focused his efforts on the latter, whom he believed to be more capable of developing socialism in Argentina. In the editorial of the first edition of *La Vanguardia*, published on April 7, 1894, Justo stated that the one and a half million European immigrants, along with the existing European-oriented elements of the country, "constitute today the active part of the population, that which will little by little absorb the old criollo element, incapable of progressing by itself toward a superior social type." [22] Two years later he reiterated the same idea when he explained that the purpose of the Socialist Party was to incorporate the hundreds of thousands of European workers into the political life of the country "in order to direct it toward a collectivist, humanitarian, and scientific organization." [23]

The logical culmination of the effort by Justo and the socialists to effect the assimilation of the immigrant workers in the country's political life was participation in elections. In 1896 the Argentine Socialist Workers' Party nominated Justo and four others to run for seats in the National Congress, but the Socialists received only 138 out of the 12,000 votes cast in Buenos Aires—the only city where they had any strength—and failed to elect any of their candidates. Although the election was notoriously fraudulent, fraud had little to do with the party's poor showing; even by Socialist estimates it received no more than 250 votes.[24]

The Socialists' campaign to assimilate the immigrant worker failed. In 1896 only 43 per cent of the 764 members of the Socialist Party were Argentine citizens eligible to vote in national elections, and it was not until 1915 that the party enforced the 1895 resolution of the Executive Committee that members must be Argentine citizens. In addition, only 1 per cent of the country's 25 per cent foreign-born population, and only 2.3 per cent of Buenos Aires' 50 per cent foreign-born population, became citizens before World War I.[25]

The Birth of Organized Labor in Argentina / 19

It seems probable that the Socialists failed to provide effective leadership for the working-class movement in large part because they attempted to use the parliamentarian methods of industrializing Germany to improve the conditions of the Argentine worker at a time when such measures could not produce the desired results.

As weak as the socialist movement was during the 1880's and 1890's, the anarchists were unable to compete effectively with it for leadership of the Argentine working class because they were divided into two factions. One faction supported the philosophy of individual action of Michael Bakunin, and the other supported the collectivist philosophy of Peter Kropotkin. They were united only in favoring direct action and rejecting the parliamentarian methods of the socialists. They sought, not to assimilate the worker into Argentine society, but to destroy the existing society and build a new one in its place.

During the 1890's the collectivist faction won control of the Argentine anarchists and prepared the way for united leadership to take over the nascent labor movement. The writings of Antonio Pellicer Paraire, a Spaniard living in Argentina, provided the anarchists with a theoretical basis for collective organization and, equally as significant in a society of economically motivated immigrants, explained how they could wage a day-to-day economic struggle while working toward long-range revolutionary goals.

In 1900 Pellicer Paraire published a series of articles entitled *La organización obrera*, in which he pointed out the ineffectiveness of individual action. "The majority of anarchists," Pellicer Paraire claimed, "are adverse to all permanent coordination of wills; they confide too much in the myth of the people and in spontaneity." But, he continued, the ruling minority dominated because of its organization, and in order to end this minority rule the workers would have to organize superior forces.[26]

He proposed an economic organization designed to improve the lot of the workers in the present society, and a revolutionary organization designed to bring about a new and better society. Every local trade group or factory unit would organize a *sociedad de resistencia*. The local sociedades would unite to form a craft federation that would fight to improve economic and social conditions. In addition to the craft federation, the sociedades were to form a local federation, or "revolutionary commune," to handle all matters of "liberty and existence" and constitute the nucleus of the future anarchist society.

The anarchists' new concern for organization and economic well-being led them in 1901 to join the socialists in establishing the Federación Obrera Argentina (FOA). Through the efforts of leaders such as the anarchist Pedro Gori and the socialist Adrian Padroni, the federation remained united for more than a year. However, at its Second Congress in April 1902, the FOA divided over the seating of delegates. Both sides denounced the "fraudulent maneuvers" on the part of the opposition, and finally the representatives of the nineteen socialist affiliates walked out.[27]

After the withdrawal of the socialists, the anarchists controlled much of organized labor in Argentina. Despite the formation of the socialist-controlled Unión General de Trabajo (UGT) in 1903, the anarchists were the strongest single faction in the labor movement until 1910, when the government suppressed their activities.[28]

Having established their control over the FOA, the anarchists converted it into a political organization to propagate their ideas. They changed the name to Federación Obrera Regional Argentina (FORA), adopted a program based on the partisan ideas of Pellicer Paraire, and in 1905 openly supported the political philosophy of anarchist communism and purged the labor federation of all non-anarchists.[29]

The anarchists' leadership of the labor movement contrasted sharply with that of their parliamentarian-minded predecessors. Instead of working to assimilate the workers into society and in this way reform it, the anarchists attempted to create a radically new "pure society." For them the nation-state was an artificial creation, as a resolution passed by the FORA in 1905 makes clear: "The frontiers that separate people are not justified, and we recognize no other country than the entire world."[30] The existing national state, they believed, was an evil that had to be destroyed before a new, regenerated society could develop. Therefore they did not hesitate to use violent, "socially unacceptable" methods to gain their ends.

The most significant new method the anarachists employed in their effort to overthrow the government and to win benefits for the workers was the revolutionary general strike. Inspired by the Barcelona general strike in 1902, the Argentine anarchists initiated a wave of local and general strikes. In the most successful of these, in May 1909, between 200,000 and 300,000 laborers stopped work in Buenos Aires for six days to protest "police murders." The strike ended when the government conceded to many of the demands of the workers.[31]

Another important technique introduced by the anarchists during this period was "propaganda by deed." This idea had developed in France, Spain, and Italy during the 1880's and 1890's, and many Argentine anarchists, familiar with the recent history of these countries, believed that individual acts of terrorism were justified when joint action failed. On August 11, 1905, an anarchist tried to assassinate President Manuel Quintana to protest alleged police brutality during the suppression of the Radical Party's attempted coup. Similarly, on November 14, 1909, a young Russian anarchist assassinated Colonel Ramón L. Falcón, the chief of police of Buenos Aires, because of his apparent ruthlessness in dealing with worker demonstrations and protests.[32]

Anarchism in Argentina had another aspect that has confused a number of writers who have dwelt only on the exercise of violence and terror. At the same time that the anarchists pursued their militant anti-government policy, they also pursued the apparently contradictory policy of trying to improve the immediate social and economic position of the worker within the society they sought to destroy. James Bryce, who visited Argentina shortly after the assassination of Colonel Falcón, commented on this paradoxical situation: "Our age has seen too many strange incidents to be surprised that these acts of violence should be perpetrated in a country where, though there is an ostentatious display of wealth, work is more abundant and wages higher than in any other part of the world. Such acts are aimed not at oppression nor at industrial conditions, but at the government itself."[33]

What Lord Bryce and others failed to understand was that because the labor movement was largely an immigrant movement confronting a hostile government, it had to be not only revolutionary but oriented toward immediate economic benefits. The worker who had the initiative to leave his native land in search of a better life wanted immediate economic gain even though he hated the government and sought to destroy it. Pellicer Paraire had suggested a means of approaching both objectives simultaneously, and so the Argentine anarchists, unlike their European counterparts, emphasized immediate economic benefits as well as revolutionary activity.[34]

Precisely because of the dual nature of their program, the anarchists were for a time able to provide more effective leadership for organized labor than the socialists. Anarchist policy and the general prosperity of the period did improve

The Birth of Organized Labor in Argentina / 23

conditions for the worker. The employers, making substantial profits, could afford to increase wages in order to end strikes and maintain order. Between 1904 and 1909 the salaries of skilled and semi-skilled workers increased more rapidly than the cost of living; the average work day of these groups was reduced by one or two hours; and rents in some working-class districts of Buenos Aires were lowered.[35]

For the most part, the conservative landed oligarchy that controlled the Argentine government from 1880 to 1916 had little understanding of or sympathy for the nascent labor movement. There were a few men—Carlos Pellegrini, Joaquín V. González, Roque Saenz Peña—who recognized the need to help the working class, but they were unable to change the thinking of their own class. At no time did the government communicate to the worker a desire to understand his social and economic problems or to help him solve them within the existing institutional framework of the country. The working class could not become part of Argentine society on terms of equality with the oligarchy.

The government was ambivalent toward the worker. In the 1890's the ruling oligarchy appeared indifferent to the labor movement, but as the increasingly militant FORA introduced new methods of fighting to gain its ends, the government matched these with new repressive measures. In response to the 1902 wave of strikes and the first general strike in Argentine history, the police began to raid union headquarters, use labor spies, jail workers on a large scale, and suspend the publication of labor periodicals.[36] The government also used the state of siege—a declaration of emergency that permitted it to suspend the normal constitutional guarantees—against the workers, setting a precedent that has been followed in Argentina every since.

For the purposes of this study, the government's most significant means of combatting the rising militancy of labor was to deport the leaders of the movement. On November 23, 1902, the National Congress passed the Ley de Residencia, which permitted the government to deport all foreigners whose conduct "compromised the national security or disturbed the public order," to prohibit the entry of foreigners who were guilty of criminal offenses, and to deport a condemned foreigner within three days.[37]

This law isolated the immigrant worker from Argentine society. Taking part in a strike made a man an "undesirable alien," a "professional agitator," or a "subversive element." The worker had no protection under the laws of the country because the courts generally would not review by *habeas corpus* proceedings the President's act of deporting "undesirable aliens."[38]

Yet a little more than a year later the government appeared to soften its attitude toward the workers. In 1904 Minister of Interior Joaquín V. González, one of the more progressive members of the oligarchy, attempted to improve labor-government relations. He presented a national labor law to Congress that provided for an eight-hour day, the regulation of night work, Sunday rest, accident insurance, regulation of women's work, and the prohibition of child labor. At the same time the law provided for government regulation of labor union activity.[39]

If the proposed Ley González had been adopted, it would have been a dramatic step forward in labor-government relations. It provided the first protective legislation for the worker in Argentine history and also attempted to establish a basis for labor-government cooperation in the settlement of disputes. Nevertheless, both business and labor opposed it. Business interests felt that the law granted the worker unheard-of and unnecessary concessions, and the labor organizations believed that it would end their independence by placing them under government regulation. This proposed legislation therefore never became law.[40]

The Birth of Organized Labor in Argentina / 25

In 1907 a few individuals in the government again attempted and again failed to establish meaningful relations with the labor movement. As a result of their efforts the Congress created a Department of Labor to handle such matters. The new Department of Labor immediately invited the FORA and the UGT to participate in a tribunal that would resolve labor-management conflicts, but both labor federations refused to support the "corrupt bourgeois government" in this effort.[41]

These and other efforts of the more progressive elements of the oligarchy to establish effective channels of communication between business, government, and labor failed because no side was willing to concede anything, and as a result the struggle ended with the forceful suppression of the labor movement. The celebration of the Centennial of Argentine Independence in May 1910 produced the final scene in the drama. The government approached the leaders of the FORA in an effort to avoid any demonstrations during the celebration. The leaders of the FORA, faced with a militant and only partially disciplined movement, hesitated. They felt they should call a strike because the workers wanted one, although they were concerned about the "inevitable reaction of [Argentine] nationalism" that their strike might provoke.[42]

The recently established syndicalist Confederación Obrera de la Región Argentina (CORA), hoping to seize the initiative from the hesitant FORA, called a general strike for May 18, seven days before the independence celebration. In order to maintain its position of leadership, the FORA felt obliged to call a general strike for the same day. Its leaders announced that unless the government freed all political prisoners and repealed the Ley de Residencia, the affiliates of the FORA would strike.

The government, denied the cooperation it had sought, moved to prevent the demonstrations by a complete repression of organized labor. On May 13 it began to arrest labor leaders and the next day it declared a state of siege. Mobs gathered and, joined by the police, attacked and destroyed nearly all union buildings and working-class newspapers. Thousands of workers were jailed and dozens deported. The government achieved its goal; there were no labor demonstrations during the Centennial celebration. But, notes the anarchist historian Diego Abad de Santillán, "history will record that to celebrate the centennial, the government had to convert Buenos Aires into an armed camp." [43]

Tension remained high throughout May and the struggle did not end until June 26. That day a bomb exploded in the empty Teatro Colón and an anarchist was accused. Within forty-eight hours the National Congress, supported by most non-working-class sectors of society, passed a law that singled out the anarchists as the cause of social unrest.[44] The Ley de Defensa Social was designed to destroy the anarchist movement. It prohibited anarchists from entering the country, propagating their ideas, or holding public meetings, and listed the penalties for various acts that jeopardized national security.[45]

With the passage of the Ley de Defensa Social, anarchist leadership of organized labor came to an end and the labor movement was severely weakened. Most of the leaders of the FORA were deported or jailed, the organization did not hold meetings for more than two years, and the two anarchist newspapers ceased publication. The local affiliates of the FORA were allowed to function, but their activities —like those of all labor groups—were sharply curtailed.

Thus, despite certain attempts to help labor, the net result of the government's policy was to isolate the worker and to label him a criminal and a subversive element. The government did not grant legal recognition to most labor unions, and instead of dealing with labor leaders in their capacity as representatives of the workers, it threatened to deport them because they were "undesirable foreigners."

The government perhaps believed that by deporting the working-class leaders it had deported its social and economic problems. These problems, of course, could not be solved in this way. The leaders were merely representatives of a new and growing, but isolated and unassimilated, immigrant working class seeking a better life. Unless the government was willing to deport all workers, it could not eliminate social unrest.

By 1910 organized labor had clearly emerged in Argentina, but it remained outside the institutional structure of the country and would remain there until conditions permitted it to use the existing institutions to help fulfill its economic and social aspirations.

2

Early Manifestations of Working-Class Nationalism

Organized labor did not fully recover from the tremendous setback of 1910 until nearly the end of the decade, when war stimulated prosperity and the relative shortage of workers gave the unions a strong bargaining position. The "revived" labor movement, however, was not the same movement the government had suppressed. In the interval, a new generation of workers, with new attitudes important for the development of popular nationalism, had come of age.

This new generation of workers was led by syndicalists and later by socialists rather than by anarchists. Syndicalism had developed in France during the 1890's as a reaction to the parliamentarianism of the socialists and the exclusiveness of the communist anarchists. Unlike anarchism and socialism, syndicalism grew out of the existing labor organizations and developed as a non-political pragmatic ideology based on the immediate needs of the worker. The goal of the movement was to unite all workers into one labor organization that would help them improve their immediate situation and would become the basic institution of society sometime in the future.

Syndicalism first appeared in Argentina at the moment when it was reaching the peak of its influence in Europe. In 1906 the syndicalists took over the Unión General de Trabajo from the socialists, and at the same time they established a group of supporters within the anarchist FORA.[1] In 1909, in an attempt to unite the labor movement, the syndicalists and the autonomous unions established a new labor federation, the Confederación Obrera de la Región Argentina (CORA), and in 1915 they disbanded the CORA and joined the FORA. At its Ninth Congress, later that year, the FORA divided into syndicalist and anarchist factions over the issue of the exclusiveness and political nature of anarchist communism. The syndicalists controlled the dominant faction which, because the Ninth Congress repudiated anarchist communism, became known as the FORA IX. The anarchist faction became known as the FORA V because at the Fifth Congress, in 1905, the federation had adopted the political philosophy of anarchist communism.

The apolitical syndicalist FORA IX, which controlled the labor movement from 1915 to 1922, was the most effective independent labor central the country had ever known. Recovering from the events of 1910 and the split of 1915, it increased its following from 51 affiliates with 3,000 members to 734 affiliates with about 70,000 members. The annual number of strikes, reflecting new union activity, increased more than five times—from 65 in 1915 to 367 in 1919—and the number of strikers increased more than twenty times, from 12,000 to 309,000. Most important for the worker, as a result of this activity, plus war prosperity and the curtailment of immigration because of the war, real wages increased. As Table I shows, real wages declined between

TABLE I

REAL WAGES OF INDUSTRIAL
WORKERS, 1914–1930
(IN PER CENT) *

1914	68	1923	86
1915	61	1924	85
1916	57	1925	89
1917	49	1926	90
1918	42	1927	95
1919	57	1928	101
1920	59	1929	100
1921	73	1930	91
1922	84		

* República Argentina, Departamento Nacional del Trabajo, División de Estadística, *Estadística de las huelgas* (Buenos Aires, 1940), pp. 21–22.

1914 and 1918, but after that they rose quickly, reaching a peak in 1923 which was 26 per cent higher than that of 1914.

A number of factors differentiated the anarchist- and syndicalist-led generations of workers, but probably the most important was the change in the composition of the working class. The anarchist-dominated FORA of the pre-World War I period received its greatest support from artisan European-born immigrants. Its membership consisted primarily of Spaniards and Italians who worked in situations of close personal contact with their employers, and its most important affiliates were craft unions—shoemakers, bakers, carpenters, and bricklayers—located in Buenos Aires and Rosario. In contrast, the labor movement during World War I and the 1920's consisted primarily of transportation workers living in all parts of the country, many of whom were the sons of immigrants who had little or no personal contact with their employers.

The rise of the transportation workers to a position of preeminence in the labor movement resulted from the rapid economic development and modernization begun in the latter part of the nineteenth century, and in particular from the dramatic growth of the railroad and maritime industries. Between 1900 and 1930 the number of miles of railroad in Argentina more than doubled, increasing from 10,375 to 23,960. The maritime industry developed in similar proportions and with similar speed. Between 1913 and 1929 the volume of internal maritime trade increased 100 per cent, from 11,800,000 to 22,700,000 tons per year.[2] As these industries grew, so of course did the number of employees working for them, and by 1920 the transportation workers represented more than half of the organized workers in the country.[3]

The growing number of Argentines born of immigrant parents in the labor movement was the result of the passage of time and of World War I. Between 1880 and 1910 more than two million immigrants came and remained in Argentina. But between 1910 and 1920 the threat of war and the war itself reduced the flow of immigrants to practically nothing; only 269,000 permanent immigrants came to the country during the entire decade.[4] On the other hand, large numbers of immigrants had been in Argentina long enough to raise families. As a result, the sons of immigrants filled the growing demand for workers and became an increasingly important segment of organized labor.[5]

A third change in the composition of the working class was the development of a small group of white-collar workers and government employees. The bank workers, the journalists, the commercial employees, the telegraph workers, and the post office employees of the federal capital all organized during this period, as did such groups as the teachers of Mendoza and the commercial employees of Rosario.[6] Although some of these unions did not survive very long, enough white-collar and government workers' unions continued to operate to exert some influence on the labor movement.

The growth of the transportation unions and the increase in the number of sons of immigrants, white-collar workers, and government employees were gradual and often uneven developments. But, by the end of World War I, these developments had progressed to the point where they had stimulated changes in the traditional attitudes of the organized worker. The leaders of the large and influential railroad and maritime unions, representing men from all parts of the country who worked in increasingly impersonal situations, began to recognize that the local union was no longer able to solve their most important problems. Local strikes were less and less effective, and alone the local union could do nothing to prevent regional wage discrimination, the high cost of living, speculation, and unemployment. These union leaders realized that their problems were national problems, and they became increasingly aware of the necessity of achieving influence at the national level. This in turn forced the workers to reevaluate traditional labor attitudes toward the government.

The psychological attitudes of the sons of immigrant workers reinforced the transportation union leaders' growing awareness of national problems. The European-born immigrant was torn by a dual loyalty, but his son—born in the country where he lived and worked—was much less involved in this emotional conflict. In most cases he was anxious to become an active an influential part of Argentine society and was perhaps more susceptible than the native worker to appeals of Argentine nationalism. Lord Bryce, echoing the opinion of many others, pointed out that "Children born in the country grow up to be Argentines in sentiment and are, perhaps, even more vehemently patriotic than the youth of native stock."⁷

Finally, unionization of some white-collar workers and government employees injected important new attitudes into the labor movement. The bank workers, teachers, and post office employees were not revolutionaries, nor were they class-oriented. They wanted to reform Argentina's capitalist system, not destroy it. They conceived of the state as a potential instrument to bring about desired social and economic change and therefore sought to gain influence within it.

New government attitudes toward organized labor also contributed to the evolution of the workers' attitudes. Prior to World War I, the government's labor policy had ranged from indifference in the 1890's to systematic persecution and isolation of the workers during the early 1900's. But with the election of Hipólito Yrigoyen to the presidency of Argentina in 1916, the government changed its traditional attitude toward organized labor.

A major difference between Yrigoyen's government and the governments of his predecessors was that for the first time in Argentine history the "middle sectors" achieved decisive influence in the direction of the country.⁸ The President's labor policy reflected this fact; he was sympathetic to the needs and aspirations of the workers because he believed they were a legitimate element of society, but there was a limit to his understanding. Between 1916 and 1919 the government supported labor in many of its demands, but beginning in 1919, as prosperity waned and fear of social revolution spread in the middle sectors, it began to curb labor's activities.

The leaders of the new government claimed that they represented all of the Argentine people and not just the landed oligarchy. The government, Yrigoyen insisted, must be impartial. It must act to end "privileges and special

Manifestations of Working-Class Nationalism / 35

rights that might weaken the principle of national unity." It must "support all classes and take care of all interests, seeking in the common good the security of each individual."[9] The government was, in other words, the political representative of the working class as well as the other sectors of society.

Yrigoyen protected the rights of labor to organize and strike, and involved the government in labor-management disputes in order to ensure justice for both sides. As a result, during the first three years of his presidency—during which the country enjoyed wartime prosperity and underemployment—the labor organizations were able to expand into new industries, geographical areas, and industries only partially organized. The meat packers of Berisso, the textile and metal workers in Buenos Aires, and the sugar workers of the north made their first attempt to organize, and the FORA IX increased its membership from 3,000 workers in 1915 to 70,000 in 1920.

In addition, the government intervened in the important maritime strike of 1916 and the railroad strike of 1917 to protect the interests of labor as well as those of the employers and the country as a whole. Both strikes were settled by granting the workers many of their demands; moreover, during the railroad strike Yrigoyen defended the rights of the workers in the face of strong business pressure to do otherwise. A number of representatives of industry and commerce asked the President to end the strike by ordering the Marines to take over the railroads. Yrigoyen, apparently upset by such a suggestion, said: "Let it be understood, sirs, that privileges have ceased in this country and that from this day on, the armed forces of the nation will be used only in its honor or in defense of its integrity."[10]

The attitude and actions of the Yrigoyen government represented a significant break with those of former conservative governments. Yrigoyen ended the systematic persecution of labor and suggested that the government had an obligation to serve and defend the workers' interests as well as those of the other sectors of society. At the same time, however, he acted in ways that strained labor's incipient faith in the government.

Underlying such lack of confidence was the fact that the President had no specific labor program and therefore dealt with organized workers on an *ad hoc* basis. This failure to institutionalize the rights of labor meant that the workers were secure only when a man sympathetic to their cause was President and only as long as that man remained sympathetic. More specifically, labor was concerned because the government did little to pass protective labor legislation. Neither Yrigoyen nor his successor, Marcelo T. de Alvear, sought to repeal the Ley de Residencia or the Ley de Defensa Social. The government also continued using the police to deal with labor, a reminder to the workers that many considered their problems to be "matters for the police." And, as we have noted, although the real wages of industrial workers increased substantially after 1919, they had declined nearly 40 per cent between 1914 and 1918.

The events of the Semana Trágica, January 7 to 14, 1919, illustrate both the government's fear and the degree of its support of organized labor. The violent outbursts by labor and the severe repressions by the government were the result of pressures built up over a period of several years. Real wages had declined and the example of the Russian Revolution served to aggravate worker-management relations. Many workers believed that this revolution furnished a precedent for their own country. Businessmen and many in government, fearing that a similar revolution might occur in Argentina, opposed Yrigoyen's efforts to protect labor and waited for an opportunity to demonstrate the "inadequate and misguided" nature of his policies.

On December 2, 1918, most of the 2,500 workers of the

Manifestations of Working-Class Nationalism / 37

Vasena metallurgic factory of Buenos Aires went on strike to protest the dismissal of several of their fellow workers for union activity.[11] When their first strike did not produce the desired results, the metallurgic workers decided to initiate another more extended strike and to broaden their demands. They submitted a petition to their employer demanding an eight-hour day and a salary increase of at least 20 per cent in addition to the reinstatement of the dismissed workers. The strike continued without incident until January 7, 1919, when strikers clashed with workers brought in by the company to replace them. The police intervened to break up the conflict and one worker was killed and many wounded. As the strike continued, other unions supported the metallurgic workers and the FORA IX took charge. On January 9, when the workers attempted to bury the victim of the January 7 conflict, another fight with the police broke out and more people were killed and wounded. The labor federation called a general strike and the chief of police of Buenos Aires was replaced by the Minister of War so that the latter could take military command of the city.

The next day, January 10, the conflict took an even more serious turn. Working-class groups attempted to assault the post office and police headquarters. Unofficial organizations such as the Liga Patriótica and the Asociación de Trabajo, both of which represented conservative business interests, joined the police and the army to curb the demonstrations.

The leaders of the FORA IX now decided to seek an immediate end to the entire conflict. They denied any responsibility for such acts as assaulting the post office and the police station and submitted their demands for settlement to the government. They asked for the approval of the petition of the original strikers, the Vasena metallurgic workers, and the release of all imprisoned workers. Representatives of FORA IX met with the President and other government officials, and although the prisoners were not released, the union was granted its wage and hour demands.

On January 12, when the strike seemed nearly settled, the police claimed that they had uncovered a Soviet-backed plot to overthrow the Argentine government. There was little evidence of such a plot, but the police, assisted by the Liga Patriótica and the Asociación de Trabajo, conducted a search of the working-class districts of Buenos Aires for conspirators. As a result hundreds of people, particularly Jews and anarchists, were killed, wounded, or jailed.

The Vasena metallurgic workers, even though they had been granted shorter hours and higher wages, refused to return to work until all of the workers, including those most recently arrested, had been released from prison. The FORA IX also supported this demand. On Wednesday, January 15, after a labor delegation had met with Yrigoyen and other government officials, the prisoners were released. By the end of the week almost all workers were back at their jobs and the crisis had subsided.

It is important to keep in mind that during the Semana Trágica the government demonstrated concern for as well as fear of organized labor. It seems clear that the middle-sector government used the police and the armed forces and permitted unofficial and anti-labor groups to intervene against the workers because it considered the situation to be potentially explosive. At the same time, by assisting in the settlement of the original dispute, the government did attempt to demonstrate its sympathy for organized labor.

Yrigoyen's attitude and policies toward organized labor, reflecting his middle-sector support, were ambivalent. Yet his actions during the Semana Trágica and other similar crises, harsh and unjust though they seemed to some, could not obscure the fact that the government considered organized labor to be a vital if little-understood part of society, entitled to equal consideration, protection, and respect under the law. Compared with previous governments, that of Yrigoyen showed some favor toward organized labor, and this fact, along with the changes in the composition of the working class, stimulated new labor attitudes important for the development of Argentine nationalism.

The shift in the leadership of the labor movement from the anarchists to the syndicalists reflected these changes in the working class and the government. The syndicalists rejected the exclusiveness of their predecessors and followed a policy of apolitical unionism that made cooperation with the government possible. In a motion made at its 1915 Congress and passed by a vote of 46 to 14, the members of the organization declared: "The FORA does not pronounce itself a partisan organization nor does it advise the adoption of philosophical or ideologically determined systems." [12]

The significance of the apolitical stand of FORA IX was that for the first time an Argentine labor federation aspired to be a genuinely national labor organization, representing all political factions and all parts of the country. Other labor federations had at times expressed similar ideas but had made little, if any, effort to carry them out. The FORA IX, by carrying out its policy of apolitical unionism, took an important step toward achieving its goal of representing the Argentine workers.

Another important response of FORA IX to the changes in Argentine society was its non-revolutionary unionism. In its statements, the federation leaders spoke of the "revolutionary struggle of classes" and the "revolutionary general strike," using the same tired rhetoric as the anarchist FORA. In its actions, however, the leaders of FORA IX supported Yrigoyen's government as no previous labor federation had ever supported an Argentine government.[13]

Sebastián Marotta, Secretary-General of the FORA IX during most of this period, insists that much of organized labor backed the Yrigoyen government. But, he points out, labor never officially supported the President, because such an act would have defied the FORA IX's ban on political pronouncements and would have divided the labor movement.[14] Nor did the workers support Yrigoyen with votes. The organized labor movement was still made up predominantly of immigrants and only a little more than 2 per cent of the foreign-born in Buenos Aires and less than 1 per cent of the foreign-born in the rest of the country were able to vote in national elections.[15]

Labor's support of Yrigoyen was manifested primarily in its cooperation with the government in times of conflict. Unlike the anarchist FORA, the syndicalist FORA IX accepted government arbitration and mediation in labor disputes. For example, FORA IX, working with the Federación Obrera Marítima, accepted the mediation of the Department of Labor to settle the maritime strike of 1916. The employers, distrustful of Yrigoyen, would not. This was a vivid contrast to a similar situation that had occured in 1907, when the employers, confident that the government was on their side, were willing to cooperate with the Department of Labor to settle disputes, but the labor federations considered such cooperation "treasonable collaboration with bourgeois capitalism."[16]

Another example of labor's cooperation with the government occurred during the railroad strike of 1917. The Minister of Public Works, while expressing his respect for the workers' rights as strikers, asked the union for permission to run trains that carried milk to hospitals. The permission was forthcoming on the condition that union members run the milk trains. Such cooperation, based on something approaching mutual respect, was not to be found in Argentina before this time.[17] For the first time in Argentine history a major labor federation was able to follow a policy of cooperation with the government because its leaders believed such a policy served the interests of the workers.

The thinking of a number of Argentine socialists was as important for the development of nationalism in the labor movement as was the FORA IX's policy of cooperation with the government. For the first thirty years of labor union activity in Argentina, the Socialist Party was the only working-class organization to express any kind of nationalism. In the 1890's Juan B. Justo, the founder and leader of the party, set forth a slightly modified form of the liberal nationalism of Sarmiento and Mitre; he sought to create a new, modern, Argentine nation by assimilating the European immigrant workers into the political structure of the country, where they might exert their influence and transform society. During the first two decades of the twentieth century, Manuel Ugarte, Alfredo L. Palacios, and others injected new ideas of nationalism into the Socialist Party and provided the working class with a much broader conception of the phenomenon. As members of the party became important labor leaders during the 1920's and 1930's, they utilized some of the ideas of Justo, Ugarte, and Palacios and in this way nationalism spread to the labor movement.

Ugarte and Palacios shared certain nationalist ideas with Justo. All three believed that nationalism and socialism were compatible and that the Socialist Party was an outgrowth of the Argentine environment and not, as the Italian socialist Enrico Ferri charged, an "exotic flower."[18] They also believed that the Socialist Party and organized labor should help create a new nation, and that the state should intervene in economic and social problems to protect the interests of all sectors of society.

Palacios held further ideas in common with Justo. Both men supported free trade, the minimization of the class struggle, and the curtailment of the power of the Church and the military. They also looked to the liberal Argentine thinkers and statesmen—Bernadino Rivadavia, Esteban Echeverría, Domingo F. Sarmiento, and Bartolomé Mitre—for their inspiration.

But Palacios and Ugarte disagreed with Justo on some significant points. They placed greater emphasis than Justo on the potential contribution of the native Argentine—the criollo familiar with Hispanic traditions and values—to the transformation of the Argentine nation. Palacios, although anxious to utilize European ideas and people in Argentina, believed that the future nation should be a synthesis of immigrants and criollos and their respective traditions. "The great patriotic task," he declared, "consists in giving the immigrant roots in our soil. . . . Our collective activity is to realize . . . the great vision of the future, without forgetting that the force [with which to create this vision] must be both natives and foreigners." [19]

Ugarte carried the argument one step farther. He insisted that the criollo must be the basic element of the emerging Argentine society because the criollo was a bastion of the traditional Hispanic values and institutions that were the essence of the Argentine nation. "Spain," he pointed out, "was the cradle . . . of our nationality. We are her affectionate children and no banner should be closer to our hearts than hers." [20]

Out of this belief in the importance of the Argentine criollo tradition emerged a new meaning of anti-imperialism that differed from the concept as stated by Justo. Justo attacked foreign political influence in Argentina, but welcomed what he considered to be the progressive ideas of Europe and the United States as a means of counteracting the backward, Hispanic, criollo traditions. He did not believe, therefore, that the United States and Britain—the Anglo-Saxon powers—were necessarily enemies of the country.

Ugarte and Palacios, on the other hand, considered the

Anglo-Saxon powers the greatest threat to the cultural as well as the economic and political independence of Argentina. Ugarte believed that the unification of Latin America was the only way to protect Argentina from North American imperialism and to guarantee its own traditional, criollo, social and political values. In 1900 he therefore initiated the campaign to unite Latin America for its own self-defense that was to continue throughout his life. In *La Patria Grande, Mi campaña hispanoamericana, El porvenir de América Latina,* and *El destino de un continente*—all written between 1910 and 1917—he argued and reiterated his case. The United States had dismembered Mexico, intervened in Cuba, Santo Domingo, and Nicaragua, and had separated Panama from Colombia. The only way to prevent the subjugation of all Latin America by the Anglo-Saxon powers was to create one great Latin American nation, conscious of its distinct Hispanic origins and traditions and prepared to defend an independent future.[21]

Palacios was not as active in the anti-United States campaign as Ugarte, but he did support the latter's effort to unite Latin America. In 1913 Palacios wrote to Ugarte, indicating this support: "My dear Ugarte: I sent to you a lecture I gave last year demanding, in the name of Latin American solidarity, the condemnation of the war debt, and the return of the trophies to Paraguay [the trophies won during the Paraguayan War of 1865–1870]. I want in this way to point out again my enthusiastic support for the campaign begun by yourself."[22]

Twelve years later Palacios was instrumental in establishing the Latin American Union, an organization whose central purpose was to create a Latin American federation capable of resisting foreign imperialism. In addition, the program of the Latin American Union repudiated Pan-Americanism—as opposed to Latin Americanism—secret diplomacy, and foreign intervention to collect debts.[23]

Ugarte and Palacios introduced other new nationalist ideas. Ugarte's was one of the earliest voices raised in favor of government protection of national industry. Argentina, he pointed out, protected only foreign industry and prohibited the development of national industry. "The country that exports only raw materials and imports foreign manufactured products," he maintained, "will always be a country in the intermediate stage of its evolution."[24] Therefore, unlike Justo and Palacios, he favored modifications of the free-trade system and extensive state protection for national industry.

Palacios took a new nationalist position with regard to war. War, he claimed, was not always the result of conflicting bourgeois interests, nor was it always detrimental to the interests of the working class. In fact, he continued, the workers might benefit from a war and might want to support their government's policies in the event of war. He therefore did not believe, as did many working-class leaders before World War I, that in the event of war the workers throughout the world should go on strike.[25]

Palacios and Ugarte injected a number of new ideas of nationalism into the Argentine Socialist Party most of which modified the liberal ideas of Justo. Despite the fact that their positions were not identical, they were similar enough so that the membership of the party attacked them both for espousing "criollo nationalism" and expelled them from the organization.

Ugarte, who had joined the party in 1904, was expelled in 1913. In the latter year, shortly after he returned from a trip throughout Latin America, Ugarte became involved in a controversy with the editors of the Socialist Party newspaper, *La Vanguardia*. *La Vanguardia* took the editorial position that Colombia, like all of the South American countries, had been plagued by civil wars and political chaos, and that the separation of Panama from the mother

Manifestations of Working-Class Nationalism / 45

country would "probably contribute to its [Colombia's] progress, bringing it into the family of prosperous and civilized nations." [26] Ugarte challenged the accuracy and the implications of the editorial. Colombia, he claimed, was "one of the most generous and cultivated" countries that he had visited. Furthermore, the separation of Panama from the rest of the nation—the direct result of Yankee diplomacy— would not in any way contribute to the mother country's progress. Such a statement, Ugarte insisted, was an attack on Hispanic values and a defense of North American imperialism and Anglo-Saxon values.[27] Shortly after this incident Ugarte was expelled from the party.

The expulsion of Palacios in 1915 was of greater significance than that of Ugarte because Palacios, as the party's first National Deputy, was more influential than his friend. Officially, Palacios was expelled because he violated the party's ban on dueling, but the real reason was his independence of action and his espousal of criollo nationalism. In a speech before the Second Extraordinary Congress of the Socialist Party in 1915, Representative Pedro Balino expressed what seemed to be the sentiment of a majority of the members when he charged: "Doctor Palacios ought to have been ejected from the Socialist Party before now, if not for having . . . continued creating and establishing false independent committees that supported his candidacy . . . [then] for his criollo nationalism." [28]

The party ejected Ugarte and Palacios largely because of their criollo nationalism, but it did not reject all forms of nationalism. The war caused many formerly indifferent socialists to support the kind of economic nationalism voiced for many years by Justo, and in 1915 the party confirmed its general concern for the assimilation of the immigrant worker by enforcing its 1896 decree requiring its members to be Argentine citizens. As German submarines began to interfere with Argentine shipping, temporarily crippling a number of industries and therefore destroying jobs, many in the party—including Justo—seemed to accept Palacios' analysis of the situation, ignored the opposition of the internationalists, forgot the "bourgeois nature" of the conflict, and talked instead of protecting Argentine commerce against the foreign threat.[29]

The issue developed into a crisis within the party at its 1917 Congress, where Justo supported military intervention by the government in order to protect Argentine shipping. The internationalists of the party were in the majority, however, and defeated his motion.[30] Disregarding this defeat, the Socialist Deputies in the National Congress—loyal followers of Justo—supported a break in relations with Germany. The party divided and the internationalists withdrew to establish the Partido Socialista Internacional, which later became the Communist Party of Argentina.

Thus, although the Socialist Party expelled Ugarte and Palacios for their criollo nationalism, it also rejected the internationalists' alternative. At the same time Justo's brand of nationalism—a modified form of liberal nationalism—became an increasingly important force within the organization.

During the 1920's, partisanship—stimulated by the Russian Revolution and the worsening economic and social situation of the worker—reappeared in the Argentine labor movement. The Russian Revolution represented an ideological issue for almost every union. Most workers applauded the ideals of the Revolution, but the partisans of Russian leadership of the international working-class movement fought bitterly with those who opposed such leadership.

After the war, the reestablishment of contact with Europe became the main cause of the worsening position of the Argentine worker. National industry now had to compete with world industry for the Argentine market, and

Manifestations of Working-Class Nationalism / 47

many Argentine workers had to compete with new immigrants for jobs. In addition, the election of the more conservative Marcelo T. de Alvear to the presidency of the country in 1922 meant that labor would receive less support from the government than it had previously enjoyed.

Thus, although organized labor reached a peak in 1920, it fragmented disastrously soon afterward. In 1922 the FORA IX disbanded and the Unión Sindical Argentina (USA) replaced it. The socialist-controlled railroad unions withdrew immediately and the syndicalists, supported by the communists, were left in control of the new labor federation. The leaders of the USA, in contrast to those of the FORA IX, interpreted apolitical unionism in such a way that they would not cooperate with the government at all. They believed that the policies of their immediate predecessors had been unsuccessful because they had not prevented unemployment and the weakening of the labor movement. Therefore they attempted to revive the discredited anti-government policies of the pre-World War I anarchists.[31]

The USA had misjudged the nature and significance of the changes that had taken place in the working class; in addition to the transportation workers, other important unions withdrew from the federation. In 1924 the municipal workers left the USA because Francisco Pérez Leirós, their Secretary-General and a National Deputy for the Socialist Party, was expelled for participating in politics.[32] The printers of Buenos Aires also left the organization because of political differences. And the communists, after failing to win control of the USA and to affiliate it with the Moscow International, withdrew. By 1925 the USA had only 1,000 dues-paying members, compared with the 70,000 members the FORA IX had had in 1920.[33]

Because of this fragmentation, the major developments of the labor movement during the 1920's took place within individual unions, and particularly within the important railroad workers' union, the Unión Ferroviaria. It had affiliates throughout the country, the largest number of members of any union, and an unequaled strategic position. In addition, it was not greatly affected by the reopening of European markets and the new influx of European immigrants.

The Unión Ferroviaria was a relative latecomer to the labor scene. The first railroad union in Argentina was La Fraternidad, the organization of firemen and engineers established in 1887. La Fraternidad had a generally successful history, but in 1912 it lost a major strike primarily because it lacked effective support from the other railroad workers. It therefore helped the non-engine railroad employees to organize. In 1922 all of these groups joined to form the Unión Ferroviaria, which from the beginning was the largest union in the country.[34]

The establishment of the Unión Ferroviaria at that particular time was important to the development of nationalism within the labor movement because it incorporated into its program the nationalist ideas and policies of previous labor organizations and of the Socialist Party at a moment when most other unions and federations were rejecting them. The Unión Ferroviaria was national in scope because the railroads operated in most parts of the country; it represented all the non-engine railroad workers; and it organized according to the centralist industry-wide principles of La Fraternidad. Its leaders followed the non-revolutionary, apolitical policies of the FORA IX, and they clearly recognized the need to establish their influence at the national level, to work within the institutional structure of the country, and to uphold the Constitution of 1853.

The leaders of the railroad unions—perhaps influenced by the ideas of Manuel Ugarte—went beyond their pred-

Manifestations of Working-Class Nationalism / 49

ecessors in that they sought to use nationalism to defend their economic position and consciously stated their case in terms of the national interest. In 1928, for example, one of the foreign-owned railroad companies attempted to reduce the number of shop men it employed for the construction of railroad coaches, claiming that there was not sufficient work for them to do. At the same time the company—in violation of a 1926 agreement with the union to construct its coaches in Argentina whenever possible—was importing coaches from abroad. The leadership of the union protested immediately and carefully pointed out: "We are defending not only our own interest . . . but also that of many other Argentine families and, indirectly, national production. We have the support of public opinion, and the government [of Yrigoyen] agrees fully with our point of view, recognizing that in such an emergency, the Unión Ferroviaria is not inspired by its own interest, but . . . by an ample criterion of general interest." [35] This use of nationalism to protect the jobs of union members was effective; the foreign coaches that had been ordered came into the country, but the company also agreed to build a minimum of two coaches a month in its own shops.

In 1926 the Unión Ferroviaria, La Fraternidad, and the Municipal Workers joined to form the socialist-oriented Confederación Obrera Argentina (COA). The COA was the most important labor federation in Argentina between 1926 and 1930, with a membership of about 70,000 workers.[36] Since the Unión Ferroviaria was the most influential member of the COA, representing about 50,000 workers, the labor federation as a whole could not help but be imbued with the railroad union's concept of nationalism.

By 1930, when the members of the COA and the USA united to establish the Confederación General del Trabajo (CGT), the railroad workers had developed a rudimentary nationalism that combined the nationalist policies of the FORA IX, the nationalist ideas of the Socialist Party, and at least an awareness of the potential force of economic nationalism. This nationalism was the basis for the liberal nationalism that emerged full-blown within the labor movement in the late 1930's.

3

The Emergence of Liberal Nationalism

September 1930 was an important month for organized labor in Argentina because a significant change of government occurred and because most of the factions of the labor movement united into one organization. On September 6, the extreme right-wing General José E. Uriburu overthrew the problem-ridden and by then unpopular government of aging Hipólito Yrigoyen and ushered in a thirteen-year period in which the government, representing a coalition of conservative forces similar to that which had ruled Argentina before World War I, was hostile to the aspirations of organized labor.

A few weeks later, the members of the socialist-controlled Confederación Obrera Argentina (COA), the syndicalist-controlled Unión Sindical Argentina (USA), and a number of autonomous unions joined together to establish the organization that has since dominated the Argentine labor movement, the Confederación General del Trabajo (CGT). The written agreement uniting these groups provided that the CGT would be governed by an annual National Congress of elected delegates and by an Executive Committee. Until formal statutes could be drawn up and approved, the CGT would be governed by a temporary National Labor Committee (Comité Nacional Sindical) composed of fifteen members each from the COA and the USA, and ten from the autonomous unions. The primary function of the National Labor Committee was to write the statutes and to convoke a formal constituent assembly to establish the organization officially.[1]

In order to maintain labor unity after a decade of division caused chiefly by partisan squabbles, the leaders of the CGT insisted that it be independent of all political parties and ideological groups. The government of General Uriburu, however, made a policy of political neutrality difficult to sustain. In a manifesto of October 1, Uriburu expressed fascist sympathies. Although he insisted that he respected the Constitution of 1853 and would uphold it, he also suggested that the Argentine political system should be drastically reformed along the lines of Mussolini's corporate state. "When the representatives of the people cease being merely representatives of political committees and occupy the benches of Congress as workers, ranchers, farmers, professors, industrialists, etc.," he explained, "then our democracy will be something more than a nice word."[2]

Many labor leaders were concerned about the anti-democratic and anti-liberal ideas of Uriburu. They did not, however, want to risk dividing the newly united labor movement or incurring the wrath of the government by joining the political opposition. Moreover, many democratic groups in Argentina accepted the new government and the Supreme Court had granted it legal recognition. Therefore, the leaders of the CGT, after interviewing a representative of the Uriburu government, issued a statement outlining what they considered to be a neutral position.

The Emergence of Liberal Nationalism / 53

It said in part: "The CGT, the representative body of the sane laboring forces of the country, is convinced that the provisional government wants to reform the administrative structure of the country and is disposed to support it . . . in its institutional and social action. . . . [It is also] convinced . . . that the provisional government maintains martial law only to assure public tranquillity." [3]

The labor leaders recognized the importance of a sympathetic government, and in return for their support of Uriburu they wanted the same kind of relationship they had enjoyed with Yrigoyen. In its Minimum Program, the CGT called for full recognition of the right of unions to exist and operate freely, the participation of unions in all public institutions related to work and living conditions, and assurance that the benefits of mechanization would be accorded to all, including the workers.[4] In other words, the workers wanted to secure their position of increasing equality with the other sectors of society.

But labor was denied its aspirations when the government introduced a program that subverted the constitutional guarantees of many citizens and granted privileges to special groups. Soon after the September 6 coup, it suppressed the anarchist- and communist-led unions and followed this with attacks on the more moderate labor elements. In addition, General Uriburu denounced the minimum wage law, interrupted labor meetings, instituted a system of labor spies, broke strikes by police action, and made no effort to fulfill existing labor legislation.[5]

The government also reverted to the pre-World War I system of ruling by fraud and force, and, as was true in the earlier period, thus denied the popular classes means of gaining influence within the political structure of the country and of bringing about peaceful change. In April 1931, the government annulled the Buenos Aires provincial election because a Radical had won, and filled the vacant office with one of its own men. The next year the government again resorted to fraud to assure the election of General Augustín P. Justo as Uriburu's successor.[6]

The leaders of the CGT vigorously protested the general disregard of legal and constitutional rights and emphasized that what they wanted was to enjoy the rights of *all* citizens. By way of an example of injustice, they noted that the government had created a ten-member National Commission of Unemployment that included only one representative of the CGT. Why, they asked, should they not have equal representation with the government and industry on this important committee?[7]

The government's refusal to curtail the activities of unofficial armed bands such as the Legión Cívica was, according to the labor leaders, another denial of equal protection under the law. These groups attacked workers, acted as strike breakers, and sometimes killed men with impunity. Yet when the CGT discussed means of disarming these bands, many moderates as well as conservative elements united in their defense for fear that labor would arm and rebel.[8]

To complicate the situation, high unemployment and the stabilization of real wages put particular pressure on the leaders of the CGT to find immediate and effective solutions to the workers' problems. By 1933 about 334,000 out of 5,000,000, or 7 per cent of the working force, were unemployed. The real wages of industrial workers, which had doubled during the decade of the 1920's, remained about the same throughout the decade of the 1930's (see Table II).

The leaders of the CGT were confronted with a dilemma. On the one hand, they had adopted a policy of apolitical unionism in order to avoid dividing the labor movement or antagonizing the government. On the other hand, they believed that the governments of Uriburu and Justo were subverting the constitutional rights of the workers by deny-

TABLE II
REAL WAGES OF INDUSTRIAL WORKERS, 1929–1939 (IN PER CENT) *

1918	42	1934	99
1929	100	1935	101
1930	91	1936	95
1931	98	1937	96
1932	104	1938	96
1933	96	1939	97

* República Argentina, Departamento Nacional del Trabajo, División de Estadística, *Estadística de las huelgas* (Buenos Aires, 1940), pp. 21–22.

ing them any significant role in society and by curtailing hard-won economic and social benefits. How, the labor leaders wanted to know, could the CGT work within the limitations of its apolitical policy to alter the attitude of the hostile government and to protect its legal rights?

The dilemma produced a serious conflict within the CGT because the syndicalists of the former USA and the socialists of the former COA proposed different solutions to the problem. The syndicalists advocated continuing the policy of apolitical unionism and concentrating on specific economic issues. The socialists in effect wanted to abolish apolitical unionism so that the CGT could actively identify itself with the political groups that were opposing the oligarchy, fascism, and the government, and were defending what they considered to be the threatened democratic state.

The struggle took place within the temporary National Labor Committee of the CGT because the syndicalists, who had gained control of the organization, had never called a

National Congress. As the struggle developed, the socialists came to believe that the landed oligarchy, the Church, the military, and foreign business had combined with international fascism to deny the workers their constitutional rights, and that the syndicalists, by maintaining their policy of complete political neutrality, were lending tacit support to the "pro-fascist, anti-labor" coalition. The syndicalists denied this accusation, but their actions plus the deteriorating position of the worker caused much of organized labor to believe what the socialists claimed.

At the November 30, 1933, meeting of the National Committee, the socialists charged that a recent manifesto of the syndicalist-controlled Executive Committee was not sufficiently anti-fascist and anti-government. After a lengthy and agitated debate, the issue was temporarily resolved by the Committee's decision to appoint a special commission to draw up a declaration on fascism. But at the same time the Committee voted against cooperating with the political parties of the left in the fight against the "reactionary elements" of society, thereby defeating the socialists.[9]

The apolitical policy of the syndicalists had the support of a majority of the National Labor Committee by the end of 1933, but they could not win the support of the large and important socialist-controlled railroad, commercial employees', municipal workers', and printers' unions. Thus, early in 1934, the commercial employees repudiated the anti-fascist manifesto of the National Labor Committee because it was not strong enough. In addition, the printers' union accused the Executive Committee of the CGT of serving the "reactionary government."[10]

The struggle continued and intensified until December 12, 1935, when the socialist leaders of the Unión Ferroviaria, La Fraternidad, the Confederación General de Empleados de Comercio, the Unión Tranviaria, the Unión Obrera Municipal, and the Asociación Trabajadores del Estado, who

The Emergence of Liberal Nationalism / 57

represented a substantial majority of the labor movement, constituted themselves the new Executive Committee of the CGT. The new Committee claimed that it had taken over because the former Executive Committee had denied the wishes of the majority of the members of the CGT.[11] Within a few months it held a Constituent Congress and formally established the federation under the direction of a Central Committee and an annual National Congress.

The socialist revolt of 1935 succeeded because the ideas of the new leaders were better suited to the political situation of the 1930's than those of the syndicalists. A policy of apolitical unionism and cooperation with the government had been able to protect the workers' interests under the relatively sympathetic regime of Yrigoyen and the Radicals. The governments of Uriburu and Justo, however, which represented different groups in society, were hostile to organized labor and were attempting to "subvert the democratic state." Under these circumstances, political neutralism or political isolation was ineffective and seemed almost suicidal.

The new socialist leaders of the CGT, who believed that the interests of the workers and of the democratic state were threatened by an alliance of international fascism with conservative and anti-democratic Argentine interests, set forth a popular liberal nationalism. This nationalism, based on the values of the European immigrant and his descendants who since the 1870's had dominated the labor movement, was the articulation of the workers' desire to protect their growing identity with the traditional liberal Argentine nation envisioned by Domingo F. Sarmiento, Juan B. Justo, and, to a certain degree, by Alfredo L. Palacios. Its primary function was to create and protect a national consensus based on certain liberal concepts under attack at the time: modernization and industrialization within a free-trade economy, "Europeanization" of the country by means of continued immigration, strict adherence to the Constitution of 1853, government by competing independent political parties, and restrictions on Church and military participation in politics.

In order to create and defend this national consensus, organized labor actively intervened in politics for the first time since the anarchists had led the movement in the pre-World War I period. The labor leaders continued to pay lip service to apolitical unionism, but in fact they became very much involved in politics.

At the CGT Constituent Congress of 1936, the leaders of the organization reaffirmed their complete independence of all political parties and ideological groups. But at the same time they noted that the CGT would "constantly intervene in all national problems that affected the worker."[12] These vague statements reflected the uncertainty of the CGT leaders with regard to a political role for the labor federation. There was no indication how labor was to intervene "constantly" in all national problems that affected the worker, nor was there any indication which "national problems" affected the worker.

An article that appeared in the newspaper of the labor federation—the *CGT*—shortly after the Constituent Congress seemed to express the views of the leaders with regard to political activity. Formerly, the author of the article noted, the politics of the working class had necessarily been syndicalist and apolitical. Now, however, the situation had changed. The workers of France and even those of Spain—the country of classic apolitical unionism—had joined the popular front against fascism. Fascism, the author concluded, so threatened the continued existence of free labor unions that they were justified in committing themselves politically to supporting the country's democratic elements.[13]

The CGT dramatically manifested the political implications of its new liberal nationalism by celebrating May Day in 1936 with all of the democratic elements of Argentine

The Emergence of Liberal Nationalism / 59

society. José Domenech spoke for the CGT, Arturo Frondizi for the Radicals, Lisandro de la Torre for the Democratic Progressives, and Mario Bravo for the Socialist Party. The theme of all of the speeches was the defense of Argentine democracy against the growing threat of fascism.

Commenting on the joint celebration, an editorial in the *CGT* explained that May 1 had been a practical demonstration of the federation's apolitical policies. Labor had a specific economic mission that could not be confused with the objectives of the political parties. But, the editorial continued significantly, the political structure of the country must be changed so that it would serve everyone, and in the present situation labor must work for the same goals as the democratic political parties.[14]

The commercial employees supported this idea of temporary political involvement in more direct language. The May Day celebration, they said, manifested the political independence of the CGT but did not alienate the federation from the forces that supported concrete and common proposals for the defense of democracy.[15]

Both international and domestic events combined to increase the intensity of the socialist labor leaders' anti-fascist campaign. For example, the Argentine workers seemed to identify their cause with that of the Spanish Republicans fighting General Franco and his German and Italian allies. To help this cause and that of the anti-fascists throughout the world, the leaders of the Argentine labor federation conducted an extensive campaign to raise money for the Spanish Republicans and attempted to counteract anti-Republican propaganda printed in many of the Argentine newspapers. From 1936 to 1939, nearly every issue of the *CGT* included at least one article and sometimes more devoted to the situation in Spain.[16]

Domestic events, particularly what labor considered to be the partiality of the government and its unconstitutional acts, also stimulated the development of labor's anti-fascist campaign. "When a man is given a public function in our country," the leaders of the CGT claimed, "it is a stamp of pride for him and a tribute from his fellow citizens to his impartiality." This principle of honorable public service, they continued, was not now being upheld by those in government.[17]

In addition, the labor leaders—threatened by the government's anti-strike activity—demanded recognition of the worker as an equal member of society, entitled to full respect and protection under the law. The author of an article in *La Fraternidad*—the newspaper of the engineer and firemen's union of the same name—argued that the workers were not the enemies of the police or the state. But he insisted that the police and the government must recognize that strikes were not necessarily aimed against the state or the police, nor were they ideological; strikes were a simple attempt to win economic benefits.[18]

However, what labor considered to be arbitrary and unconstitutional acts continued. As a result of a bricklayers' strike, the government arrested and deported five labor leaders under the provisions of the Ley de Residencia. This law, argued an editorial in the *CGT*, was not only unconstitutional, but contrary to the Argentine traditions of democracy and hospitality. With this law, the landowners were attempting to dispossess the workers of their *Patria*.[19]

Despite the fraudulent presidential election of 1937, there was some hope among the democratic elements that the newly elected president, Roberto M. Ortiz, would return the country to its democratic tradition, as had President Saenz Peña twenty-five years before. President Ortiz supported the Congressional investigation of fascist penetration in Argentina that the Socialists and the Radicals had called for. He intervened in the fraudulent gubernatorial elections in the province of Buenos Aires in 1940. And he seemed to be sympathetic to the aspirations of the popular classes.[20]

The leaders of the CGT recognized the difference between President Ortiz and his immediate predecessors and began to reassert the necessity for government-labor cooperation. The future of organized labor, they noted, was "intimately bound up with the highest and most permanent interests of the country." [21] And the increasingly influential commercial employees expressed their desire to "continue collaboration [with the President] in the difficult task of improving the future of the Patria." [22]

Despite this apparent resurgence of the desire of some members of organized labor to achieve their goals through government cooperation, implementing such a policy proved impossible. Many of the same elements that had supported Uriburu and Justo supported the Ortiz government, and the good intentions of the President were often nullified by opposition within the governing coalition. Existing labor laws were ignored and anti-labor sentiments in the government remained strong.[23]

The liberal nationalism that emerged within the labor movement between 1935 and 1939 became more pronounced during the next four years because it was used for new purposes. The nationalism of the socialist-led CGT emerged in the early period as a means of defending both the interests of labor and the country's threatened democratic institutions, but after 1939 nationalism was used by the socialists to attempt to maintain their leadership of the labor movement.

In 1935 the socialists successfully challenged the syndicalists for control of the CGT because the syndicalists had failed to protect the worker against the hostility of the Uriburu and Justo governments. As leaders of the labor movement after 1935, however, the socialists were unable to do much better than their predecessors. Between 1930 and 1935 the real wages of industrial workers remained the same. Between 1935 and 1939 they fluctuated, but ultimately declined a bit (see Table II). In addition, many workers were unorganized, and discontent among the lower class remained high.[24] Under these circumstances, the newly organized communist unions and the displaced syndicalist unions challenged the socialists for the leadership of the labor movement.

The growth of communist influence in the labor movement was closely related to the growth of industrial unions. During the 1930's, Argentine industry developed rapidly because the world depression had reduced the country's capacity to import goods and had forced it to rely on domestic companies for its needs. As national industry grew, so did the number of industrial workers, and between 1935 and 1939 the population of the country increased 6 per cent while the number of persons employed in industry increased 31 per cent.[25]

The persistent and militant communists were the only ones to organize any of these new industrial workers. In 1935 and 1936 they led a series of strikes to gain recognition of their unions. This campaign culminated in the construction strikes of 1936, which in turn led to the establishment of the eventually powerful communist-dominated Federación Obrera Nacional de la Construcción (FONC).

The establishment of the FONC and its incorporation into the CGT gave the communists significant influence within the labor movement and changed the balance of labor power. In 1935 the transportation unions—the Unión Ferroviaria, La Fraternidad, and the Unión Tranviaria—had more than 100,000 members; the commercial employees had about 15,000 members; the municipal employees, about 10,000; and the textile workers, about 5,000. The construction work-

The Emergence of Liberal Nationalism / 63

ers were only partially organized and possessed very little strength.

By 1940, however, the transportation workers had increased their membership from 100,000 to 115,000, while the formerly unrepresented construction workers numbered about 50,000. At the time of the First Ordinary Congress of the CGT in 1939, the communist-led FONC had 19 of the 138 representatives, when previously it had had none.[26]

The growth of the communist-led industrial unions was important for the development of liberal nationalism in several ways. First, the leaders of these unions, following the policy of international communism, sought to form a popular front to defend Argentina's democratic institutions from the attacks of the "conservative-fascist" alliance. In 1929 the communists had established their own labor federation, the Comité de Unidad Clasista. This federation was never very successful and in 1935, in response to the new Comintern policy of cooperation with the democratic left, the Argentine communists dissolved the Comité de Unidad Clasista and joined the CGT. A popular front like the ones that developed in France or Chile never materialized in Argentina, but for a time the popular front atmosphere pervaded the Argentine left and the communists were working with the socialists in their anti-fascist campaign.

In August 1939, when Hitler and Stalin signed a non-aggression pact, the popular front atmosphere in Argentina abruptly ended. The communists and socialists, former partners, now attacked each other violently, and in response the socialists used liberal nationalism to defend their own position and discredit the communists.

At the May 1940 meeting of the Central Committee of the CGT, Secretary-General José Domenech—a member of the Socialist Party—argued that the issue in the current European struggle was a question of fascism or democracy, and that the interests of Argentine labor would best be served by a democratic victory. He therefore proposed a declaration that would "energetically repudiate all totalitarian expansion."

Pedro Chiaranti, one of the leaders of the communist-controlled FONC who had previously supported the ideas of Domenech and the socialists, now argued that the issue of the war was one of rival imperialisms and not one of democracy or fascism. Argentine labor had no interest in the matter, he declared, and so he proposed a counterdeclaration repudiating war because of its imperialistic nature and supporting Argentine neutrality. The Domenech resolution passed, but the vote of 25–17–1 indicated the relatively equal strength of the socialist and communist factions within the Central Committee.[27]

The split between the socialists and the communists involved more than a difference of opinion with regard to the Hitler-Stalin pact and the developing European conflict. The struggle was fundamentally one for control of the labor movement. The socialists controlled the older, more highly skilled, and more conservative transportation unions—La Fraternidad, the Unión Ferroviaria, the Unión Tranviaria—as well as the commercial employees and the municipal workers. Many of these unions had obtained property in the form of union buildings, vacation colonies, and hospitals. Some had social security and pension systems and others were seeking them. All had a growing number of full-time salaried union officials. These unions were non-revolutionary and believed that government cooperation—though temporarily frustrated—was essential to protect their interests.

The communists, on the other hand, represented the newer industrial unions—the construction, textile, and metal workers. They had few buildings, vacation colonies, hospitals, or pension funds to protect. They had little or nothing to conserve, and their leaders came from a younger, more aggressive, generation of workers who were not committed

The Emergence of Liberal Nationalism / 65

to the idea of cooperation with the government as the best way to protect the workers' interests. Thus the communist-socialist struggle was also one between the haves and the have-nots of the labor movement.

While the socialists fought with the communists, they also had to combat the minor challenge of the syndicalist unions displaced from a position of leadership in 1935. These unions, primarily those of the telephone and maritime workers, reestablished the Unión Sindical Argentina (USA) in 1937 and once more opposed the increasing influence of the Socialist Party in the labor movement. Nevertheless, the leaders of the USA were also concerned with the growing fascist threat to the country's democratic institutions and late in 1940, Luis Gay, Secretary-General of the USA, sent a note to the CGT suggesting "common action in defense of the liberties and conquests of the labor movement threatened by the possibility of a reactionary *coup d'état.*" [28] But because the USA had only minor influence within the labor movement, the CGT could with little danger to its position of leadership demand unity on its own terms or not at all. This position made the achievement of unity impossible.

The socialist leaders of the CGT concentrated their efforts on discrediting the communists and in so doing frequently appealed to the liberal nationalism of the workers. In August 1940, the CGT held an anti-fascist rally in Luna Park to oppose Hitler's occupation of Europe as well as pro-Axis Vice-President Ramón S. Castillo's assumption of power from the ailing President Ortiz. Ángel Borlenghi, Secretary-General of the commercial employees' union, indirectly attacked the communists by discussing organized labor's dependence on a democratic system and its obligation to unite the democratic elements of the country in defense of such a system.

Francisco Pérez Leirós, Secretary-General of the municipal workers, elaborated on the same theme. "Nothing," he declared, "is superior to the interest of the Nation." Union members must defend the democratic and representative institutions of the country because they aspired to a better life, and democracy was the most perfect instrument known of to achieve it. They could fulfill their aspirations within the law, he concluded, and their problems could be worked out within the framework of the national constitution.[29]

In a speech before an Acción Argentina demonstration in Luna Park later that year and in an interview with representatives of Argentine Libre—both non-partisan political groups opposing fascism—CGT Secretary-General José Domenech reiterated the same points. According to him, the present struggle was not one between rival imperialisms, as the communists maintained, but a struggle for existence. If the fascists won in Europe and America, Domenech warned, free and independent trade unionism would come to an end. Labor, therefore, must unite the democratic elements in defense of traditional constitutional government.[30]

When Germany invaded Russia in mid-1941, the communist labor leaders switched from a position of neutrality to fanatical support for the Allied and the Russian cause. Instead of criticizing the socialist leaders of the CGT for supporting the democratic elements in Argentina and the world in the fight against fascism as they had previously done, the communists now criticized them for not giving more assistance to the anti-fascists.

The socialists responded by challenging the sincerity of the communists as anti-fascist fighters. At the end of June, the *CGT* printed an editorial entitled "The Weather Vane of the Comintern." When the Red International was established, the editorial began, the communists attacked all other sectors of labor. With the growth of fascism, however, they established a new line of cooperation with all democratic sectors to fight against fascism. Then when the Hitler-Stalin pact was signed, the communists defended Hitler and Mussolini as victims of English imperialism and

The Emergence of Liberal Nationalism / 67

attacked democracy as a fraud designed to make the world fight an imperialist war. Most recently, Hitler's attack on Russia had produced another line that favored cooperation. What, asked the editorial, did the communists really believe?[31]

The communist-socialist conflict for control of the labor movement manifested itself clearly again in the October 1942 meeting of the Central Committee of the CGT. The Committee expelled a communist leader of the construction workers' union who had written an article attacking the socialists, and it also condemned the communist newspaper *La Hora* for repeated attacks on the CGT.[32]

The communists, now back on the side of the democratic countries fighting fascism, retaliated by attacking the CGT for not doing more against fascism in Europe and Argentina. The position of political neutrality of the CGT, they charged, was in reality an expression of solidarity with the "fascist" government of President Castillo.[33]

Secretary-General Domenech once more attempted to use nationalism to bolster his case. Originally, he noted, the socialists and the communists had worked together in the CGT. What then, he asked rhetorically, had happened? The communists had changed their policy because "foreign elements" had infiltrated their unions.[34]

In December 1942—with the two major sectors competing with each other to be the most anti-fascist—the Second Ordinary Congress of the CGT articulated its nationalism in precise terms. There the labor leaders observed that since 1930 the economic and democratic evolution of Argentina had been stunted by the ruling landed oligarchy and that the working class had suffered most during this period. To correct this situation, they claimed, the country must return to democratic constitutional government, and they insisted that labor was uniquely qualified to unite the country in defense of such a government. In their view, the labor movement, "because it is independent of all partisan and political interests, possesses the necessary conditions to stimulate the unification of all the political and economic sectors of the Republic concerned with reestablishing honest elections, permitting the representatives of the genuine majorities access to the direction of the state, guaranteeing constitutional liberty for all the inhabitants of the country, and supporting the democratic countries fighting totalitarianism. . . ."[35]

This clear expression of liberal nationalism could not obscure, even temporarily, the well-developed partisan divisions within the labor movement, and the struggle continued until the CGT formally split into two organizations. But the division of the CGT between communists and socialists was not in itself enough to divide the labor movement, because the socialists had a substantial majority on the Central Committee. Within the socialist element of the CGT, however, there was a growing rift that contributed significantly to the open division of the labor movement. One group of socialists was led by José Domenech and other leaders of the powerful Unión Ferroviaria. The other group was led by Francisco Pérez Leirós of the municipal workers and Ángel Borlenghi of the commercial employees.

A combination of reasons caused this division, including personal hostility and rivalry, and resentment of the Unión Ferroviaria's domination of the CGT. The most important reason, however, was mutual distrust of the political intentions of the opposition. The Domenech group wanted to make the CGT into a labor party, or to create a separate labor party, either of which could assume leadership in uniting the democratic elements of the country. The Pérez Leirós-Borlenghi group wanted the Socialist Party to represent the political interests of labor and feared that the Domenech group would develop the CGT into a rival political organization to replace the Socialist Party.[36]

This split among the socialist members of the CGT contributed decisively to the schism in the whole organization. At the October 1942 meeting of the Central Committee mentioned above, Domenech resigned as Secretary-General ostensibly because the Committee had permitted the Federación Gráfica Bonaerense to continue in the CGT even though it was behind in the payment of its dues. Technically Domenech was correct; the statutes of the federation specifically forbade a member to continue on the Central Committee if it fell behind in payment. But his resignation in order to enforce his point of view made this minor conflict a major issue. A vote to reconsider the original motion that permitted the printers to continue on the Committee went against the Domenech faction 22–19–1, and the socialists Ángel Borlenghi, Francisco Pérez Leirós, and José Argaña voted with the communists in opposition to Domenech, thus establishing the alliance that was to divide the labor federation.[37]

The actual division occurred at the March 1943 meeting of the Central Committee, at which the members were to elect new officials. Two lists of candidates were presented. List Number One was headed by Domenech. List Number Two, headed by Pérez Leirós, was supported by the communists and the anti-Domenech group of socialists. When Marcos D. Lestelle of the Unión Ferroviaria voted for List Number Two, the Unión Ferroviaria replaced him with Juan Rodríquez, who then voted for List Number One. With the vote of Rodríquez, the Domenech group won by a single vote, 23–22. The opposition charged that the elections had been fraudulent and withdrew.[38]

Because both Domenech and Pérez Leirós were members of the Socialist Party, the party's Executive Committee attempted to resolve the problem. But the split came about precisely because Domenech and his followers were more loyal to labor than to the Socialist Party, and so the latter could not possibly settle the matter. The CGT therefore divided into two hostile camps with about equal numerical strength: the CGT Number One, composed of the unions whose first loyalty was to labor—the Unión Ferroviaria, the Unión Tranviaria, and the Sindicato de Cerveceros; and the CGT Number Two, which included the unions whose first loyalty was to the Socialist or the Communist Party—La Fraternidad, the commercial employees, the municipal workers, the printers, the state workers, and the FONC.[39]

On the eve of the Perón era, organized labor was in an ambiguous position. On the one hand, the CGT had approximately 331,000 members, out of a total of 547,000 organized workers in the country. Furthermore, by actively participating in the anti-fascist campaign of the late 1930's and early 1940's, the CGT had for the first time identified labor with substantial segments of Argentine society. On the other hand, less than a third of the country's industrial workers and about a tenth of all persons employed in some capacity were organized, and the overwhelming majority of them were concentrated in Buenos Aires and Rosario.[40] Organized labor had produced a liberal nationalism to defend its interests, but it was divided and certainly not a genuinely representative or national movement.

4

Labor's Nationalisms and the Rise of Perón

Since 1943 the history of Argentine labor and nationalism has been intimately bound up with the career and personality of Juan Domingo Perón. Perón was the first influential Argentine leader to recognize the potential political significance of the workers' frustrated aspirations, as articulated in their developing nationalisms, and between 1943 and 1946 he skillfully used the ideas and groups within the labor movement to help him obtain political power. On the one hand, he undermined the influence of the Communist and Socialist Parties by asserting that they were foreign to the Argentine tradition. And, on the other, he supported those who believed that labor should be an independent political force and encouraged the development of criollo nationalism among the rapidly growing number of internal migrant workers. As a result, Perón was able to gain political power, and in the process labor achieved new status within Argentine society.

Perón was only one of a number of pro-Axis colonels and

generals who participated in the June 4, 1943, coup to overthrow President Ramón S. Castillo and prevent his succession by pro-Allied Patrón Costas. He did not at first, however, control the new government and after several days of political struggle, General Pedro P. Ramírez emerged as Provisional President. Ramírez assured the Argentines that the armed forces had acted only to defend the honor and traditions of the country and to end government by fraud and corruption.

Although it was short-lived, organized labor's initial reaction to the Ramírez government was favorable. Since Yrigoyen's first presidency, many labor leaders had understood the necessity of working with the government to protect their economic and social gains and to promote their identity as part of the national community. They had had some success with this policy during the Yrigoyen era, but very little from 1930 to 1943. Therefore, when the armed forces overthrew President Castillo, the labor leaders were willing to entertain the idea of cooperating with the new government on the grounds that any government would be better than the previous ones. An editorial in the *CGT* criticized the old rulers for failing to satisfy the aspirations of the people, return the country to constitutional rule, and solve the major economic problems of the country. The declarations of the new government, the editorial concluded, had led to high expectations on the part of organized labor.[1]

In mid-July the government disbanded the CGT Number Two because it was an "extremist organization," and many of its affiliates reluctantly rejoined the CGT Number One. This encouraged and pleased the leaders of the CGT Number One and throughout July and August they continued to support the government. They did not protest the passage of the Ley de Asociaciones Profesionales, which provided for government regulation of the activities of the labor unions.[2] And in a *CGT* editorial, the leaders of the federa-

Labor's Nationalisms and the Rise of Perón / 73

tion suggested that the traditional working-class suspicion of all government intervention in the development of the labor movement was unnecessary because in many cases state intervention could benefit the workers.³

It soon became evident, however, that the Ramírez government—like the government of José E. Uriburu thirteen years before—was anti-labor. In August, the large and important Unión Ferroviaria and La Fraternidad were subjected to intervention and forced to withdraw from the CGT. As a result, Secretary-General Domenech, a member of the Unión Ferroviaria, resigned his position and issued a manifesto demanding the return of independent trade unionism. The Executive Committee of the CGT transferred the records and funds of the organization to the homes of several members, and the furniture to the Unión Tranviaria building. It adjourned indefinitely until the remaining Committee members could decide whether or not to continue the federation.⁴

The members did decide to reconstitute the Central Committee of the CGT despite the forced absence of the railroad unions and within three weeks elected a new Executive Committee. The CGT leaders now attacked the Ley de Asociaciones Profesionales, which many had formerly accepted. This law, they now insisted, imposed unionism on workers, discriminated against immigrants, and denied some persons the freedom to organize.⁵

A direct attack on the government followed the attack on the Ley de Asociaciones Profesionales. Union organization had increased as industrialization had progressed, a *CGT* editorial stated. Now, however, the government had begun an illogical attack on unionism in Tucumán, Santa Fe, Córdoba, Entre Ríos, and Corrientes that left business free to exploit the workers. "The country does not belong to the privileged minority," the editorial concluded, in a manner reminiscent of the pre-1943 period, "and cannot be governed entirely for its benefit."⁶

Labor unrest and strikes increased during the month of October 1943, and the government responded by arresting dozens of labor leaders. In December, the government further antagonized the liberal labor leaders by reinstating Catholic religious instruction in the public schools, outlawing political parties, and establishing rigid control of the press. Within seven months, Ramírez had completely alienated organized labor.

Colonel Juan D. Perón was watching closely the developments of labor-government relations. Despite his collaboration with the right-wing military faction, at some point during this period he recognized that the present government could not, as the governments of the 1930's had attempted to do, maintain its position by force alone. He understood that to survive it would have to have broad popular political support and he determined to use the labor movement as the basis of this support. Thus, while the Ramírez government was frustrating the aspirations of labor, Perón was establishing a personal relationship with a few of its leaders.

Perón's first contact with labor leaders was in early July 1943, when he and his close friend Colonel Domingo Mercante met with Ángel Borlenghi and José Argaña, the representatives of the Pérez Leirós faction of the CGT. Although the CGT Number Two was intervened in a few weeks later, these men continued to meet with Perón and became personally attached to him. Juan A. Bramuglia, a lawyer for the Unión Ferroviaria, Francisco Pablo Capozzi of La Fraternidad, and others were added to this group. From these meetings Perón learned what the labor leaders wanted: equal status with all other groups as part of Argentine society and a government that represented their interests and aspirations. More specifically, they wanted freedom to organize throughout the country, an effective Ministry of Labor, pension and social security systems, and an end to government intervention in the unions.[7]

Perón, anxious to associate himself with the aspirations of labor, used his influence within the new government to fulfill some of these demands. He indicated his support for labor's right to organize by aiding the packing house workers in their strike of September 1943. Through Perón's influence the strike was settled and the workers signed their first collective bargaining contract. In addition, Perón walked down the streets of Berisso, one of the centers of the meat-packing industry, with his arm around the shoulders of Cipriano Reyes, the leader of the workers. For the first time since the Yrigoyen period, the workers had the active support of an important government official.

On October 27, 1943, the government appointed Perón to the apparently insignificant post of head of the Department of Labor and Social Security. Within a month he succeeded in elevating the importance of his new post by transforming the department into an independent secretariat whose head had cabinet rank. In his new position as Secretary of Labor and Social Security, Perón was better able to meet the demands of the labor leaders. Although he did not end the intervention in the railroad unions, he changed interventors—government-appointed officials to run the unions. The original interventors were strongly opposed by the unions, but the new appointee, Colonel Domingo Mercante, the son of a railroad engineer, was well liked by both the leaders and workers. And in December 1943 Perón's efforts led to the suspension of Ramírez' now strongly opposed Ley de Asociaciones Profesionales.

In addition to fulfilling many of their specific demands, Perón understood that fundamentally the labor leaders wanted government help to achieve a new status within society. In a *CGT* editorial, the labor leaders stated that in the past state intervention had been despotic, instituted for the benefit of a small minority. Now, the editorial continued, the need was for state intervention in collaboration with the people for the benefit of all.[8]

In his speech at the establishment of the Secretariat of Labor, Perón appeared to respond to the *CGT* editorial. "I have never believed that the problems of labor and management were private matters," he began. In the past, "the state remained aloof from the working population. It did not regulate social activities, as was its duty; it only had contact [with labor] . . . when the fear of seeing the apparent order of the street upset obliged it to descend from . . . its ivory tower." Now the government must encourage a labor organization with "a deep-rooted love of the Patria and absolute respect for law," Perón concluded, "and we must be able to count on the loyalty and support of all the workers as we move along the road toward the greatness of the Patria."[9]

Continuing his effort to give labor new status within the emerging Argentine nation, Perón spoke of the virtue of work. "Work, after the home and school, is an irreplaceable molder of the character of individuals," he declared. Work molds individual character, plus "collective habits and customs," and therefore "the national tradition."[10]

The leaders of the CGT were delighted. Perón, an important government official, was suggesting a role for labor of which they had only dreamed. He was helping them to achieve new status and influence by protecting their rights to organize, by establishing a Secretariat of Labor, by arguing that labor should be a partner with the government in the development of the country, and by saying that work was the molder of the national tradition. By the end of 1943, Perón had laid the foundation upon which to build an enduring personal relationship with labor.

Before Perón could proceed with his plans, he had to gain greater influence within the government, and during the first six months of 1944 he was able to do so. On February 24, the unpopular General Ramírez was forced to retire and a close associate of Perón, General Edelmiro Farrell, replaced him as Provisional President. At the same time Perón became Minister of War. His influence continued to grow and in early July he became Provisional Vice-President of the country. By mid-1944, as Secretary of Labor, Minister of War, and Vice-President, Perón was the most powerful man in the government.

Once in a secure position within the government, Perón intensified his efforts to win the personal support of the workers. He stated and restated the important idea that the interests of the nation should be the same as those of labor, and he promised all workers new status, dignity, and influence within Argentine society. Specifically, Perón again stressed the dignity of work. The Leaders of the Revolution have divided the country into two groups, he explained. One group consisted of the men who worked; the other group consisted of the men who lived off those who worked. "We have placed ourselves openly at the side of the men who work." [11]

In addition to seeking support through his speeches, Perón competed for the nationalist mantle by carrying out a program that substantially benefited the workers. He encouraged and assisted the organization of the long-exploited sugar workers of the north, the wine workers of Mendoza, the wood workers and others. He demanded that existing laws such as those providing for paid vacations, for protection against arbitrary job dismissal, and for restricting monopolies be enforced. He initiated new legislation to establish much needed labor courts in all parts of the country, price controls on articles of primary necessity, and protection for rural workers. And he helped the commercial employees to establish a pension system, and the railroad workers to improve their existing pension system, raise money

78 / Labor, Nationalism, and Politics in Argentina

for a clinic, win increased salaries, and terminate government intervention in their unions.

One of Perón's most popular acts was to appoint labor leaders to important government positions. For example, he made Juan A. Bramuglia, a former lawyer for the Unión Ferroviaria, federal interventor in the important province of Buenos Aires. For a long time, noted a writer in *La Fraternidad*, men from the upper classes had held high government positions, particularly in the province of Buenos Aires. Now, however, a man of humble background, familiar and sympathetic with the workers, had become the interventor.[12]

At the same time that he appealed to the economic interests and psychological aspirations of labor, Perón sought to win the political support of the workers by undermining the influence of the Socialist and Communist Parties. The government intervention in the CGT Number Two in July 1943 weakened the traditional working-class parties' hold over the labor movement, but they managed to maintain some strength within the CGT Number One. In mid-1944 Perón openly attacked these groups. "Foreign ideologies," he explained, with reference to socialism and communism, "constitute without doubt . . . the worst sickness of the working masses. The politicians have always exploited this factor to divide the working classes and to use them for their benefit." The present government, he warned, would not permit any foreign element to develop in the labor organizations.[13]

Perón's policies were successful to the extent that a majority of the liberal workers supported him because he had done more for labor than any other individual in Argentine history. A few liberals—those most closely identified with the Socialist Party—opposed the government, but whenever a specific issue arose, the CGT followed Perón and most of the liberal leaders of the federation seemed to move closer to some of his positions.

The CGT's support of government protection of industry is an interesting case of the liberals' *rapprochement* with Perón. To protect and encourage industry, the government established a Bank of Industrial Credit, a Secretariat of Industry and Commerce, and protective tariffs on certain items. The traditionally free-trade-oriented CGT went along with this program, including the protective tariffs. Argentina could not base its economic independence on agriculture and livestock alone, a *CGT* editorial explained, because it would always be subject to the whims of foreign manufacturers for its needs. The country must defend its national industry against the "improper" use of freedom of trade.[14] This was not a wholesale endorsement of protectionism, but it was a significant modification of labor's traditional concepts of free trade.

The CGT's endorsement of the government's neutral foreign policy is another important example of the liberals' modification of their traditional ideals. Up to that time, the labor organization had strongly supported a policy of cooperation with the democratic countries of the Western Hemisphere and the world. But the liberal leaders of the CGT now explained that neutrality did not mean opposition to or isolation from the democratic countries. It was simply a policy of support for the government against foreign pressure that might "frustrate the national will."[15]

By the end of 1944, the CGT and many of the leading unions of the country supported Perón and the government because together they had given labor new status within society. Perón had won popular support, the leaders of the CGT explained, because of his active sympathy for the working class. It was for the good of the country that the *de facto* government had replaced the clique that ruled by fraud and "institutional subversion."[16]

The leaders of La Fraternidad expressed similar views. The Revolution of June had been Argentine in all of its phases and for this reason the foreign trusts had opposed it. Most important, they continued, the Revolution had begun "the era of achievement" and improved the worker's position in the country. The worker was no longer an outcast.[17]

The leaders of the Unión Ferroviaria criticized the "unjust intervention" of the Ramírez regime in their union, but pointed out that such intervention had served to end the myth that the railroad workers were "professional agitators." Perón, they noted with obvious pride, now the most important member of the government, had publicly proclaimed that the railroad workers were the country's model union. The new government had revolutionized the social panorama of the country. "Today the force of the State is at the service of social justice," and the voice of the worker had the same authority and respect as others.[18]

At the same time that he was courting the members of organized labor and particularly the liberals of the CGT Number One, Perón sought the support of the unorganized workers from the interior, who were becoming an increasingly important part of the working force in the cities.

The world depression and World War II stimulated the process of industrialization in Argentina by once more isolating her from the European countries that had traditionally supplied her with manufactured goods. The corresponding demand for industrial workers, the mechanization of agriculture and the relative decline in the number of agricultural jobs, and the government's restrictive immigration policy caused a large migration of workers from the rural areas of the interior into Buenos Aires and the other cities of the country.

Although there had been some internal migration in Argentina for many years, it was not until the late 1930's that it reached significant proportions. In 1914 11 per cent

Labor's Nationalisms and the Rise of Perón / 81

of the population of greater Buenos Aires had been born in the interior and 49 per cent had been born abroad. By 1936 still no more than 12 per cent of the population of the federal capital had been born in the interior, and 36 per cent came from abroad. By 1947, however, 29 per cent of the city's population had been born in the interior and only 26 per cent abroad. In absolute terms, an average of 8,000 persons born in the interior arrived in Buenos Aires each year between 1896 and 1936. This number increased to 72,000 annually between 1936 and 1943, and to 117,000 annually between 1943 and 1947.[19]

Migration destroyed the traditional communal ties of the rural peon, as it had those of the European worker, and caused him also to seek a new communal identity in the urban environment. Before 1943, however, his efforts to do so were frustrated. The government ignored him and the socialist leaders of the CGT did not incorporate him into the labor movement or attempt to help him in any way.

The leaders of the pre-1943 CGT were aware of this migration, but apparently failed to grasp its significance for the future of labor and the political development of the country. As early as June 1938, the author of an article in the *CGT* complained that before the labor organization had been able to absorb the unemployed from the world depression, it was being threatened by the rural peons who were fleeing to the centers of population in search of work. Between 1938 and 1943, the CGT leaders continued to indicate their awareness of the increasing numbers of migrants from the interior, but they did little or nothing about them.[20]

The internal migrants and the organized workers viewed each other with hostility and suspicion. The members of the CGT unions were largely of European immigrant stock, skilled or semi-skilled workers, and they lived in Buenos Aires or one of the other cities on or near the east coast. The new workers came from the rural areas of the interior;

they were illiterate, unskilled, and unorganized. They had no knowledge of socialism, fascism, democracy, or the Constitution of 1853. Their conception of government was the paternalistic, authoritarian, patrón-peon relationship of the *estancia*.[21]

The socialist labor leaders of the pre-1943 CGT, inheritors of much of the liberal democratic tradition of Domingo F. Sarmiento and Juan B. Justo, associated the internal migrant with what they believed to be the anti-democratic, anti-progressive, Hispanic criollo tradition of the interior. The internal migrant associated the labor leaders with abstract foreign ideas and with efforts to obliterate his criollo traditions and values. And as the internal migrants became the largest single element of the working class, the nationalism of the socialist labor leaders became the doctrine of an elite.

Under these circumstances, Perón had little difficulty appealing to the internal migrants. He helped them organize unions to protect their economic interests, attacked what they considered to be the "foreign" ideologies of socialism and communism, defended the Church and religious education, and articulated many of their criollo ideals. In the process, the uprooted workers from the interior identified personally with Perón and came to envision him as something of a new patrón who was their labor leader, their government, and the embodiment of their nation.

Ángel Perelman, Secretary-General of the Unión Obrera Metalúrgica (UOM) from its establishment in 1943 to 1946, clearly articulated this criollo, or anti-liberal, nationalism. He claimed that the Socialist and Communist Parties, along with the CGT, had betrayed the interests of the workers and the nation and therefore should be replaced by genuine national workers' organizations. These groups, he maintained, were European imports which, because they did not protest the overthrow of the authentically Argentine and popular government of Hipólito Yrigoyen and because they supported the "bourgeois policy" of free trade, were nothing more than the left wing of the liberal oligarchy.²²

What seemed to bother Perelman most, however, was the exclusiveness and elitism of the traditional workers' organizations. Like Manuel Ugarte and Alfredo Palacios, he believed that the criollo tradition was a fundamental element of the emerging Argentine nation. Therefore, he insisted, the CGT was not a genuinely national organization; it represented only the "aristocracy of labor," the skilled European immigrant stock organized in unions that served the foreign-owned public services. Why, he wanted to know, did the CGT not organize the unskilled criollo workers who were filling the jobs in Argentina's new industries?

What Argentina needed, Perelman suggested, was a truly national labor party and federation that together would seek to incorporate the criollo worker, protect Argentine industry, and destroy the power of the liberal bourgeoisie, the landowners, and the foreign capitalists. Such organizations would be important for the development of a new Argentine nation, faithful to its Hispanic-criollo traditions.

Hilario Salvo, who in 1946 succeeded Perelman as Secretary-General of the UOM, commented further on some of these ideas. He pointed out that the criollo nationalists were anti-liberal and anti-democratic because liberal democracy in Argentina had resulted in the exploitation of the powerless masses by the wealthy landed oligarchy. Therefore the criollo nationalists wanted an all-powerful government, capable of curbing the power of the oligarchy and protecting the interests of all members of society. Civil liberties should be protected, Salvo concluded, but in cases of conflict the government should intervene to make sure that the rights of society as a whole predominated over those of the individual.²³

Thus the criollo nationalism that would become the dominant concept of the labor movement was an articulation of the hostility and fear that the workers from the interior felt toward the traditional ruling groups of society, plus an expression of their desire to protect their own traditional values and way of life.

Although Perón had won the support of a majority of labor by the end of 1944, this support was not as absolute as it first appeared to be. In mid-1945 the termination of World War II and the preparation for national elections led to an easing of government restrictions on the activities of political parties and labor unions. As a result, considerable labor opposition appeared. The increasingly isolated socialists of the former CGT Number Two openly broke with the leadership of the existing CGT and attacked Perón and the government for "perverting" the liberal democratic system. This split was a continuation of the split in the CGT in March 1943. On the one hand, there was a minority of socialists and communists who believed that their parties should represent the political interests of the worker, and who opposed Perón as a fascist. On the other, there was a large majority of syndicalists and socialists whose primary loyalty was to the labor movement, who believed that labor needed a new, independent, political party to represent its interests, and who supported Perón. From 1945 on, the former were called "liberals" and the latter "laboristas," even though both groups continued to hold many liberal ideas in common.[24]

The liberal unions that opposed Perón were La Fraternidad, the shoemakers, the textile workers, a segment of the commercial employees, and a segment of the Unión Tranviaria. Concerned about the government's limitation of the right to strike, the intervention in the municipal and metal workers' unions, and what they considered to be other restrictions on labor freedom, these unions joined together in mid-1945 to protest the government's actions.

Although in 1944 it had apparently supported Perón, in May 1945 the Executive Committee of La Fraternidad passed a series of resolutions attacking the "undemocratic actions" of the government. Appealing to labor's liberal nationalism, the Committee demanded the reestablishment of the constitutional rights of freedom of the press, freedom of speech, and freedom of association. It also called for termination of the state of siege, reestablishment of "institutional normality," and an end to isolation from the democratic countries of the world.[25]

In mid-1945 Perón, uncertain as to its extent, attempted to head off the liberal labor opposition to the government by responding to a number of its demands. On June 9 the government freed all political prisoners of democratic persuasion. On July 7 President Farrell announced that presidential elections would be held in the near future. On August 6 the government lifted the state of siege that had been in effect since the end of 1941. And in an important speech at the Colegio Militar in mid-August, Perón defended the social and economic revolution before his military colleagues. "Government of the popular mass is beginning," he declared. "It is a fact that the army must accept. If we do not bring about a pacific revolution, the people will initiate a violent one."[26]

Despite these efforts, Perón was unable to satisfy his liberal labor critics, and in September and October this dissident group increased its attacks on the government. Perón, fearful of the political effects of this continuing labor opposition, decided to end it by whatever methods were necessary.

The laboristas, although they constituted a substantial majority of the CGT, found themselves in an uncomfortable position. They supported the achievements of Perón and wanted more of them, but they also agreed with many of the criticisms of the liberals. Without attacking the government, they began to talk of the need to reestablish constitutional rule and maintained that the Argentine workers were united by their sense of democratic responsibility. They felt the same responsibility as did Argentines on May 25, 1810— as did Mariano Moreno and later Esteban Echeverría and Roque Saenz Peña.[27]

The laborista leaders of the Unión Ferroviaria reiterated these ideas. In their view, the Argentine nation was fortified by common sentiments of democracy and liberty that identified it with the ideals of the founding fathers. Therefore, the government should release all political prisoners, terminate the state of siege, and return to constitutional rule.[28]

In addition, the laboristas were anxious to be on the winning side and were afraid that the labor liberals, united with the non-labor democratic opposition, might win the struggle against the regime. Therefore, they attempted not to alienate themselves from either group.

The liberals made their most decisive move early in September when La Fraternidad, the textile union, and the shoe workers withdrew from the CGT. They were supported by wildcat groups within the commercial employees' union and the Unión Tranviaria. Jesús Fernández, president of La Fraternidad, justified the withdrawal by once more appealing to liberal nationalism. "The so-called CGT does not actually represent the authentic labor movement," he began, "inasmuch as its leaders . . . have placed themselves at the service of foreign causes that are in conflict with the [Argentine] labor tradition." The CGT, he charged, "has remained indifferent to the closing of and intervention in unions, the detention of leaders, the assaults on workers, the . . . creation of divisionist unions, the proscription of union liberty and democracy, international isolation, the high cost of living . . . [and] inflation." [29]

This attack came at a time when general opposition to Perón was reaching a climax. There was growing hostility toward the government among nearly all the political parties, principal newspapers, intellectuals, and university students, not to mention business and financial organizations. Shortly after the new United States Ambassador, Spruille Braden, arrived in May 1945, he openly supported this opposition and took a leading part in it. The lifting of the state of siege in August gave the opposition greater freedom to work and it made the most of the opportunity. The culmination of this effort was the September 19 March of the Constitution and Liberty, in which more than 250,000 persons took part. Many thought it meant the end for Perón.[30]

With the liberals openly opposing him and many laboristas waiting to see who would win the struggle, Perón acted to ensure his control of labor. Late in September he precipitated a change in the leadership of the CGT, replacing Secretary-General Alcides Montiel with the more "reliable" Silverio Pontieri, and a few days later the government reimposed the state of siege. Finally, on October 2 the government decreed a new Ley de Asociaciones Profesionales that permitted only unions with government-granted legal recognition (*personería gremial*) to bargain with the state and the employer.[31]

As Perón attempted to consolidate his labor support, the struggle with non-labor opposition became more intense. On October 9, the Campo de Mayo garrison, led by its commander General Eduardo Ávalos, moved on Buenos Aires and forced Perón to resign from all three of his offices. Both the pro- and anti-Perón forces were confused by this development, but the latter were more confused. For example, General Ávalos permitted Perón to speak to the workers on October 10 and to remind them that he had signed an order for a general pay increase that he hoped the new government would grant. In addition, the opposition rather foolishly proposed solutions that only antagonized and frightened labor. One group argued that the conservative, anti-labor Supreme Court should take over the country. And business, with Perón out of office, refused to grant the workers the officially recognized paid holiday, Día de la Raza, on October 12.

Everyone in the labor movement except the small group of liberals felt threatened by the Ávalos coup, and while the opposition groups argued among themselves, most of labor united and organized for its self-defense. An *ad hoc* committee of five laboristas, including CGT Secretary-General Silverio Pontieri, Ángel Borlenghi, Alcides Montiel, Luis Gay, and Néstor Álvarez, met to decide how best to preserve the gains made during the past two years. They visited Perón who, according to Luis Gay, was of little help because he was afraid and did not know what to do.[32]

After October 12, when the Ávalos government arrested Perón and confined him on the island of Martín García, the labor leaders acted on their own. On October 14 the CGT declared a strike and the next day Cipriano Reyes, the head of the recently established but nevertheless powerful meat packers' union, appeared before the leaders of the federation and demanded immediate implementation of the strike declaration. On October 16, the Central Committee of the CGT, composed primarily of laboristas and a few anti-liberals, met to decide what specific action they should take. The labor leaders were uncertain as to the best course and therefore took nearly ten hours to make up their minds. The representatives of the older unions—the printers and the railroad workers—argued against the implementation of the general strike call on the grounds that General Ávalos was in effective control of the country and had given labor adequate guarantees that the gains of the past two years would be maintained. The representatives of the newer industrial unions supported the general strike because they claimed that labor could not trust General Ávalos. The latter group, although few in number, was the most persuasive and at one o'clock in the morning the Central Com-

Labor's Nationalisms and the Rise of Perón / 89

mittee voted 21 to 19 to declare a revolutionary general strike for October 18.[33] After the vote was taken, all groups within the CGT actively supported the strike

On the day after the CGT meeting, October 17, Eva Duarte, Perón's mistress and future wife, Cipriano Reyes, Colonel Domingo Mercante, Hilario Salvo, Luis Gay, Ángel Perelman, and others went about urging the laborista and anti-liberal workers to converge on the presidential palace in anticipation of the general strike.[34] Tens of thousands of workers, particularly the meat packers and the metal workers, responded to this call, and by late afternoon the Plaza de Mayo in front of the Casa Rosada, the presidential palace, was filled to its capacity of approximately 100,000 persons. The pro-Perón police and armed forces restrained objectors from interfering with the demonstration. In the early evening the laborista committee met with President Farrell, who apparently was waiting to see what was going to happen, and arranged for Perón to be released and permitted to speak from the balcony of the Casa Rosada. At midnight Perón appeared and gave a short speech, devoted mainly to telling the workers to go home, but it was enough to convince them that he had been restored to power and that the gains of the past two years would be protected.[35]

October 17 was significant for many reasons. Perhaps most important was the fact that it intensified the workers' growing feelings of national identification by making them aware of their own political power. By their presence in the Plaza de Mayo they had forced what they considered to be the conservative anti-labor opposition to restore Perón —the symbol of the egalitarian nation they envisioned—to power. Now, after years of frustrated attempts to establish their influence within Argentine society, they had succeeded, and they were determined to enjoy and protect their new status.

October 17 also enabled Perón to consolidate and reassert

control over both his military and his labor supporters. The military, faced with the alternative of civil war or Perón and his social and economic program, chose the latter. The laborista leadership of the CGT, faced with the alternative of Perón's sometimes undemocratic methods plus his social and economic program or no social and economic program at all, also chose Perón.

In addition, the events of October 17 solidified the realignment of the labor power structure; the laborista leadership joined with the anti-liberal workers to gain nearly absolute control of the labor movement, and the formerly influential liberals, who did not participate in the demonstrations, were left with but a small following and no influence. In response to a suggestion in the conservative press that the demonstration was an "artificially stimulated demagogic trick," *El Obrero Ferroviario,* the newspaper of the laborista-controlled Unión Ferroviaria, pointed out that labor had not responded to demagoguery, but had defended its legitimate conquests, goals it had fought for over many years.[36]

Finally, October 17 was significant because it fixed the name *descamisados,* or "shirtless ones," upon the masses who supported Perón. The term had been used by the well-to-do to indicate their disgust for the masses, but after October 17 the latter willingly accepted this label to indicate their pride in being poor but hard workers who were the basis of the emerging nation. The descamisados even claimed to be the heirs of the *sans-culottes* of the French Revolution. They were the new "criollo sans-culottes," a *CGT* editorial proudly proclaimed, and on October 17 they had saved the Perón Revolution.[37]

Shortly after October 17, the laborista leadership of the CGT—familiar with the history and recent electoral victory of the British Labour Party and anxious to institutionalize the political power of the workers—established the

Partido Laborista Argentino, formulated a program, and elected Luis Gay and Cipriano Reyes as president and vice-president of the organization.

The election of Gay and Reyes as leaders of the new party was logical. Both men had won the respect of the antiliberal as well as the laborista sectors of the movement; they had been strong supporters of Perón from the beginning; and they had been among the most active in the events of October 17. In addition, Gay had been urging the formation of just such an independent non-partisan labor party for many years.[38]

Gay and Reyes rejected the elitism of the discredited liberals and the latter's identification with the Socialist Party because they conceived of the Partido Laborista as an independent political counterpart of an independent CGT. "We are a national party, . . . by our scope, by our roots, and by the earnestness with which we seek national solutions to national problems," Reyes explained. The party expressed the "national collectivity. . . . We reject and combat the pretended irreconcilability" between workers and intellectuals. It proclaimed the "essential virtue of work, fountain of all success, basis of all conquest, and rock of human virtues, including knowledge, wisdom, and the spiritual values. We believe and proclaim that . . . [all groups] —workers, students, producers, and professionals—are part of the people." [39]

Nevertheless, Gay and Reyes accepted most of the ideas of liberal nationalism and incorporated them into the party's program: constitutional government; restrictions on the political activity of the Church and the military; industrialization based on a free-trade economy; continued European immigration to help meet the demand for labor; agrarian reform without abolishing the right to private property; nationalization of public services and a few basic industries owned in large part by foreigners; rent, property, and inheritance taxes; profit sharing; and social security. It was a program for a national social revolution, but significantly this revolution was meant to be carried out by democratic means.[40] Thus, although it was supported for a time by the anti-liberals, the Partido Laborista with its philosophy of *laborismo* was a political expression of liberal nationalism.

In retrospect it is possible to accuse the Laborista leaders of unpardonable naïveté. They were confronted with an unsolvable dilemma, but they refused to recognize it as such. They thought they could support Perón and the social and economic revolution without supporting his undemocratic methods or losing their independence. Only time could convince the party leaders that it was impossible to do both.

On January 15, 1946, the Partido Laborista freely nominated Perón as its candidate for the presidency in the February elections on the grounds that he had done more than any other individual for labor. Although there was some resentment when Perón insisted that the party accept the dissident Radical J. Hortensio Quijano instead of Colonel Domingo Mercante as its candidate for vice-president, the resentment was not profound and had little or no consequence on the outcome of the election. Perón, by running with a Radical, was making an obvious bid for the mantle of Hipólito Yrigoyen, the only Argentine President who had manifested any sympathy for the working class, and most of the workers did not object.

During the campaign, the Laborista-backed Perón appealed both to the laborista variety of liberal nationalism and to criollo nationalism. He portrayed himself as the protector of labor and as the defender of the Constitution and the laws of the land. In this campaign he was greatly assisted by the ineptness and the disunity of the opposition.

Labor opposition continued to manifest itself between

Labor's Nationalisms and the Rise of Perón / 93

October 1945 and February 1946, but it only strengthened Perón's hold over the majority of the workers. At the International Labor Organization (ILO) meeting in Paris in late 1945, the socialist and former head of the CGT Number Two Francisco Pérez Leirós and the communist Rubens Iscaro, supported by the pro-communist Mexican labor leader Vicente Lombardo Toledano, claimed that the Perón regime was fascist-inspired and that the CGT was not an independent labor organization. Because of these attacks, the CGT delegates were not admitted to the ILO Congress that year.[41]

The labor opposition, still fighting the battles of the late 1930's and early 1940's, attempted to discredit Perón by calling him a fascist. But Perón skillfully linked this opposition to the conservative European-oriented elements in Argentina and thus sought to undermine whatever appeal it might still have had for the workers. In November 1945, the Socialists and Communists along with their labor following had united with the Radicals and some of the Conservatives to establish the anti-Perón Unión Democrática. Perón had merely to allude to this fact to convince most workers that the traditional workers' parties were allied with the "reactionary elements" to overthrow the regime of social revolution.

The laborista leaders of the CGT attacked both parties for supporting the oligarchy. CGT Secretary-General Pontieri explained that when the Socialists and Communists were unable to control the syndicalist FORA IX during the Yrigoyen period, they had charged that the organization was subservient to the government. Today, he concluded, they were making the same baseless charge against the CGT because they could not admit that the workers simply preferred the government to them.[42]

At first the campaign focussed on Decree No. 33,302 of

December 20, 1945, which provided for salary increases for most workers and a month's pay as a Christmas bonus. Business responded promptly and decisively to the challenge. At a meeting on December 27, the members of the Unión Industrial Argentina, the leading industrial association in the country, declared that the Christmas bonus was unconstitutional, that salary matters were an exclusive part of the deliberative process between business and labor, that financially it was impossible for business to meet the demands of the decree, and that the latter imposed a false economic solution to Argentine problems that would have "detrimental moral consequences." To dramatize their protest, the industrialists closed their factories and shops for three days.[43]

The CGT immediately sent a note to President Farrell saying that under no circumstances would the workers permit the decree to go unenforced, that labor supported the government measures to enforce it and to break the "reactionary lock-out" of the employers, and that labor stood behind the government's plan for industrial development.[44]

At the height of this controversy the Supreme Court declared unconstitutional the decree that authorized the Secretary of Labor to appoint provincial and territorial delegates with the power to levy fines against those who did not obey labor laws. Most of labor feared that the gains of the past two years would be critically undermined because the employers could now with impunity disobey the decrees of the Secretary of Labor.[45] It appeared to many people that the only way to protect their interests was to elect Perón President.

The campaign reached a peak two weeks before the election when the United States issued its "Blue Book" on Argentina. This document accused Perón and his associates of collaborating with the Nazis and claimed that the CGT

Labor's Nationalisms and the Rise of Perón / 95

was nothing more than a puppet of the government.⁴⁶ Perón exploited this attack by representing the elections as a choice between himself and Braden, the former United States Ambassador and at that time the Assistant Secretary of State, who prompted the release of the "Blue Book." It was not difficult for the workers to conclude that a foreign enemy—Braden and the United States—had joined with the internal enemy—the oligarchy and the Unión Democrática—to attempt to destroy Perón, the social and economic revolution, and the egalitarian nation they envisioned.⁴⁷

This combination of events was all that Perón needed. In the February elections, which the opposition at first admitted were fair, Perón defeated his colorless opponent by 300,000 votes: 1,527,230 to 1,207,155. He won 56 per cent of the popular vote and 304 of 376 votes in the electoral college. His supporters won two-thirds of the seats in the Chamber of Deputies, 28 of the 30 seats in the Senate, and all of the provincial governorships. Perhaps his most significant victory was over the old workers' parties; neither the Socialists nor the Communists won a single congressional seat.⁴⁸

Sometime later, Perón explained what he understood to be the significance of the period: "Revolutions may be legitimized by the consensus of public opinion and because they are considered as having served lofty aims or put an end to a corrupt political situation. Regarding at least my personal participation in the movement of June 4, 1943, it is indisputable that it has been legitimized by the popular demonstration of October 17, 1945, and by the elections, free, completely free, of February, 1946." ⁴⁹

Between 1943 and 1946 Perón skillfully appealed both to the laborista variety of liberal nationalism and to criollo nationalism, won the support of a large majority of the organized and unorganized workers, and became the first freely elected President of Argentina in nearly twenty years. Labor, with Perón's assistance, had become largely independent of the traditional workers' parties and assumed a significant role in the new national community. But or- ganized labor was still independent of the government to a considerable degree, and this Perón could not tolerate for long.

5

The Triumph of the Criollo Nationalists

When he first became President in February 1946, Juan D. Perón could have ruled Argentina democratically in accordance with the country's liberal tradition. But he probably never considered this alternative, because for many years he had associated with the anti-liberal elements, accepted their Hispanic-criollo values, and subscribed to their authoritarian concepts of government. At times Perón utilized such democratic devices as elections, but he believed that the state, with himself at its head, should be all-powerful and take on many of the functions hitherto carried out by other institutions. And he also believed that in case of conflict the rights of the state, representing the will of the people, should predominate over the rights of groups or individuals.

Therefore, during his first administration, Perón overcame the opposition of the liberal democratic sectors of Argentina and established an anti-liberal authoritarian regime. He restricted the activities of the political parties, intervened in the universities and expelled many professors, replaced all but one member of the Supreme Court, and curtailed the freedom of the press. What is most important for this study, he destroyed the power of the laborista leaders of the labor movement.

During the mid-1940's, the anti-liberal internal migrants became the largest element of the working force. Nevertheless, in early 1946 the major labor organizations were still controlled by the democratically oriented and independent laboristas, who espoused a modified form of liberal nationalism. The laboristas had supported Perón up to this point, but the President recognized that there were limits to this support. He therefore set about to discredit the laboristas as he had the liberals, and to replace them with anti-liberals who were personally loyal to him and whose criollo nationalism coincided with his own ideas.

As President of Argentina, Perón continued the social and economic revolution he had begun more than two years before in order to ensure the loyalty of the workers. This revolution, which appealed to laboristas and anti-liberals alike, did improve the total wages and position of the workers during this period, but it also made them economically dependent upon the state and Perón.

During most of this period prices rose rapidly, but until 1949 wages increased even more rapidly. Between 1943 and 1946 real wages fluctuated somewhat, but for the most part stayed the same. After 1946, they increased until 1948, when real wages for unskilled workers were 37 per cent higher than in 1943. After 1948 they began to decline, and by the time of the presidential election in November 1951, they had dropped below the 1943 level (see Table III).

Fringe benefits increased steadily throughout this period, and added from 30 to 50 per cent more to total wages. The government increased the number of paid legal holidays, established paid vacations, and provided accident

TABLE III

REAL WAGES OF INDUSTRIAL WORKERS, 1943–1951
(IN PER CENT) *

Year	Unskilled Workers	Skilled Workers
1943	100.0	100.0
1944	104.0	—
1945	—	—
1946	96.0	91.0
1947	108.5	105.0
1948	137.0	127.0
1949	133.5	120.0
1950	127.0	113.0
1951 †	115.0	99.9

* United States Department of Commerce, Bureau of Foreign and Domestic Commerce, Foreign Service Report Series, *Economic Review of Argentina* (Washington, 1951, 1953); United States Department of Commerce, Business Information Service, World Trade Series, *Economic Review of Argentina* (Washington, 1951). For different figures that nevertheless indicate the same trend, see Confederación General Económica de la República Argentina, *Informe económica* (Buenos Aires, 1955), pp. 181–192.

† Average for the first ten months of the year.

and sickness insurance for most workers. In addition it began a social security program. In 1943 only half a million workers were eligible for social security, but by 1946 the number had increased to more than a million and a half, and by 1951 about five million workers, approximately 70 per cent of the total working population, were covered by social security.[1]

Perón's wife Evita greatly helped the workers win economic benefits. She had taken a leading part in the organization of a national union of radio employees and had also been active in the demonstration of October 17, 1945. But it was not until the inauguration of her husband as President of Argentina in June 1946 that Evita began to play a leading role in the labor movement. She moved her office to the Secretariat of Labor and took over all of the governmental agencies that had anything to do with labor matters. She handled all collective bargaining, all disputes, all contracts, all pensions, and she encouraged leaders and individual workers to come to her with their problems, attended personally to many of them, and in this way built up her own loyal following.

In addition to dominating the governmental agencies that regulated organized labor, Evita established a nominally private welfare foundation in June 1947. Under the aegis of the President's wife, this organization collected what amounted to forced contributions from many sources, including business firms and all members of the CGT. With this money Evita built schools, hospitals, and playgrounds, and she bought medicine, food, and clothing to distribute to needy people all over Argentina. How much was collected and distributed is unknown, since Evita kept no records. The amount was substantial, however, and provided aid for the needy not available elsewhere.[2] All things considered, the workers financially were better off in 1951 than they had been in 1943.

Moreover, Perón's revolution concerned itself with more than simple economic gains, and the President continued in a variety of ways to satisfy the workers' demand for dignity and equal status within Argentine society. Most important, he reiterated his statement that the workers were the essence of the new Argentine nation and that his government was a government of the masses. This regime, he insisted, "is one with a profoundly proletariat and worker base, and our acts of government are inspired by this mass."[3]

For the first time in the history of the country, workers

held some of the important cabinet positions. Ángel Borlenghi, Secretary-General of the commercial employees, became Minister of Interior. Juan A. Bramuglia, former lawyer of the Unión Ferroviaria, became Minister of Foreign Affairs. José María Freire, ex-official of the glassmakers, served as Secretary and later Minister of Labor. And Ramón Cereijo, a labor leader, became Minister of Finance.

Perón also continued to protect the workers' right to organize throughout the country and actively encouraged them to do so. When he was elected President in February 1946, there were approximately half a million organized workers in Argentina. By the end of 1951, when he was reelected, this number had increased approximately five or six times, to about two and a half or three million.[4]

To ensure continued broad labor support, Perón initiated new campaigns to increase the workers' growing feeling of dignity, equal status, and communal identity. None was more important than the incorporation of labor's rights into the Constitution of 1949. Article 37 of the Constitution listed the following rights of the worker: (1) the right to work; (2) the right to a fair reward; (3) the right to acquire skill; (4) the right to good working conditions; (5) the right to the preservation of health; (6) the right to well-being; (7) the right to social security; (8) the right to protection for the family; (9) the right to economic advancement; and (10) the right to the defense of occupational interests.

The new Constitution also protected the workers' rights by making private property, capital, and natural resources "subject to the national interest." Article 38 stated in a manner similar to the Mexican Constitution of 1917 that "Private property has a social function and, in consequence, it shall be subject to the obligations that the law may establish for the purpose of the common good." Article 39 pointed out that "Capital must be put at the service of the national economy and must have social well-being as its principal objective." And Article 40 stated that "The organization and exploitation of wealth has as its goal the well-being of the people." [5]

The workers' response was almost unanimously favorable. For the first time in Argentine history their rights were protected by the Constitution. No longer could anyone dismiss them as "professional agitators," deny the legitimacy of their demands, or deny them equality. Because of Perón, the law and the government finally guaranteed the workers a meaningful identity as part of society.

Perón also found favor with most sectors of labor through his campaign for national economic independence. He attempted to place essential industries and the public services under state control in order to free Argentina from the pressure of foreign business and to permit the workers to serve the country and themselves instead of a private employer. The government nationalized the telephone, gas, electricity, and water companies as well as the Central Bank. It created the Instituto Argentino de Producción e Intercambio (IAPI) to control the country's foreign trade, established a National Economic Council to coordinate all of the financial and economic activities of the regime, developed the merchant marine, promulgated a Five-Year Plan for industrial development, and paid the foreign debt.[6]

Organized labor shared the satisfaction and pride of many sectors in the country as the government pursued this program of economic independence. CGT representatives were present at the well-publicized ceremony in historic Tucumán, where Perón proclaimed Argentina's economic independence. On July 9, 1947, the one hundred and thirty-first anniversary of the country's declaration of political independence, Perón declared Argentina's "economic emancipation from the foreign capitalist powers which have exercised tutelage, control and dominion over her." [7]

The Triumph of the Criollo Nationalists / 103

The nationalization of the railroads, however, seemed to give the workers their greatest satisfaction. The early Argentine railroads had been owned and operated by the state as well as by British and French businessmen, and by 1890 the government and private foreign concerns each owned about 2,900 miles of railroad. After 1890, however, this balance changed drastically, and in 1943 the British alone owned more than 18,000 miles, or about 70 per cent, of the Argentine railroads.[8]

Labor's desire for nationalized railroads was not new. As early as 1917 the railroad workers had proposed the nationalization of the railroads as the "best guarantee for the progress of the country." In 1938 the Unión Ferroviaria passed a resolution asking for the nationalization of the Ferrocarril Central de Córdoba, and in 1942 La Fraternidad suggested that the state purchase the railroads in order to provide incentive for "the development of the nation that would benefit the people in general." [9]

Soon after the Revolution of June 4, 1943, the government began the negotiations that eventually led to the purchase of the railroads. On February 13, 1947, an Anglo-Argentine agreement was signed, but because the purchase was related to the renegotiation of the meat and wheat agreement, the details could not be worked out until February 1948.[10]

On March 1, 1948, hundreds of thousands of Argentines filled the enormous square and park in front of Retiro Station to hear Perón, Evita, and a number of labor leaders eulogize the nationalization of the railroads. The reaction of most of organized labor was expressed by a note the commercial employees sent to Perón, thanking him for buying the railroads and thus realizing "a profound aspiration of the Argentine people." [11]

The liberal and laborista railroad workers in particular expressed their delight. An editorial in *La Fraternidad* entitled "Ya Son Nuestros" explained that during the past twenty-five years "the railroad companies have not satisfied any of the innumerable local and national interests. . . . Without denying what they did to help the economic and moral development, let us suggest that . . . the railroad companies have completed their mandate in this country." [12]

Under a half-page headline, "Perón Cumple," a writer for *El Obrero Ferroviario* pointed out that the nationalization of the railroads gave the workers economic independence, dignified their work by making them their own bosses, and placed the railroads at the service of the nation instead of foreign interests. Therefore, the author concluded, this was one of the greatest days in Argentine history.[13]

Nationalization continued to be a popular achievement with the workers. A year later, Jesús Fernández, the liberal anti-Peronist president of La Fraternidad, wrote an article in the union's newspaper praising the nationalization program. Economic independence had originally been demanded by Mariano Moreno, he noted, but the first real step to achieve it was the nationalization of the railroads. Now the Argentine railroad workers were their own bosses and therefore no longer outcasts in Argentina. The railroads, he concluded, could stop serving their own profit interests and start seeking the good of the nation.[14]

The chief significance of the revolution during this period was that, in satisfying some of the economic and psychological needs of all sectors of the labor movement, it brought the workers increasingly under the influence of the state and Perón. Perón and Evita raised total wages, appointed labor leaders to cabinet posts, protected the worker so that he could organize throughout the country, insisted that labor's demands be incorporated into the new Constitution, and nationalized the industries that made hundreds of thousands of workers employees of the state. The workers there-

The Triumph of the Criollo Nationalists / 105

fore came to look to Perón and Eva, rather than to the unions, as the source of all social and economic betterment.

At the same time that Perón was carrying out this revolution, he was destroying the power of the democratic labor leaders and the independent labor organizations. In 1946 the major labor groups—the Partido Laborista, the CGT, and most of the important unions—were led by laboristas who believed that an independent labor movement was the best guarantee for the continuation of social and economic progress. Perón, however, feared the power of these organizations because they were, to a considerable degree, independent of himself and the government, and were a significant barrier to his assumption of control over the labor movement.

Perón used a variety of methods to destroy the independence of the movement. By making the workers look to the state and to himself for the improvement of their situation, he gradually undermined the power of the democratic labor leaders. But his most effective technique was to do what he had done to defeat the Socialists and the Communists: to make every issue one of national loyalty. He defined each issue in such a way that what he wanted appeared to be for the good of the nation and what his opponents wanted was un-Argentine. To be more specific, he identified the democratic leaders with foreign interests, treated unauthorized strikes as acts of treason, and expanded the membership of the labor organizations with anti-liberal workers who accepted him as the labor leader, the embodiment of the government, and the national patrón.

Perón's first target was the recently established Partido Laborista. He had succeeded in minimizing the influence of the Socialist and Communist Parties in the labor movement, but the Partido Laborista emerged from the presidential election as a strong independent organization whose leaders conceived of it as the Argentine equivalent of the British Labour Party. Its leaders supported Perón, but they intended to maintain their independence and insisted that the country be run democratically.

A number of incidents revealed the difference of opinion between the President and the leaders of the Partido Laborista. For example, Perón wanted Ángel Borlenghi to be president of the party, but the party convention elected Luis Gay. Perón also wanted to pick the Laborista candidates for the national and provincial offices. The party refused to permit him to do so and respected the choices of its provincial and national conventions. The party did bow to Perón's wishes and accepted J. Hortensio Quijano instead of Domingo Mercante as its vice-presidential candidate, but it submitted to this change primarily because Mercante withdrew and asked the organization to support Quijano.[15]

Soon after the election of 1946 there were rumors that Perón would do away with the party, but it was not until May that he made his intentions clear. In a radio speech the President announced without warning that he would dissolve his electoral coalition and establish in its place the Partido Único. The Laboristas understood the implication; there would be no room for an independent labor party in the new political scheme. The National Executive Committee met and, supported by 83 of the 101 Laborista Deputies, refused to disband the party. Within two days, however, 30 of the Laborista Deputies had defected to Perón and soon more left the party. Luis Gay, president of the Partido Laborista, resigned his post rather than vote to dissolve the party, but he did not openly break with Perón at this time. Finally only Cipriano Reyes, the party's vice-president, remained to oppose Perón openly.[16]

It is not exactly clear how Perón persuaded the Laborista Deputies to join him. Certainly it was not out of character

The Triumph of the Criollo Nationalists / 107

for the President to use bribery and force when he deemed it necessary. Most likely, however, the situation determined the choice of many, as it did for Luis Gay. Although the leaders believed in a genuine, independent, working-class political party, once Perón had made clear his stand they saw no meaningful alternative to supporting him. Under his leadership the social and economic revolution was progressing and an increasingly large percentage of the workers were identifying their interests with those of the President. It was felt that this was not the time for a break with Perón, because more could be gained by continuing to go along with him.[17]

In August 1946, the Partido Laborista, shorn of its congressional following and its president, held a National Congress to decide upon its future. The remaining members agreed to keep the party in existence and to make Cipriano Reyes the new leader. But Perón would not permit even this skeleton of the party to exist. On July 4, 1947, an attempt was made to kill Reyes that may or may not have had the backing of the President. More important, on January 30, 1948, the government withdrew legal recognition from the party, which disqualified it for participation in the March elections or any future ones.[18]

By February 1948, the only remnants of the once flourishing Partido Laborista were a few party leaders, and Perón soon imprisoned or exiled them. On September 24, 1948, the President claimed that there had been an attack on his life. He accused Cipriano Reyes, Walter Beveraggi Allende, and the other Laborista leaders of plotting with John Griffiths—a former cultural attaché in the United States Embassy in Buenos Aires—to murder him and turn the country over to foreign interests. Reyes was imprisoned without a trial and remained there, with the exception of one brief period of freedom, until the overthrow of Perón. A few leaders were able to escape into exile, but most shared the fate of Reyes. As a result, by the end of 1948, Perón had eliminated labor's only remaining political organization.

At the same time Perón sought to establish absolute control over the CGT. The laboristas who led the organization had supported him on October 17, 1945, but their backing had been equivocal and the vote in favor of the general strike had been extremely close. They clearly supported Perón in the presidential election of February 24, 1946, but because their statutes prohibited political involvement they could make no direct endorsement of his candidacy.[19] And although they did not openly protest when the President destroyed the Partido Laborista, many still believed labor should have its own independent political party as well as an independent economic organization.[20]

In November 1946, Luis Gay, former president of the Partido Laborista, once again defeated Perón-supported Ángel Borlenghi in an election, but this time for the secretary-generalship of the CGT. Although he had supported Perón on October 17 and February 24, Gay must have worried the new President because he was a liberal nationalist, popular with the workers, incorruptible and independent. As soon as he was elected Secretary-General, Gay spoke with Perón and told him that the labor federation must be independent of the government and that he would fight to keep it that way.[21] As the author of an article in the *CGT* explained, Gay belonged to the syndicalist school that believed organized labor should give directions to political parties and the government, not vice versa.[22]

Apparently it was Gay's personal popularity with the workers that concerned Perón most. The new Secretary-General was liked and respected by almost all sectors of labor, as a writer for the *CGT* pointed out. The country needed more men like Gay, the author of the article began, men who would accept important labor positions and responsibility

The Triumph of the Criollo Nationalists / 109

without seeking money. Gay was President of the National Postal Savings Bank, Vice-President of the Argentine Telephone Company, and Secretary-General of the CGT, but he took a salary only for the first job. Gay had learned to be personally disinterested and to repudiate ambition. The old labor leaders, the author concluded, had carefully cultivated the Spartan spirit and everyone might profit from their example.[23]

Because of his popularity and integrity, Gay was a difficult man to attack. A visit by a delegation of United States labor leaders in January 1947, however, gave Perón the issue he needed to link Gay with foreign opponents of the regime and in this way to undermine his reputation and influence in the labor movement. Perón had invited the American labor leaders to visit Argentina, but because they refused to come unless they were also invited by the labor organizations of the country, the CGT and the government jointly sponsored the visit. Angered by this arrangement, Perón was further annoyed by the fact that the American delegation announced that it had come to conduct an investigation of the controversial Argentine labor movement.[24] The CGT held a reception for the American labor leaders the night they arrived in Buenos Aires. Gay, as Secretary-General of the organization, was the official host and spent a considerable time talking with his guests. Later that evening, the Executive Committee of the CGT met at the request of Perón and removed Gay from office for "collaborating" with the foreign critics of the regime.

Nevertheless, because Perón wanted the workers to believe that the Americans supported him, the United States delegation received favorable publicity in the Argentine labor press. For example, the *CGT* printed the American delegation's message to Perón in which the leaders thanked him for the opportunity to see Argentina and expressed a desire for further cooperation between the United States and the Argentine labor movements. Another article in the same issue even noted that the Americans took off their coats and became "perfect descamisados." [25]

After the labor delegation returned to the United States, it published an extremely informative report on Argentine labor in which it concluded that while little formal government action had been taken to suppress civil liberties, an atmosphere of fear interfered with the exercise of those liberties; that while the government, taking advantage of the country's favorable economic situation, was instituting overdue social and economic reforms, in general it was using them for political purposes; and that while a small independent group of opposition labor unions existed, the CGT was not free to elect its officers, to carry on private collective bargaining with the employers, or to administer its own internal affairs.[26]

The American labor leaders claimed that the resignation of Luis Gay as Secretary-General constituted one significant indication that the CGT was not free from government domination. They had met Gay for the first time at the CGT reception on the night of their arrival and were surprised to learn the next day that the recently elected Secretary-General had resigned without warning. "We found it difficult to believe," they explained in their report, "that such could be the fate of the leader of an organization of more than 500,000 workers just because he had allegedly disagreed with the trade-union plans of the president of the country." [27]

The by then captive CGT responded promptly to the report and used it as "evidence" to prove that Gay was in fact a traitor. The report of the North American labor delegation was absolutely false, the new leaders claimed. Luis Gay, the Argentine collaborator in this attack, had betrayed his country and the workers to the Yankee imperialists and therefore had been replaced. The doors of the presidential palace were open, they continued. If Gay felt the need to correct certain things, he could have and should have discussed them with Perón.²⁸

Aurelio Hernández, the trusted Peronist who replaced Gay, carried on an active campaign to end the last vestiges of independence within the CGT. In an obvious attempt to appear as devoted and disinterested as his predecessor, Hernández refused to accept any salary for his new job. Of more consequence, he expanded the coverage of the *CGT*, increased its circulation from 10,000 to 45,000, and made it a propaganda sheet for the government.²⁹ An analysis of the content of the paper from 1943 through 1947 reveals that before 1947 there were very few articles about Perón or Evita that were not directly related to labor matters; there were no full-page pictures, no slogans, no headlines, and no big articles devoted to the presidential couple. As soon as Hernández became Secretary-General, the labor content of the *CGT* decreased and the political content increased. On March 1, 1947, there appeared the first full-page picture of Perón and Evita with appropriate slogans. From that time on, the *CGT* was at the service of the Peróns.

Perhaps the most significant thing Perón and Hernández did to end the independence of the labor movement was to stimulate an incredibly rapid expansion of the labor federation by organizing many of the hitherto unorganized workers. Before 1947, the CGT remained in the hands of the leaders of the older unions, most of whom were laboristas. By expanding the movement to include anti-liberal, non-skilled workers in the cities and the interior, Perón was able to reduce to insignificance the numerical importance of the laboristas.

The available figures on the growth of the CGT, although not entirely reliable, at least suggest the dimension of the rapid expansion of the organization in 1947. At the beginning of the year, the CGT had approximately 500,000 members, by the end of the year, it numbered about 1,500,000. Until 1947, most of the growth of organized labor was due to an increase in the size of the old unions. In 1947, however, the growth was caused primarily by the organization of new unions of unskilled, anti-liberal workers.[30]

Hernández had served his master well; by the end of 1947 Perón had gained control of the CGT and had destroyed its independence. But even the faithful Hernández did not remain leader of the CGT very long. Because of a disagreement with Evita Perón, he was soon replaced by José Espejo. The name of the new Secretary-General, Sr. Mirror, was appropriate. His major qualification for the job was that he had been the janitor in the apartment house in which Eva Duarte and Juan Perón occupied joint suites in 1944 and 1945.[31] He did what he was told and did not offend the President and his wife. The CGT, like its Secretary-General, had become a mirror for the Peróns.

Perón's third object of attack was the individual unions. This was his most difficult task, because there were so many unions all over the country that no centralized or uniform campaign was possible. His technique of winning control varied with each organization. The continuing social and economic revolution won support, but it did not necessarily win absolute obedience. Perón therefore bribed some labor leaders, offered others government jobs, intimidated still others, and jailed or exiled a few. Also he denied legal recognition to certain recalcitrant unions, such as the textile and shoe workers' unions.

The President's major technique of gaining control of unions, however, was direct intervention by the government or the CGT, allegedly to protect the interests of the working class and the nation. Some reason was always found, such as corruption within the union, to "justify" intervention and give Perón's actions a semblance of legality.

The Triumph of the Criollo Nationalists / 113

Once in charge of the union, the government-chosen interventor could and did manipulate its affairs at will, expel uncooperative leaders and members, and continue to hold elections until the results satisfied him.[32]

The President tried to win the support of some unions by means of elections, but in many cases this technique was at best only partially successful and he had to resort to direct intervention. For example, in March 1947, the Federación Gráfica Bonaerense, the printers' union, held an election to choose its Executive Committee. The election itself was free and the Peronist candidate, winning a few more than half of the 8,000 votes, proclaimed it a great democratic victory. Such elections were technically free, but the campaigns were not. Anyone could run for office, but the Peronist candidate received unlimited funds from the government and other assistance, such as the exclusive use of the cars of the Ministry of Labor.[33]

Despite the Peronist victory in the elections of 1947, the printers retained some independence and Perón once more reverted to intervention. In February 1949, they went on strike for higher wages, the strike was declared illegal, and the union was subjected to intervention by the CGT. To justify this action the new authorities of the union explained that the CGT had taken over to begin the "Argentinization of the organization of the syndicate contaminated during so many years by influences foreign to the country." They had given the union an "Argentine spirit," they continued; they had taken down the pictures of Marx and Stalin, replaced them with a bust of San Martín, and burned all of the literature that contained "foreign ideas." [34]

As part of his campaign to destroy the independence of the individual unions, Perón limited the right to strike in a manner reminiscent of the pre-World War I governments. Since that time, the strike in Argentina had been used by the workers to put economic pressure on their employers in order to win specific benefits. In very few cases were strikes politically motivated and, with the exceptions of some of the communist-inspired strikes and the workers' demonstration on October 17, 1945, none could have been interpreted as a revolutionary attack on the government. Perón, however, fearful of the potential political significance of this kind of independent labor action, began to claim that unauthorized strikes were acts of treason and that the leaders of such strikes were traitors to their country.

Perón initiated his attack on the right to strike even before his election to the presidency. In January 1945, the government issued a decree that made an illegal strike—a strike declared without government permission—a crime against the state. In the Rights of the Worker, first announced on February 24, 1947, and later incorporated into the Constitution, Perón significantly did not include this right. A strike, he argued, was no longer necessary in Argentina, because the government protected the interests of the workers. In addition, such action could disrupt the economy and hurt the national interest. The strike, therefore, was an extreme measure to be used only when all the legal means for settling a dispute had been exhausted and when permission from the government had been granted.

The CGT reiterated the Perón theme with regard to strikes. In February 1947, the captive organization issued a warning to those calling strikes without first consulting the Secretariat of Labor and explained that such wildcat action was not in keeping with the "recent Argentine labor tradition." Strikes were extreme measures to be used only when all legal means had failed, the leaders stated. In Argentina strikes had practically lost their meaning because the present government fulfilled the demands of the workers.[35]

Anyone who called an unauthorized strike was attacked as a communist or a socialist working in alliance with foreign interests. In October and November 1949, the Perón-organized sugar workers of Tucumán struck for higher wages without government permission. The strike was declared illegal and the leaders arrested, but the only way the government could settle the dispute was to grant the workers a 60 per cent wage increase.

This strike so disturbed Perón that he addressed the country on the radio to explain why it had occurred. He insisted that it was a politically motivated protest inspired by unpatriotic leaders. Three conclusions could be drawn from this incident, the President pointed out. First, the directors of the sugar workers had betrayed the general interests of the working class for their own personal political objectives. Second, in opposition to the principles of Justicialism,[36] the directors of the union had entered into conversations with the opposition political parties, ending the possibility of a negotiated solution. And third, the Communists, Socialists, Radicals, and Conservatives had approved of this betrayal of the workers' interests and thus showed their lack of patriotism.[37]

The railroad strikes of late 1950 and early 1951 were handled in the same manner. The workers demanded higher wages and more responsive union leadership, but Perón attacked them as traitors working for foreign interests. In a speech before a meeting of the CGT in January 1951, he explained that the Communists had planned a world-wide uprising in the transportation industry, as nearly simultaneous strikes in England, the United States, Chile, and Brazil illustrated. Bands of Communists, Socialists, and Radicals, he continued, had gone through the workers' districts of Buenos Aires and punished the women and children of workers who wanted to work. He promised to follow the precedent set in England and the United States, and to apply every legal means to contain the illegal activities of the un-Argentine leaders of the strike.[38]

The culmination of Perón's attack on the independent labor unions was intervention in La Fraternidad in May 1951. Early in 1951 the CGT sent notes to all of the unions asking them to designate four delegates to coordinate labor's efforts to reelect Perón. La Fraternidad refused to participate and pointed out that its statutes prohibited political involvement of any kind. After a series of notes and violent denunciations by the CGT and Evita, La Fraternidad was intervened in because it had not "fulfilled the will of the Argentine workers."[39] This act abruptly terminated the independence of the last free labor organization in Argentina.

During the six years of his first presidency, Perón destroyed the Partido Laborista, and subdued the CGT and the individual unions in the labor movement. All opposition to this campaign was provoked, he claimed, by foreign interests allied with renegade Argentines who had betrayed their country. The success of the campaign was unquestionable. Between 1946 and 1951 the number of union meetings per year held in the greater Buenos Aires area declined from 759,497 to 167,676, reflecting the growing uselessness of such expressions of labor democracy.[40] By 1951 there were no labor institutions independent of the government, and in all cases the labor leaders were anti-liberals whose primary loyalty was to Perón.

The destruction of the liberals and the laboristas left a leadership vacuum in the expanding labor movement that Perón with the help of his wife personally sought to fill. With the use of symbols and ritual he continued his effort begun in 1944 to transfer the patrón-peón relationship of the estancia to the national political scene and to make the recently organized internal migrants believe that Perón was the embodiment of the criollo nation, and that through

The Triumph of the Criollo Nationalists / 117

him they had achieved a new communal identity and a significant voice in the direction of the country.

The most important symbols of the regime were Perón himself and his wife Evita. Perón was the symbol of the nation and Evita the symbol of the descamisados. In his speech at the celebration of the nationalization of the railroads on March 1, 1948, Perón made his position clear: "In this celebration today I want you to forget that I am General Perón, and that before your conscience, before the conscience of all Argentines, before the conscience of all the world, I might be the material representation, the living incarnation of the . . . Argentine nation."[41]

A year later, the CGT Secretary-General José Espejo reiterated the same theme. No one, he declared, could stop the great work of Perón, not even Braden and his Argentine collaborators. But to defend this great revolution the nation must be loyal. It must have "loyalty without limits to the leader—that is, loyalty to ourselves because he is our incarnation in this great cause, the cause of the Patria itself."[42]

Perón was the incarnation of the nation, the national patrón, and as such the representative of labor. But Evita was labor's particular symbol—a closer daily contact, a special channel to Perón. Her role in filling the institutional and psychological needs of organized labor increased as the independence of the old labor organizations declined.

Evita was uniquely qualified for her new role. She had learned the problems of the poor firsthand. She was the youngest of five brothers and sisters, all of whom had been born out of wedlock. Her father died, leaving them nothing. There were many years of poverty and misery. What others read in books, Evita knew from personal experience.[43]

Evita played an important part in building up the image of her husband as the national patrón from whom all benefits had come and toward whom all loyalty must go. In her book, *La razón de mi vida*, she expressed the themes that she had repeated time and time again in speeches before the descamisados: "I was not, nor am I, anything more than a humble woman . . . a sparrow in an immense flock of sparrows. . . . All that I am, all that I have, all that I think and all that I feel, belongs to Perón. . . . But I do not forget, nor will I ever forget, that I was a sparrow, nor that I am one still. If I fly higher, it is through him. If I walk among the peaks, it is through him. If sometimes I almost touch the sky with my wings, it is through him." [44]

Evita also explained the relationship of Perón and herself to the workers. There are ordinary men who move along the paths already explored by others, she told them, and there are extraordinary men who see the future and lead others toward it. In the second group she placed Alexander the Great, Columbus, Napoleon, San Martín, and Perón. When Perón became President he could no longer devote as much time as he wanted to the people. Therefore, Evita revealed, her mission was to maintain close contact with the people. There could be no separation between the people and the government, she concluded, because "in order to divorce himself from his people, the head of the government would have to begin by divorcing his own wife." [45]

The symbols of the nation were well defined, but to give the workers the feeling of active identification with these symbols and participation in the direction of the country, the Peróns developed an increasingly elaborate system of rituals. The most important annual ritual was the celebration of Loyalty Day, the anniversary of October 17, 1945. Each year the CGT began Loyalty Day preparations earlier than the previous one, and by 1950 the publicity first came out in the beginning of August. The ceremony was similar every year: a few labor leaders would speak, but the show was highlighted by the speeches of Evita and Juan Perón

The Triumph of the Criollo Nationalists / 119

to thousands of workers crowded into the Plaza de Mayo. The speeches also were similar every year: loyalty to Perón, to the revolution, and to the nation was the greatest of all human virtues.

The government also planned many special celebrations for the workers and other sectors of society. The Declaration of Economic Independence and the nationalization of the railroads were the occasion for important celebrations that furthered Perón's image as the protector of the nation and the worker. But the celebration of the Year of San Martín in 1950 was an unparalleled opportunity for Perón to develop his own image as the second liberator of Argentina. He proclaimed it the Year of the Liberator General José de San Martín and took every opportunity to identify himself with the national hero. The *CGT* was filled with articles on Perón and San Martín and with full-page pictures of the two in identical poses, looking very much alike. Long articles appeared stating that if San Martín were living today, he would be fighting for social justice with Perón and the descamisados.[46]

In addition to the annual and special celebrations, Peronist ritual included songs, poems, and slogans. After 1948 "Perón Cumple, Evita Dignifica" began to appear at the top or bottom of each page of labor newspapers. "Santo" and "Santa de Trabajo" and "La Dama de Esperanza" were frequently used sobriquets, and other familiar slogans included "Argentines should be neither excessively rich nor excessively poor" and "The land belongs to those who work it." In its November 1950 issue, *El Obrero Ferroviario* published a poem to Evita by Dr. Raúl Mende. Its opening verse is sufficient to indicate the kind of poetical adulation that flourished:

> Todas las primaveras de la Patria
> florecieron en ella. Todo el pueblo
> se dió cita en su nombre . . .
> Evita! . . . para el sueño

de todos los humildes de mi tierra,
para la fe de todos los enfermos
para todas las lágrimas,
para el dolor de todo desconsuelo:
estrella, corazón, ángel y verso
lo mejor de la tierra
y lo mejor del cielo! [47]

During his first presidency Perón helped the anti-liberals, who had become the largest sector of the working force, take over the labor movement. He organized the internal migrants, who were unfamiliar and unconcerned with the Argentine tradition of independent democratic unionism or with liberal nationalism. He also destroyed the independent labor organizations, replaced their liberal and laborista leaders with anti-liberals personally loyal to him, and became the exclusive source of social and economic benefits for the worker. Finally, he skillfully employed symbols and ritual to help fill the leadership void, establish himself as the national patrón, and make criollo nationalism the ideology of the labor movement.

6

Labor Opposition to Perón

During Perón's first presidency there were two kinds of labor opposition to the government: the ideologically motivated opposition of certain leaders fighting for independent unionism, and the purely pragmatic opposition of workers fighting for economic benefits. Opposition developed as some leaders and workers began to realize that the interests of labor, the nation, and Perón were not, as he had repeatedly assured them, always the same.

Liberal, laborista, and even anti-liberal leaders protested to varying degrees the government's increased restrictions on union activity, and attempted unsuccessfully to justify their protests in terms of nationalism. They claimed that Perón, by denying them their independence, was betraying the interests of the nation and frustrating the will of its members.

The liberals were the first to oppose the regime. They openly broke with Perón in September 1945 when La Fraternidad, the shoemakers, and the textile workers withdrew from the CGT.[1] Under the leadership of Cándido Gregorio of the textile workers and Alfredo Fidanza of the shoemakers, they joined together shortly after Perón's election to form the Comité Obrero Argentino de Sindicatos Independientes (COASI). COASI was small and not particularly effective, but it was annoying to the regime. For example, in 1949 a COASI rather than a CGT representative was seated at the organizing meeting of the International Confederation of Free Trade Unions (ICFTU) because COASI's members convinced the international organization that the CGT was not independent of the government. Shortly after this, Perón forced the COASI leaders into exile in Montevideo.[2]

The most significant liberal labor opposition in Argentina came from the leaders of La Fraternidad, the prestigious union of railroad engineers and firemen. La Fraternidad supported much of the social and economic revolution of Perón. It strongly approved of the Rights of the Worker, the nationalization of the railroads, the government's reaffirmation of Argentine sovereignty over the Islas Malvinas and Antarctica, and the numerous wage increases. The union's support of the government was limited, nevertheless, because it was not willing to exchange its independence for the benefits of the revolution; its leaders believed that no permanent benefits could be won and no genuine revolution could take place if the independence of labor were sacrificed. In an editorial in *La Fraternidad*, the union leaders expressed their philosophy. They had a tradition of "sane patriotism" and of concern for the general economy of the country, they explained. Their patriotism, however, did not exclude independent action to win increased salaries or to defend their own interests.[3]

Throughout the period the railroad workers used liberal nationalism to defend independent, apolitical unionism. In the name of traditional Argentine liberties they demanded the repeal of all laws that restricted the right to strike and they denounced all state intervention in unions. One of the major objects of their attack was the Ley de Residencia, the law that permitted the government to deport foreigners whose conduct "compromised the national security." The members of La Fraternidad stated their case most forcefully in 1948 just after the government had invoked the Ley de Residencia to detain and deport a number of workers involved in a strike. This use of the law, the railroad engineers and firemen claimed, was unconstitutional. The law was "oligarchical and reactionary" in origin and it contradicted the fundamental liberties guaranteed by the Constitution. The deportations, they declared, must be stopped immediately and the law repealed.[4]

In addition to opposing government restrictions on labor independence and democracy, the leaders of La Fraternidad attacked what they believed were government encroachments on other Argentine democratic institutions. The liberal members of the union demanded the reinstatement of secular education to ensure the impartiality and freedom of Argentine public education. In 1946 they applauded the free press for defending democracy and liberty, and in 1950 —after the government had closed down dozens of newspapers—the union Congress passed a resolution insisting that freedom of the press was "the most eloquent expression of democracy" and demanded that the publication of all newspapers be resumed.[5]

An article in *La Fraternidad* in late 1950, entitled "Rosas and the Revisionists of History," seemed to capture the essence of the liberal union's protest against the anti-liberal Perón government. Attacking Perón by indirectly equating him with the nineteenth-century anti-liberal *caudillo*, Juan Manuel de Rosas, the author of the article suggested that it was difficult to understand how citizens of Argentina, with its "liberal, democratic and progressive tradition," could support a "disgraceful 'revision' [of history] that wants to make Rosas the archetype of our people." He was a caudillo, he turned the government over to the landed aristocracy, and he offered the Islas Malvinas to England for money. Argentina's heroes, the author of the article concluded, were Manuel Belgrano, Mariano Moreno, Bernardino Rivadavia, Esteban Echeverría, Domingo F. Sarmiento, and Juan Bautista Alberdi.[6]

The opposition of La Fraternidad was annoying, but Perón hesitated to intervene in the union because of its prestige and its long tradition of leadership. In December 1950 and January 1951, however, the members of La Fraternidad actively participated in the "illegal" railroad strikes, and a few months later refused to support Perón for reelection. Provoked by these incidents and firmly in control of the rest of the labor movement, Perón instructed the CGT to intervene in La Fraternidad and thus silenced the major remaining source of liberal opposition to his regime.

Until late 1946, the laborista leaders of the labor movement identified their interests with Perón. Gradually, however, they came to believe that the President, by restricting the actions of the labor organizations and by attempting to establish a personalistic regime, had betrayed the social and economic revolution and the Argentine liberal constitutional tradition. More specifically, they protested Perón's destruction of the Partido Laborista, and his curtailment of the independence of the CGT and the individual unions.

The ideas of Luis Gay and Cipriano Reyes, leaders of the Partido Laborista, were similar to those of many of the laboristas and provide some indication why they originally supported Perón and then opposed him. Gay, as leader of the telephone workers and Secretary-General of the Unión Sindical Argentina during the 1930's, was disgusted with the fraud, corruption, and attacks on labor of the Uriburu, Justo, and Castillo governments. He therefore believed that the Revolution of June 4, 1943, would bring a change for the better. Many did not completely trust Perón during the 1943–

1946 period, Gay maintained, because they understood that fundamentally he was a "criollo" fascist; but he did bring about a social and economic revolution and there was no alternative to supporting him if the revolution were to continue.

Gay somewhat naïvely insisted that he had supported the ideas that Perón represented, not Perón the man. For example, he maintained that the October 17, 1945, demonstration was intended to defend the achievements of the past two years against the threat of a counterrevolution and was not primarily an uprising to defend Perón. Similarly, he insisted that the election of 1946 was a victory for the Partido Laborista and the social revolution, and not a personal victory for Perón.[7]

Cipriano Reyes, the ambitious vice-president of the Partido Laborista and one of the chief organizers of the October 17, 1945, demonstrations, explained how Perón had "violated" the laborista concept of nationalism. In his book ¿Qué es el laborismo?, published in late 1946, Reyes charged that Perón had totally ignored the national will.[8] The government of Perón claimed that it had "forged the national unity," he began. But what kind of unity was that? Why did Perón refuse to accept the "genuine unity" established at the polls on February 24, 1946? Why had he destroyed the Partido Laborista, which won two-thirds of the seats in the Chamber of Deputies and 85 per cent of the popular vote? Either the revolution was popular or it was not a revolution, concluded Reyes. The country would have unity, but "Unity betraying the masses is not unity. Unity ignoring the popular mandate is subversion. Unity [achieved] behind the backs of the people and for the purpose of frustrating the express desires of the people is politically fraudulent and venal, as fraudulent and negative as were the most ominous periods of oligarchical rule."[9] Perón, Reyes clearly intimated, had betrayed the revolution and the nation.

Many laboristas criticized Perón for betraying the revolution, but because they saw no meaningful alternative, most of them continued to support him for some time. They may have been naïve to believe that it was possible to separate Perón from the revolution, but they were sincere in their desire to fight for social and economic change, an independent labor movement, and for a new egalitarian and democratic Argentina.

Although the anti-liberals developed a close personal identification with Perón and became the backbone of the government-controlled labor movement, some of their leaders at times opposed the regime. In general, they believed that the social and economic revolution should proceed, whatever the cost. The government should play a major role in the revolution to make sure that the greater good of the national community prevailed over the narrow desires of individuals and groups. Nevertheless, a number of the leaders recognized the need for independent action to protect their interests.

One of the leading government critics among the anti-liberals was Hilario Salvo.¹⁰ Salvo, who was Secretary-General of the metallurgic workers' union (UOM) from 1946 to 1951 and a Peronist Deputy in the National Congress from 1951 to 1954, believed himself to be a loyal Peronist even though he was expelled from the party in 1954. Salvo argued that Perón's most significant contribution to Argentine society was the social and economic revolution from 1943 to 1946. After Perón became President, he concentrated on politics instead of the revolution, and for political reasons destroyed the independence of labor. Unfortunately, Salvo pointed out, Perón did not understand that opposition could be loyal, and that constructive opposition could be helpful to growth and development. He therefore attempted to destroy all manifestations of opposition to the government, loyal or otherwise.

Although Salvo objected to some of Perón's actions, he did little to protest them openly. He opposed the dissolution of the Partido Laborista and the expulsion of Luis Gay as Secretary-General of the CGT. But he made no significant gesture or statement of protest until 1949, when he resigned from the Central Committee of the CGT. From 1949 to 1954 —when he was expelled from the party for "disloyalty"— Salvo demanded the restoration of the independence of the labor movement and the revival of the original revolution. However, he never advocated, as did the liberals, the overthrow of the government or opposed the "undemocratic" practices of the regime.

Salvo's position and that of the anti-liberal opposition in general was paradoxical. These leaders were more sympathetic to the ideas and methods of Perón than any other group of labor leaders, but they found it necessary at times to oppose him. They wanted a strong anti-liberal government that would sacrifice everything else for the criollo revolution, but they wanted some say as to whose interests would be sacrificed first. They wanted to be able to oppose Perón as members of the loyal opposition, but Perón would not permit them this luxury.

The problem of the anti-liberals was basically the same as that of all opposition labor groups; they were ineffective because Perón had carefully placed them in an apparently insolvable dilemma. On the one hand, they supported to varying degrees what he was doing because he had accomplished more for the workers than any other individual in Argentine history. On the other hand, they objected to his personalistic approach and to some of his techniques of governing. They realized too late that for the large majority of workers Perón, the social and economic revolution, and the nation were too intimately associated to be separated. Under these circumstances nationalism could not be used effectively to justify opposition to Perón or his government.

Between 1949 and 1951 another and more effective kind of opposition developed in the labor movement. After 1948 real wages began to decline and the new Peronist leadership of the labor movement, more loyal to Perón than to the workers, did little to halt this decline. In a number of instances, therefore, the workers ignored these leaders and used the strike—the only means still available to them—to defend what they understood to be their legitimate economic interests. Most of these workers were loyal Peronists who did not think of themselves as opponents of the regime and certainly would not have supported efforts on the part of any group to replace Perón. Nevertheless, by striking without government permission, they implicitly rejected Perón's attempt to equate independent action with treason and thus maintained their right to determine in part the national interest.

During the period from 1946 to 1948 there were many more strikes than during the three-year periods immediately preceding and following it. From 1943 to 1945 there were approximately 50 strikes per year in the federal capital, involving 20,000 workers.[11] From 1946 to 1948, however, there were approximately 100 strikes per year, involving 400,000 workers, or twice as many strikes per year involving twenty times as many workers. And from 1949 to 1951 there were approximately 30 strikes per year, involving 50,000 workers.[12]

The reasons why so many strikes occurred during the three-year period from 1946 to 1948 were that the rapidly expanding labor movement still enjoyed a considerable degree of autonomy and that Perón, in accordance with his plan to organize the anti-liberal workers, encouraged and approved of many of the strikes. For example, the government supported strikes that were called to win union recognition from an employer and to force an employer to comply with new labor legislation. Thus the government supported the strikes of the sugar workers and the meat packers in 1946 because they were called to force the employers to pay the workers the controversial Christmas bonus.

Although the number of strikes declined in the period from 1949 to 1951, it was still remarkably high in view of the fact that by this time Perón had consolidated his hold over the movement and forcefully discouraged such independent action. For the most part, the government at this time opposed all strikes, and if a strike were called without prior government approval, the CGT or the government itself would intervene in the union and end the conflict. Recalcitrant leaders were replaced, jailed, or exiled.

The major strikes during this later period were those of the printers, the sugar workers of Tucumán, the meat packers, the maritime workers, the bank employees, and the railroad workers. The details of each strike were different, but significantly they all had many characteristics in common. The major cause of each was the decline in real wages. In most cases, the leaders of the unions either signed a contract or made an agreement with the government or the employer, the workers repudiated the agreement and charged that the leaders were not fighting for them, and then the workers went on strike to protest both their low wages and the subservience of their leaders to the government. In all cases, the government declared the strikes illegal because the workers had not obtained government approval for such action. Then either the government or the CGT intervened in the union involved and the strike was suppressed. In the end, however, the workers received most of the benefits for which they had struck.[13]

In none of these cases was the strike a revolutionary act

intended to overthrow the government. A few workers attempted to capitalize politically on the discontent created by the decline in real wages, but the large majority of them struck only for higher pay and attacked, not the government or Perón, but their own inactive leaders. They demanded the freedom to strike because they were learning through experience that although the government had given them much, they had to maintain a certain degree of independence in order to protect their interests.

The series of railroad strikes in November and December 1950 and in January 1951 illustrate the nature of most strikes during this period. The Unión Ferroviaria, with approximately 150,000 members, was the largest union in the country. It represented workers in a strategic industry and it included groups from all ideological sectors of the labor movement. The railroad union had strongly supported the social and economic revolution of the government and particularly the nationalization of the railroads. But when real wages began to decline, the workers, despite the disapproval of the government, felt compelled to protest.

Until mid-1948 a great majority of the union's leaders were laboristas. In 1946, 1947, and 1948, its General Assembly passed a resolution demanding the repeal of the Ley de Residencia, and in 1948 the Assembly protested the deportation of workers involved in a strike.[14] The General Assembly also paid homage to the liberal Domingo F. Sarmiento, attacked the tyranny of the anti-liberal Juan Manuel de Rosas, repudiated violation of freedom of expression, and reaffirmed its support for the democratic tradition of the country. Perhaps most important was the passage by the Assembly in 1948 of a resolution demanding the immediate "normalization" of the CGT and the convocation of its executive bodies on a regular basis.[15]

Although the laboristas were in the majority, there was also a small group of liberals in the Unión Ferroviaria. One of the most important members of this group was Antonio Scipione, a Radical who since the overthrow of Perón has led the union. Until mid-1948 the liberals represented about 15 per cent of the membership, and perhaps more, as the vote on certain issues at the annual meetings of the General Assembly suggests. For example, in 1946 the Assembly passed a resolution to pay homage to the national authorities. Scipione opposed the resolution because he believed that such an endorsement, even of a pro-labor government, violated the organization's ban on political involvement of any kind. The vote on the resolution was 76 for, 16 against, 5 abstentions, and 5 absent, indicating that there were at least 16 liberals among the 102 Assembly delegates.[16]

In 1947 the liberals fought a resolution to support the work of *El Obrero Ferroviario* because they claimed that the newspaper did not confine itself exclusively to labor news. The vote was 72 for the resolution, 10 against it, 1 abstention, and 19 absent.[17] And in 1948, the liberals were even able to muster 5 votes in opposition to a resolution to donate money to the Evita Perón Welfare Fund.[18]

There were also anti-liberals in the Unión Ferroviaria, particularly after 1948. The strongest anti-liberal group consisted of the followers of Evita Perón.[19] On August 25, 1948, in an election of dubious honesty, Pablo C. López, a railroad worker with little union experience but one of Evita's favorites, became Secretary-General of the union, and other supporters of the President's wife took over the Executive Committee. With the election of López, the Unión Ferroviaria changed considerably. In elections that were probably fraudulent, none of the 16 liberals were returned to the General Assembly. In addition, many of the laboristas were silenced and the Executive Committee, the General Assembly, and *El Obrero Ferroviario* became forums for political propaganda.[20]

As real wages began to decline, there was growing unrest

among the workers and they demanded action from their leaders. López and his followers, more loyal to Evita and her husband than to the workers they were supposed to represent, did nothing. The workers therefore took the matter into their own hands. They formed an Emergency Committee to coordinate their activity and on November 15, 1950, struck for higher wages. The leaders of the Emergency Committee were called before the Secretary of Transportation, Lt. Col. Juan F. Castro, who, by promising them a wage increase, ended the strike.[21]

The Executive Committee headed by Pablo López attempted to undermine this support for the extra-legal Emergency Committee. The members of his committee submitted their resignations and then held a meeting of many of the local section leaders, who predictably rejected the resignations. On November 27, Perón openly intervened to support López and declared that the Executive Committee of the Unión Ferroviaria was made up of the "most faithful Peronists that exist in this movement." With Perón's personal endorsement, López issued the following warning: "Attention railroad workers. All who support actions and attitudes not approved by the Unión Ferroviaria [which meant, by the Executive Committee] commit unforgivable treason against General Perón and his wife Eva Perón." [22]

The workers were not impressed by the show of support nor intimidated by the threat. The Emergency Committee did not consider the wage increase promised by Lt. Col. Castro adequate either in amount or in scope. In mid-December, therefore, it held a meeting outside the Unión Ferroviaria building to demand an appropriate wage increase and the resignation of the "inactive" Executive Committee. The meeting led to a second strike. At that point Perón intervened again, and when he learned that his Secretary of Transportation had been dealing with the extra-legal Emergency Committee he forced him to resign. Then the CGT, following his instructions, intervened in the Unión Ferroviaria and ended the strike. Later the CGT promised across-the-board wage increases and free elections for a new Executive Committee.

By mid-January the government still had not put into effect the wage increases promised in December. The Emergency Committee, somewhat intoxicated by its successful demonstrations of independence, issued an ultimatum to the government. It demanded the promised wage increases and, most significantly, the right to appoint a committee to supervise the coming elections. The government did not even answer the ultimatum, and on January 23 nearly all of the 150,000 members of the Unión Ferroviaria went out on strike.

Perón responded promptly and decisively. He summoned the Central Committee of the CGT, demanded and received their support, and on January 25 issued a decree that permitted him to draft the railroad workers for national service. Hundreds of workers were arrested and as many as 2,000 were suspended from their jobs.[23] The next day, January 26, the other members returned to work.

Perón tried to separate the workers from the leaders and to blame the strike on the Communists and, to a lesser degree, on the Socialists and the Radicals. He insisted that the strike was the work of "one or two thousand agitators and of 148,000 uncertain men."[24] Roberto Testa, a Socialist and a former official of the Unión Ferroviaria, claimed that the Socialists with the help of a few Communists had provoked the strike.[25]

There is some evidence that others too were involved in the strike. Domingo Mercante, Juan Bramuglia, and Juan Castro all disliked Evita and her disciple Pablo López and therefore may have supported or even joined with the opposition to embarrass both. Domingo Mercante, as governor of the province of Buenos Aires, where most of the activity took place, could have minimized the extent of the strike, but did nothing at all to stop it. Juan A. Bramuglia made more than his usual number of visits to Mercante during the period of the strikes. And Minister of Transportation Juan Castro dealt with the extra-legal Emergency Committee that obviously threatened Pablo López's position of leadership and his control over the union.[26]

Very likely the Communists, the Socialists, the Radicals, and some of the disgruntled factions of the Peronists participated to a greater or lesser extent in the strike, and some undoubtedly did so for political reasons. But this cannot obscure the fact that the vast majority of workers were motivated primarily by economic reasons. Politically they opposed the subservient Peronist leadership, but they did so because they wanted a wage increase and not because they wanted to overthrow the government. They demanded the freedom to strike and although the strike was forcefully put down, the workers did achieve their objectives: López was expelled from the union and wages were raised.

Thus, during Perón's first presidency the opposition of the labor leaders to the government was limited and ineffective, for the simple reason that the large majority of workers associated Perón with the social revolution and the nation, and were loyal to all three. These dissident leaders were unable to change the course of the revolution they thought Perón had betrayed and were unable to maintain their positions of leadership for very long.

The pragmatic opposition of the workers was rather widespread after 1948 and in a measure effective, but it lasted only as long as the government refused to grant their demands. The government could arrest a few leaders and call them traitors to the nation, but it could not arrest thousands of workers striking for higher pay and maintain that they were traitors. Perón therefore blamed most of the strikes on "foreign agitators," arrested a few Socialists and Communists to "prove" his charge, and when the strike was over granted the workers most of the things for which they had struck.

This record of labor opposition to the government suggests how completely Perón had assumed the mantle of popular nationalism. Individual leaders attempted to cast doubt on Perón's loyalty to labor and the nation, but with no success. The only effective labor opposition to the government was that of loyal Peronists demanding and receiving economic benefits that they believed the subservient union leadership —not Perón—had denied them.

7

Perón Abandons the Workers' Nation

By the end of his first term as President of Argentina, Perón had apparently achieved his objectives with regard to labor: he had undermined the influence of the liberals and laboristas, made criollo nationalism the dominant nationalism of labor, and had identified himself and his government with the nation envisioned by the anti-liberal workers who controlled the movement.

During his second term, however, economic and political necessity forced Perón to adopt measures that most workers considered to be contrary to their interests, and therefore brought into question the assumption that the interests of labor were in fact identical with those of the nation. The workers were loyal to Perón and to what they conceived to be the interests of the nation, but now apparently the two were not exactly the same. The workers were in conflict, and because Perón never resolved the conflict, they became confused, frustrated, and even resentful. They never openly blamed Perón, but they did attack his lieutenants in the

138 / *Labor, Nationalism, and Politics in Argentina*

labor movement and became less effective supporters of his regime at a time when he needed all the support he could get.

Until 1948, Perón attempted to strengthen the industrial sector of the economy at the expense of the agricultural sector; to reduce foreign investment, particularly in public services and railroads; to give the state a decisive role in regulating the economy; and to redistribute the gross national product in favor of the working class. He was able to pay for this program with the revenues accumulated during World War II.

After 1948 the country's financial reserves began to dwindle and inflation became rampant. Argentina lacked the necessary foreign exchange to import needed materials and equipment for continued industrial growth, and the agricultural sector, which provided most of the foreign exchange, was unproductive. Therefore, in 1949, the government initiated a new economic policy designed to stop inflation, to attract foreign investment, and to restore the agricultural sector of the economy.[1]

To stabilize prices Perón reduced the amount of public expenditure, restricted credit, stimulated productivity, and contained real wages. A decree of 1948, providing that wage increases must be absorbed by profits and not be allowed to cause commodity price increases, was not immediately enforced. Beginning in 1949, however, labor became aware of the changing emphasis of government policy. Perón designated 1949 as the Year of Productivity, and the meaning of the slogan became clear when a labor court in Azul refused to reinstate a worker who had been fired for negligence. Such unprecedented action in Perón's Argentina was justified, the CGT leaders explained, because everyone had an obligation to produce for the good of the nation.[2]

In 1950 the government initiated a new wage policy that compelled the major unions to sign contracts for two years instead of one, but in most cases inflation forced Perón to grant wage increases before the termination of these contracts. In June 1950, for example, the textile workers signed a two-year contract granting them a 30 per cent wage increase. A sharp rise in the cost of living, however, particularly in 1951, forced the employers to renegotiate the contract before the expiration date. Intent upon doing everything possible to hold down inflation, the government worked out a formula with the employers whereby they would grant the textile workers a 30 per cent attendance bonus instead of a wage increase. This meant that if a worker had perfect attendance during a two-week period and thus produced the maximum amount, he received the full bonus. If he were absent, he received only part of the bonus.[3]

The anti-inflationary productivity campaign developed slowly until the presidential elections in November 1951. After that Perón apparently felt secure enough to initiate stricter measures of control. In December 1951, he helped establish the Confederación General Económica (CGE) to represent business interests, and asked the CGE, the CGT, and the National Economic Council to stabilize prices and wages.[4] Thus, through these organizations the government determined prices and wages and tightened its control over the entire economy.[5]

The captive CGT predictably supported the government's anti-inflation campaign. In 1952 the newspaper of the federation began to print slogans at the top of each page urging the workers to produce more, to spend only what was necessary, and to save as much as possible.[6] By 1954 the leadership was urging a new kind of restraint on the workers. The labor organizations, a *CGT* editorial explained, were designed not only to guarantee unity and collective discipline, but also to make sure that the workers, "who have received the logical and necessary social justice, do not extend their demands beyond that which is reasonably just." The worker who wanted his just demands respected, the editorial concluded, must be reasonable and must realize that collective contracts were intended to protect both parties.⁷

The anti-inflation campaign reached a climax in March 1955, when the CGT and the CGE jointly sponsored the National Congress of Productivity and Social Well-Being. The theme of the Congress was productivity, but the emphasis was on worker-management cooperation for the good of the country. This series of meetings, the author of the summary report of the Congress explained, "ends the epoch of struggle and the labor movement returns to collaboration with the productive factors of the country. . . . Now the representatives of the workers act with the representatives of the employers' organizations." ⁸

Another part of the new economic program—the campaign to attract private foreign investment to Argentina—conflicted with Perón's earlier economic nationalism. Beginning in 1950 the government attempted to ease restrictions on the importation of machinery and equipment and on the withdrawal of profits from the country. In addition, it tried to guarantee investors repayment of their losses in the event of nationalization.⁹

It was not until 1954 and 1955, however, that these efforts produced tangible results. In 1954 Fiat established a factory in Córdoba, and in 1955 a number of foreign concerns built plants in Argentina or signed contracts to do so. Kaiser opened a car assembly plant in Córdoba and a subsidiary of the Standard Oil Company of California signed a contract that would enable it to explore and develop the oil fields of Patagonia. And, finally, the government negotiated a $60 million loan with the Import-Export Bank in order to construct a steel plant.

The Perón propaganda machine took up the new line immediately and explained to the workers that there had been no change in policy. "Foreign investors," the CGT argued, "are a danger for the country of investment only when those countries lack legislative norms to regulate their activities adequately." Foreign capital, the article continued, had an important mission in the development of Argentina because the country possessed adequate regulations to control its activity.[10]

The propaganda machine could not, however, destroy the evidence that the government had in fact embarked on a new economic policy. In addition to the physical presence of new private foreign companies in Argentina, the government modified its policy toward the principal source of foreign capital, the United States. In July 1953, Milton Eisenhower—the brother of the President of the United States—received an enthusiastic official welcome when he visited Argentina. In October of the same year Perón praised President Eisenhower and spoke of his warm friendship with the United States. More tangibly, Perón permitted the distribution of sixteen United States periodicals in Argentina that he had previously banned, and made a gesture to limit the activities of the Communists.

A major part of the new economic policy was the government's effort to bolster the badly deteriorating agricultural sector. During his first administration, Perón had kept prices on agricultural commodities low and credit tight. Because of the resulting loss of incentive and because of droughts in 1950 and 1951, agricultural production declined sharply. In 1952, however, the administration granted the producers their first substantial price increase since 1946 and liberalized farm credit.[11]

Despite the commitment on the part of the government, the new economic policy failed. The productivity of the agricultural worker increased slightly between 1950 and 1955, but the productivity of the industrial worker stayed about the same. In addition, the net gold and foreign exchange reserves of the Central Bank declined from 5,646 million pesos in 1947 to 1,485 million pesos in 1955, and the money in circulation increased from 8 billion pesos in 1945 to 60 billion pesos in 1955. Finally, the hoped-for flow of foreign capital was small and confined to a few industries.[12]

Significant for this study is the fact that the new economic policy forced the government to curtail the social and economic revolution on behalf of the workers. Fringe benefits remained substantially the same as before, but real wages dropped sharply between 1949 and 1952 and recovered only slightly during the 1953 to 1955 period (see Table IV).

TABLE IV

REAL WAGES OF INDUSTRIAL
WORKERS, 1949–1955
(IN PER CENT) *

1949	105.0
1950	100.0
1951	92.6
1952	82.0
1953	86.3
1954	97.1
1955	97.0

* Confederación General del Trabajo, *Boletín Informativo Semanal*, June 17, 1963, p. 5.

The industrial workers resented not only the decline in real wages, but also the favoritism shown the agricultural sector of the economy, the invitation to foreign capital to invest in Argentina, and the development of more friendly relations with the United States. The new economic policy failed to achieve its objectives but nevertheless made much of organized labor wonder whose interests the government and Perón represented. By and large, the workers went along with these programs, but this was because of their personal loyalty to Perón. They did not fail to notice that participation in what many thought were anti-labor programs reduced them to one among several influential elements in society, whereas formerly they believed they had been the most important representatives of the Argentine nation.

Perón's attacks on the Catholic Church in 1954 and 1955 also apparently offended a number of those in the large anti-liberal sector of the labor movement. Few of the workers were practicing Catholics who attended church services or participated in other religious affairs.[13] Nevertheless, the Church had exercised considerable influence over the rural peons and had been one of the few familiar and friendly organizations that the internal migrants had encountered in the city. Moreover, the Church had been a silent partner of the government during the early years of the Perón regime. As a result many workers felt some loyalty to the Church, and Perón's attacks therefore added to their growing confusion about the true nature of the government.[14]

Relations between Church and state were good from 1943 until sometime toward the end of Perón's first administration. The *de facto* government, by permitting religious instruction in the schools, reversed a half-century-old policy of separation of Church and state. The Church responded by supporting the regime. During the presidential campaign of 1946, the Argentine bishops issued a pastoral letter that advised Catholics not to vote for candidates whose platforms permitted the legalization of divorce, a ban on religious instruction in the schools, or a separation of Church and state. Since every party belonging to the opposition Unión Democrática advocated one or more of these ideas, the letter constituted indirect support for Perón.[15]

The government's subsequent involvement in social welfare and its attempt to substitute Peronist for religious education led to a less cordial relationship with the Church. In 1950 the conservative, anti-liberal Padre Julio Meinvielle attacked the Perón regime for attempting to create a "godless socialist Argentina."[16] In 1951, the editor of the important Catholic magazine *Criterio*, Monsignor Gustavo J. Franceschi, also a conservative anti-liberal, indirectly attacked the Perón regime. Franceschi claimed that in Stalinist Russia, in Hitler's Germany, and in Mussolini's Italy conformity had developed because of a mistaken belief in the power of one individual and because for many conformity was the safest way to obtain material benefits. But conformity of this kind, he concluded, with an implicit reference to the Argentine situation, would not save man or the world.[17]

The less influential liberal elements of the Church had quietly opposed Perón from the beginning, but their opposition became more pronounced with time. Monsignor Miguel de Andrea, Bishop of Temnos and the outstanding Church opponent of the regime, claimed in 1946 that he was neither for nor against Perón. He declared, however, that he believed in freedom of speech, democracy, independent unionism, Christianity, and the Argentine Constitution, and that when any of these ideals were attacked he would speak out.[18]

Andrea did not exactly "speak out" against Perón, but as adviser to the Federation of Catholic Workers' Associations —a women's trade union group in Buenos Aires—he indirectly opposed the regime. For example, in response to the government's campaign to destroy labor independence, he publicly stressed the necessity of independent unionism for the development of a democratic Argentina. And in 1950 he was instrumental in the establishment of the Instituto Cultural Gremial. The purpose of the Instituto was to train union leaders so that when they confronted Peronists or

Communists, they could effectively argue Christian labor doctrine with them.¹⁹

The Church's disenchantment with Perón had developed sufficiently by 1951 so that it did not support him for re-election, as it had done indirectly in 1946. From then on, relations between the Church and state deteriorated rapidly and in November 1954, in speeches to the governors of the provinces and to the CGT, Perón launched an open attack on the Church.²⁰ He accused the Church of infiltrating the popular movements with the intention of turning the workers against the government. In all organizations, Perón explained, there were good men and bad men. In Argentina there were 16,000 clergy and only 20 or 30 of them were disturbing the public order. His regime was not attacking the Church, he insisted, but it would move against the few bad priests who were conspiring with the Communists to overthrow the government.²¹

Between November 1954, when Perón delivered these speeches, and June 16, 1955, when he was excommunicated, the government attacked the Church continually. It passed a law to legalize divorce, it forbade religious festivals in the streets, it suspended religious instructions in the schools, and initiated the process of separating Church and state. In May there was a series of demonstrations against the Church and an attack on the palace of the Archbishop. And in June, the Corpus Christi procession, which had been prohibited by the government but which the Church held anyway, led to a public riot. To punish the Church for holding the procession without his permission, Perón expelled two Catholic prelates. Several days later the Vatican excommunicated him.²²

It is not entirely clear why Perón attacked the Church, but there are a number of reasons why he might have done so. First, the President needed to draw attention away from the deteriorating economic situation, the influx of foreign capital, and his declining popularity. Possibly he believed his attack on the Church would provide such a diversion. Second, some of his close advisers—Ángel Borlenghi, Juan Isaac Cooke, Méndez San Martín, and others—were anti-clerics and probably counseled such an attack. Third, Perón may have been concerned about the competition between the liberal Catholic organizations and his own organizations. Bishop Andrea had some influence among the workers; Acción Católica and the Asociación Democrática de Estudiantes Secundarios (ADES) had competed effectively with the government-sponsored Unión de Estudiantes Secundarios; and the proposed Christian Democratic Party could certainly win the support of a number of Peronists, especially among the workers. And, fourth, as a dictator Perón probably could not tolerate the continuing independence of the Church.[23]

What is clear, however, is that Perón misjudged the effect that his attacks on the Church would have on Argentine society in general and on the labor movement in particular. Instead of strengthening the position of the government, his policy transformed the Church into something of a symbol of independence and a rallying point for the opposition to the regime. In the labor movement an anti-clerical tradition did exist, but ironically it was for the most part associated with the liberals and laboristas whom Perón had replaced. Many of the new anti-liberal leaders were nominal Catholics and several of them believed that the attacks on the Church cost Perón considerable support among the workers.[24]

Perón's attacks on the Church never had widespread labor support. They did not win liberal or laborista backing because what members these groups still possessed were too embittered by previous incidents to consider any kind of support for Perón. And to many anti-liberal workers these attacks reversed previous government policy without sufficient justification and, along with the new economic policy, were cause for concern about the future direction of the government.

Perón attempted to dispel the growing doubts of the workers in a number of ways. For one, he used symbols and rituals to help convince the workers that nothing had changed. He continued to portray himself as "the material representation, the living incarnation," the national patrón of the Argentine nation. But the death of his wife Evita removed an important contact with labor and forced him to attempt to fill her place as the special symbol of the descamisados. From the end of 1951, when Perón first knew that his wife would soon die of cancer, until her death on July 26, 1952, the CGT carried on an intensive propaganda campaign designed to help the President accomplish his objective. And late in 1951 Evita's ghost-written book, *La razón de mi vida*, was published to communicate to the workers the need for absolute loyalty and obedience to Perón.

Not wishing to leave anything to chance, Evita made her views absolutely clear in a dramatic final speech to the descamisados gathered in the Plaza de Mayo on May 1, 1952, in which she exhorted them: "My dear descamisados, . . . be on your guard. The enemy are preparing an ambush for us. Stand by Perón, who stands by you, and then we can never be defeated, for we are the real Argentina. . . . We will never again let ourselves be kicked around by the traitorous and corrupt oligarchy and their foreign masters. Woe be to them the day they lift a hand against Perón. For that day . . . I will go out into the streets with the workingmen, with the women of the people, with the descamisados, and we will not leave one stone upon another that is not Peronista." [25]

Immediately after her death, Perón strengthened his position by taking over Evita's former jobs. He became head of the Eva Perón Social Welfare Foundation and the

Peronista Women's Party. And, most important, he replaced his wife at the frequent meetings with the leaders of the CGT.

The propaganda campaign also increased after Evita died. The mourning period stopped all civic activity for more than a week and the *CGT* printed a new series of slogans to match the event: "From immortality, Eva Perón will continue being the Guardian Angel of her people," "Eva Perón will continue to be the bridge of love between General Perón and his people." [26]

The climax of the campaign to transfer the people's personal love for Evita to her husband came on October 17, 1952. On this Loyalty Day, the descamisados filled the Plaza de Mayo to honor Perón and especially Evita. CGT Secretary-General José Espejo explained that the workers had come to support Perón once again, but this time with more desire than ever to pay homage to the memory of Evita.

The most important event of the day was the reading of Evita's will. After a moment of silence to evoke her presence the will was solemnly read: "I want to live eternally with Perón and with my people. If I die before Perón, I want this will read to the descamisados in the Plaza de Mayo on October 17. I want them to know how much I love Perón. While Perón is alive, he is my heir and after him the people." [27]

In addition to his reliance on charisma to hold the support of the workers, Perón attempted to draw their attention away from the national situation by promising them international recognition and leadership. He tried to make the Argentine workers believe that they had created a workers' nation and therefore were uniquely qualified to help the rest of Latin America achieve the same thing. He attempted to change the focus of the workers' nationalism from the internal social and economic revolution to an international revolution that would rid the continent of foreign influences and would give

Argentine labor hegemony over the labor movements of the area.

Argentine labor attachés, working in most Latin American countries since 1946, had had some success in winning support for Perón. But until 1952 there was no attempt to coordinate their efforts or to provide them with any regional support. In February 1952, 133 delegates representing nineteen countries met under the tutelage of Perón in Asunción, Paraguay, to establish the Comité de Unidad Sindical Latinoamericana (CUSL). The avowed purpose of the new international labor organization was to fight against misery, exploitation, and colonialism in America, and above all to rid Latin America of all foreign influences.[28]

In the months following the establishment of the CUSL, the anti-liberal CGT leaders set forth their objectives in greater detail. Justicialism, the CGT newspaper pointed out, had become the ideal of all Latin America. The Confederación de Trabajadores de América Latina (CTAL), the Confederación Interamericana de Trabajadores (CIT), and the Organización Regional Interamericana de Trabajadores (ORIT) had been unable to serve the needs of the workers of America because they had been puppet organizations since their establishment.[29] They had been dominated by the Communists or by the North American labor movement, which was subservient to Wall Street. The CUSL would be different, the CGT leaders concluded, because it would follow Perón's Third Position between collectivism and capitalism in the international labor field.[30]

Perón participated in the *CGT* propaganda campaign to make the workers believe they had an important international mission. For example, in May 1952 he explained that he did not want to impose Peronism on anyone. At the same time, he could not prevent others from adopting it, because "The doctrine of the Peronist movement is not the absolute property of Perón, of Peronism, or of the Argentines. . . . It belongs to all men and to all peoples who want to use it as a road to liberation." [31]

In November 1952, the members of CUSL met in Mexico to enlarge the organization, broaden its appeal, and change its name to Agrupación de Trabajadores Latino Americanos Sindicalizados (ATLAS). The leaders of ATLAS claimed that it represented eighteen million workers in Latin America and, in addition to attacking United States labor as the "tool of Wall Street" and ORIT as the "tool of United States labor," it projected Eva Perón as the saint of all of the American workers.[32]

ATLAS was a creature of the Argentine CGT and of Perón and remained so throughout the Perón period. Its first Secretary-General was José Espejo, the former Secretary-General of the CGT. Perón and the Argentine labor movement provided almost all of the funds for the organization. And the Argentine labor attachés in the Latin American countries provided much of the stimulus for the establishment of affiliate organizations.

ATLAS was most successful in countries ruled by dictators, although it did have some success in others. It won labor support in the Colombia of Gustavo Rojas Pinilla, the Chile of Carlos Ibáñez del Campo, the Nicaragua of Anastasio Somoza, the Peru of Manuel Odría, the Haiti of Paul Magloire, and the Guatemala of Jacobo Arbenz. It also received support from groups in Costa Rica, Cuba, Mexico, Puerto Rico, and Uruguay.[33]

The organization was supported by many dictators because it was useful to them. After June 1953, when General Gustavo Rojas Pinilla overthrew the government of Laureano Gómez in Colombia, Perón's labor attaché was encouraged to infiltrate the labor movement in order to establish a progovernment rival to the Church-influenced Unión de Trabajadores de Colombia. After failing to take over the organization, the Rojas Pinilla-Perón sympathizers established the

Confederación Nacional de Trabajadores (CNT) and affiliated it with ATLAS. The same element also attempted to take over the other major Colombia labor federation, the Confederación de Trabajadores de Colombia, but failed to do so. The CNT leaders claimed a membership of 120,000, but this figure was greatly exaggerated and despite ample funds the organization never exerted much influence within the Colombian labor movement.[34]

Carlos Ibáñez del Campo also attempted to use ATLAS to help him establish pro-government rivals to the existing Chilean labor federations. In 1948 the sugar workers, led by Rubén Hurtado—who supported Perón and later became an important official of ATLAS—brought together a number of unions to form the Confederación Nacional de Sindicatos Obreros de Viña del Mar. When Ibáñez, who was sympathetic to the labor policies of Perón, was elected President of Chile in 1952, Hurtado and the Peronists were encouraged. Two weeks after Ibáñez had come to power, María de la Cruz, a staunch supporter of Ibáñez and Perón, announced the formation of two new pro-Perón labor federations. Ibáñez also appointed Jorge Ibarra, a pro-Peronist, as one of his labor advisers and later exchanged visits with Perón.[35]

Perón's support among the Chilean workers was nominal, but in February 1953 most of the country's labor organizations joined together to establish the Central Única de Trabajadores de Chile (CUTCH), in part to prevent the Ibáñez government from creating a single government-controlled labor federation like the Argentine CGT. The anti-Peronist CUTCH has dominated the Chilean labor movement since 1953 and therefore ATLAS, despite the support of Ibáñez, was unable to make any significant impact on Chile.[36]

In democratic Uruguay, ATLAS managed to win the support of 5 or 10 per cent of the workers. In 1950, the

Uruguayan Peronists, under the leadership of the metallurgic worker Omar Díaz, established the Movimiento Nacional Revolucionario La Escoba. The movement had approximately 20,000 members, mostly from the metallurgic and meat packers unions, and from 1950 to 1955 published the newspaper *La Escoba*. When ATLAS was established in 1952, this group became its Uruguayan affiliate, but it at no time had anything like a mass following.[37]

Despite the support of various dictators and the establishment of affiliates in several democratic countries, ATLAS was never a strong and representative international organization. At no time did it present a challenge to ORIT. Obviously its claim to eighteen million members was completely false. Its major strength was the Argentine labor movement and the best evidence indicates that outside of Argentina it had about 166,000 members in 41 federations, confederations and locals.[38] After the fall of Perón the organization dwindled to practically nothing.

ATLAS was a failure and so were Perón's efforts to bolster the workers' fading sense of national mission by making them leaders of a continental revolution. No worker could forget the Argentine problems that affected his daily life, regardless of what the *CGT* said about his importance in the international field. Thus at critical moments Perón attempted to use other means to divert the worker's mind from the domestic situation.

For example, in April 1953, when real wages reached their lowest point during the entire period, mobs attacked and burned the Jockey Club, the Casa del Pueblo, and the headquarters of the Radical Party while the police stood by. And on May 13, 1953, Perón reverted to the oratorical style of his deceased wife in a speech before the garment workers. Quoting Evita directly, he said: "The class struggle will end only when one class disappears." The Peronist movement would, he insisted, "destroy the oligarchy" because in Argentina there could only be the class that worked.[39]

Although most workers continued to be loyal Peronists from 1952 to 1955, they became increasingly unwilling to accept the President's redefinition of the national interest. On pragmatic grounds they demanded more freedom to fight for what they understood to be their interests, and they insisted upon more responsive, efficient, and honest leadership much as they had during the latter years of the first Perón administration. But the decline in real wages, the influx of foreign capital, the new attitude toward the United States, the attack on the Church plus the increasing subservience of the labor leadership to the government all added a feeling of urgency to the protest that turned discontent into frustration and then resentment.

The liberals, exiled in Montevideo, futilely attempted to attack Perón for violating the national tradition and pointed out that he had betrayed his own ideals. In 1953 they noted that the anti-Yankee Perón had now become friendly with the United States. In 1954 they attacked the government for returning the industry of the country to private business. And they also warned that Perón was turning Argentine oil over to foreign capitalists and was favoring North American over Argentine businessmen.[40] Their attacks, however, had little effect across the river.

In Argentina the ideological lines separating the various groups within the labor movement—particularly the laboristas from the anti-liberals—became somewhat blurred during this period. The leadership of all unions was subservient to Perón and followed the changing party line rather than its own ideological inclinations. This did not, however, eliminate important manifestations of worker discontent. Such manifestations continued as before to be directed at the subservient leadership, but now, because the leaders were even more closely tied to Perón, some of the protests indirectly challenged Perón.

For example, during the 1953 General Assembly of the Unión Ferroviaria, one of the delegates, Juan de Dios Obregón, openly criticized the government. The Assembly repudiated his speech and expelled Obregón from the meeting, but it is significant that the organization permitted him to finish such a long speech and published it in the minutes of the meeting for all the workers to read.[41]

Both the government and the Executive Committee of the railroad union, Obregón charged, had failed to develop the railroads of the country. The railroads were completely disorganized and would remain so as long as they were run by inexperienced people, "men who have come off the street." The union must collaborate with the government, he continued, but "collaboration is based upon holding high the truth, pleasant or unpleasant, to the powerful, not upon always saying yes. . . . The Executive Committee, with Perón at its head, has the world in its hands, but up to now they have not known what to do with it." [42]

The same General Assembly of the Unión Ferroviaria discussed a pamphlet that also attacked the Executive Committee. As with the speech of Obregón, the Assembly repudiated the pamphlet, but it nevertheless discussed it in detail and printed it in the minutes. The pamphlet, which attacked the union's president, Rosales, because he was "afraid to speak openly," was signed by the Central Peronist Commission of the Mitre, Roca, San Martín, Sarmiento, Belgrano, and Urquiza Railroads. "We are with Perón and Evita," the pamphlet stated, but the Executive Committee, "the traitors to the nationality," were not. This Committee had acted without the support of the workers, it had illegally extended its term of office from two to four years, it had collaborated with the Communists, and it had unjustly punished members and intervened in sections of the organization. And, the pamphlet concluded, several of its members were agents of Spruille Braden and the Unión Democrática.[43]

Many metallurgic workers also protested against the policies of their union leadership and the government during this period. The metallurgic workers were divided into several groups, two of which opposed the government's policies. The first group was led by Secretary-General Abdula Baluch and completely supported the government. The second group was led by former Secretary-General Hilario Salvo and strongly opposed Baluch because of his "Trotskyite sympathies" and his subservience to the government. The third group was led by communist sympathizers in Rosario and joined with Salvo to oppose Baluch.

The struggle among these groups took various forms. For example, in September 1952, an armed group of Salvo's supporters attacked the union's headquarters. With outside help, the Baluch group was able to repel the attack, but at the same time the Rosario affiliate declared itself autonomous and separate from the general organization. The CGT intervened in the union to support Baluch, and eventually he was able to persuade the Rosario section to rejoin the central organization. But a number of leaders were dismissed and the incident left bitter feelings among the workers.[44]

Discontent with the subservient Baluch increased and in May and June of 1954, when the union was renegotiating its contract with the employers, it erupted into a violent protest. The workers asked for a 30 per cent wage increase and the employers offered them 10 per cent.[45] To back up their demand, the workers began a series of strikes and slowdowns. Early in June Baluch announced that the strike was over because the employers had offered a 16 per cent wage increase and he urged the workers to return to their jobs. A large number refused to accept this settlement and attempted to march to the Casa Rosada to present their grievances to Perón, whom they still believed would settle the matter in their favor. A fight broke out between the supporters and opponents of Baluch, the police attempted to stop it, and three people—including an officer of the union—were killed.[46]

The next day the workers established a strike committee to guide the continuing protest and issued a manifesto outlining their grievances. They demanded salaries high enough to support themselves and their families, accused Baluch of negotiating secretly with the employers, claimed that the union leadership had fired at them with guns, and insisted that they had the right to elect responsive leaders.[47]

CGT Secretary-General Eduardo Vuletich warned the strike leaders that they were "acting contrary to the interests of the government," and when they continued their activity the police intervened to "settle" the conflict. Predictably, the CGT and the union leadership claimed that the strike was communist-inspired and that it was an attempt to divide the union. Nevertheless, the demands of the workers were met: wages were increased and Baluch was replaced as Secretary-General.[48]

Labor opposition to low wages and ineffective leadership was openly expressed. Labor opposition to the attack on the Church was more subtle. The CGT, the Unión Ferroviaria, and most other labor organizations echoed Perón's charges against the Church, but at the same time they indicated their awareness of the influence the Church still had with many workers by insisting that they were attacking only a few "bad Catholics" and not the Church as a whole.

In November 1954—just after Perón's initial attack on the Church—the CGT leaders issued a declaration maintaining that the workers believed in God and that the labor federation did not close its doors to religion. But, the leaders insisted, the workers would not permit "bad Catho-

Perón Abandons the Workers' Nation / 57

lics" to infiltrate and subvert their organizations.⁴⁹ What was perhaps most significant was that the anti-liberal metallurgic workers remained silent during the government's anti-Church campaign, while the CGT and many other union leaders actively supported Perón in this effort. Silence in this case suggested sympathy, if not outright support, for the Church.

Between June 16 and September 16, 1955, all of the conflicts that had developed during Perón's second administration reemerged. The military uprising of June 16 failed to overthrow the government, but it did frighten Perón sufficiently so that he permitted the military to curtail further labor's influence and power. The military took over the CGT's remaining arsenal of 5,000 rifles and revolvers. The *CGT* printed editorials urging the workers to respect the law for the benefit of labor and the nation. Ángel Borlenghi and Eduardo Vuletich—since the death of Evita, the leading "rabble-rousers" of the labor movement—resigned their respective jobs as Minister of the Interior and Secretary-General of the CGT. And on July 15 Perón announced the end of his revolution.⁵⁰

In his July 15 speech, Perón explained that the Peronists had been the originators of a revolutionary movement and that such movements had rights that political parties did not. The regime had limited liberties when necessary to achieve its revolutionary objectives, but it had never resorted to terror. All revolutions, Perón continued, must come to an end: "The Peronist revolution has ended; now begins a new constitutional stage, without revolutions, because the permanent state of the country cannot be revolution. . . . I cease being the head of a revolution and become the president of all the Argentines. . . . Never has Peronism been stronger than at the present and it is for this reason, because we are strong, that we must be noble in the fulfillment of our mission to the Republic." [51]

The government's conflict with the Church also intensified. On June 16, 1955, the Vatican excommunicated Perón in retaliation for his expulsion of the two Argentine prelates. Then in July the Argentine Catholic hierarchy published *The Episcopal Declaration Denouncing the Religious Persecution in Argentina*, which made it clear that it was not just a few clerics who were opposing Perón, but the entire leadership of the Church. The declaration reviewed Church-state relations during the past year and pointed out how the government had made cooperation impossible. It claimed that the government had attacked the Church in the press, had accused the Church of infiltrating and interfering in non-Church movements, had permitted divorce, had suppressed religious festivals, had ended religious instruction in the schools, and had initiated proceedings to separate Church and state.[52]

At this point the non-Peronist working-class opposition began its attack on the regime. The Partido Concentración Obrera, a small pro-communist party, openly protested the lack of freedom in the country. The Socialist Party demanded the elimination of Peronism. The tiny remnants of the once-powerful anarchist FORA demanded union independence and liberty in addition to freedom to strike, associate, and speak.[53]

Perhaps the most damaging attack on the regime by working-class elements was a declaration published by fifty-six former labor leaders of liberal and laborista persuasion. It stated in part: "One of the fundamental factors of the present national crisis is the loss of autonomy by the labor movement and the denial of individual rights of its members. . . . Inflation has annulled our wage increases. We need leaders whose term of office is not measured by their enrichment and ostentation, but by austerity, abnegation, and moral leadership in order that they might be representatives of the working class before the government and the patrón class and not government agents before the people."[54]

As the opposition both within and without the labor movement increased, Perón attempted to defend his position. In mid-August he announced the end of the political truce he had declared a month before. The *CGT* began to print inflammatory editorials attacking all opposition to the regime and also began an intensive campaign to reidentify Perón with his deceased wife.[55] Finally, on August 31, Perón attempted to reenact the dramatic days of October 1945 that had brought him to power. He began the carefully staged drama by announcing his resignation. "Men are guarantees of nothing permanent for the nation," Perón explained to the CGT and the Peronist Party. "Only organizations and institutions are permanent and in them the country must find its security."[56]

The CGT and the Peronist Party rejected the renunciation according to the script, and in an attempt at a complete parallel to October 17, 1945, workers were brought in on trains and buses for a big demonstration in the Plaza de Mayo. At the "insistence" of the crowd, which was much smaller and considerably less enthusiastic than ten years before, Perón withdrew his resignation and delivered the most inflammatory speech of his life. He had offered peace and a truce to his opponents, he began, but they did not want it. Instead they had responded with violence: "To violence we have to answer with a greater violence. With their exaggerated violence we have the right to repress them violently. . . . When one of ours falls, five of theirs will fall. . . . The dilemma is clear: either we fight and conquer in order to consolidate the conquests obtained, or the oligarchy will destroy them for good. . . . Today begins for all of us a new vigil in arms."[57]

Shortly after this speech the CGT Central Committee met and adopted a motion proposed by Secretary-General Di Pietro to put the voluntary reserves of the workers at the disposition of the army. The army, disturbed for some time by the prospect of a workers' militia, rejected the offer and on September 16, 1955, General Eduardo Lonardi began the Revolución Libertadora that overthrew Perón.[58]

Perhaps the most significant thing about the overthrow of Perón is that organized labor did very little to defend him. Secretary-General Di Pietro went on the radio to urge the workers to fight for Perón, but only isolated groups in Buenos Aires, Rosario, and a few other cities responded to the call of the CGT leader.[59]

There are a number of reasons why the workers did not fight. According to the Peronists José Alonso and August Vandor, Perón never gave the order to fight and labor had no weapons. In addition, Perón was tired and he loved Argentina; therefore, he left the country to avoid a bloody civil war that would have destroyed it.[60] The anti-Peronist, Riego Ribas, suggested another important point. Under Perón, few labor leaders had developed any influence and prestige of their own, and hence at the time of the Revolución Libertadora there was no one to provide effective leadership. The discredited lieutenants of Perón occupied the union offices, but the workers would not follow them.[61]

Perhaps the most accurate interpretation is that given by the Peronists Daniel Vukasovich and Juan Carlos Loholaberry, the dissident Peronists Luis Gay and Hilario Salvo, and the anti-Peronist Sebastián Marotta, who all suggested that in addition to the above reasons the workers did not fight because Perón had terminated the revolution and had compelled them to question the assumption that their interests were the same as those of the new Argentina.[62] They had supported Perón because he had identified them with an egalitarian criollo nation in which the workers were equal,

Perón Abandons the Workers' Nation / 161

respected, and influential citizens. But Perón's policies of holding down wages, of encouraging foreign capital to invest in Argentina, of friendship with the United States, and of opposition to the Church seemed to deny this vision. Perón had done much to create a workers' nation, but now he seemed to have abandoned it.

A comparison of September 1955 and October 1945 illustrates the difference in the workers' attitudes at the beginning and the end of the Perón era. In 1945 labor united to defend Perón, the social and economic revolution, and the emerging workers' nation even though Perón had given no order to fight and they had no weapons. The military, however, was divided, uncertain whether or not to support Perón, and unable to win civilian backing. This combination favored labor and produced the workers' victory of October 17.

In September 1955 the situation was quite different. The military was more united than ever before in opposition to Perón and it had civilian backing. Labor was divided and uncertain about what Perón stood for. The majority of workers remained personally loyal to Perón, but they were resentful and did not fight. Under these circumstances the military had little difficulty overthrowing Perón.

8

The Resurgence of Criollo Nationalism

The most difficult problem confronting the successful leaders of the Revolución Libertadora was what to do about the Peronist CGT with its membership of 2.5 million. The leaders of both the anti-liberal and the liberal military factions agreed that they must end Perón's influence in the labor movement, but they disagreed as to how this might be accomplished. The anti-liberals wanted to wean the workers away from Perón by continuing much of the social and economic revolution, under their own direction. The liberals felt it necessary to purge the labor movement of all those closely associated in any way with Peronism.

General Eduardo Lonardi, Provisional President from mid-September to mid-November 1955, attempted to be neutral in the conflict between the two military factions and at the same time avoid recriminations against the Peronists. He sought to pacify the country on the basis of compromise and took as his motto that of Justo José Urquiza, the caudillo who defeated Juan Manuel de Rosas in 1852: "Ni vencedores ni vencidos"—neither victors nor vanquished. He sought a reconciliation with the Peronist-dominated labor movement because he believed that the support of the CGT was essential if he were to turn the government over to civilians in the near future. "With the support of the CGT," he remarked, "there will be no more problems."[1]

Organized labor as well as the military was divided into two broad factions. First, there were the Peronists, who controlled most of the unions and represented about 70 per cent of the workers. Within this sector was a small group of high-ranking labor leaders who would accept nothing short of the return of Perón. In addition there was another group of younger, less influential, Peronist leaders who, apparently supported by a large majority of the workers, were more willing to compromise with the government in order to protect labor's gains of the past twelve years. The second broad group within the labor movement was the "independents." This group included all types of anti-Peronists, including Socialists, Communists, Radicals, and some former Laboristas.[2]

Lonardi for the most part ignored the independents, attacked the uncompromising Peronists, and attempted to woo the moderate younger generation of Peronists. The issue that most concerned the Peronist workers was whether or not the gains of the past twelve years would be maintained. Would their status, somewhat undermined during the second Perón administration, be protected by the Revolución Libertadora? Specifically, they wanted to know who would control the CGT, the individual unions, and the labor newspapers *La Prensa* and *El Lider*. Lonardi immediately assured the workers that their legitimate interests would be protected, and after several crises he managed to settle the important issues to the satisfaction of the majority of them.

On September 25 Lonardi initiated his campaign to win

the support of the CGT by conferring with its Secretary-General, Hugo Di Pietro. As a result of the meeting, the government pledged to honor all social legislation and collective bargaining agreements, to respect the rights of the CGT and its affiliates, to prohibit any legal injunction against the labor federation, and to permit the CGT to continue to publish the newspaper *La Prensa*.[3] The next day Lonardi further enhanced his popularity with the Peronist workers by appointing as Minister of Labor Luis B. Cerrutti Costa, a Catholic nationalist labor lawyer who had strongly supported Perón during his early years.[4]

Within a week, however, the first of two major labor-government crises erupted. For one thing, the government initiated a campaign to discredit Perón and to disassociate him from the social and economic revolution of the workers. It opened up and filmed the luxurious Buenos Aires apartment hideout of the former President in order to suggest that he had not been much of a poor descamisado. It publicized the fact that in the apartment were 400 suits, 60 pairs of shoes, 10 television sets, furs, jewels, gold, and cash, besides 14 cars in the garage. Two days later, the police released several intercepted letters from Perón to his mistress, "Nellie" Rivas, the sixteen-year-old daughter of a janitor. One letter, reprinted widely in the anti-Peronist press, was addressed "My dear child" and signed "Your Daddy."[5]

Of greater concern to the Peronist workers was the fact that armed bands of independents forcefully seized a number of union headquarters, including that of the large and important Unión Ferroviaria. On October 3 the CGT leaders protested to the government and were quickly assured by Minister of Labor Cerrutti Costa that Lonardi intended to keep his promise to respect the unions' rights and to prevent their violent seizure.

Nevertheless, that same evening the Executive Committee of the CGT wrote a letter to Lonardi that condemned the violent assaults on the unions and asked for protection against future ones, committed the leaders to hold immediate free elections and to declare an amnesty so that all workers could participate regardless of ideological affiliation, and asked the government for money to pay for the elections. Lonardi met with the CGT Executive Committee, received its letter, and again assured the leaders that he would protect labor's interests.[6]

During the next few days an important rank-and-file Peronist revolt broke out and led to the ouster of the older generation of uncompromising Peronist leaders. Clearly the Peronist workers were no longer willing to tolerate the old corrupt, subservient leadership. As a result, on October 5 two young Peronists, Andrés Framini of the textile union and Luis Natalini of the light and power workers, replaced Hugo Di Pietro and his Executive Committee as leaders of the CGT.[7]

The change in leadership, which brought to power the moderate Peronist element the government believed it could work with, represented a triumph for Lonardi. Therefore, the Minister of Labor quickly recognized the new leaders and immediately concluded an agreement with them on October 6 in order to strengthen their position. According to the new agreement, all CGT affiliates would hold elections within 120 days; there would be a complete amnesty so that all workers could participate in the elections; the newly elected authorities would select representatives to the Central Committee of the CGT, who in turn would elect the Executive Committee and the Secretariat of the federation; and the Minister of Labor would oversee the elections and protect all labor organizations from further armed attack by opposition groups.[8]

When this agreement had been reached, the government intervened in a number of unions that had been violently seized by the independents—including the railroad, meat-packers', telephone, and maritime unions—and returned them to their Peronist leaders. For a brief period of about a week, labor union activity seemed to stabilize, with the various labor factions and the government apparently accepting the *status quo*.

The temporary calm was deceptive, however, because the second major labor-government crisis of the Lonardi period was already developing. In mid-October, the government invited newspapermen from all over the world to view the jewels, furs, and dresses collected by Evita Perón, and at the same time accused the Perón administration of committing widespread electoral frauds. In addition, anti-Peronist elements again attacked several union headquarters and ejected the CGT interventors.[9]

At first the new CGT leaders, anxious to work with the government, responded with restraint. For example, they advised the workers to heed the advice of the government and report to their jobs on the traditional Peronist holiday, October 17. They also petitioned the government, asking that their demands as stated in the October 6 agreement be fulfilled.

Nevertheless, the crisis augmented rapidly. On October 19 a group of independent labor leaders met and issued a statement that was critical not only of the Peronists, but of the Minister of Labor as well. The independents claimed that Cerrutti Costa did not understand the democratic principles for which the Revolución Libertadora had been fought, denounced the "compromising actions" of the Minister of Labor—particularly his plan to hold union elections within 120 days—and demanded fulfillment of the "genuine objectives" of the revolution.[10]

During the next week the attacks on the unions continued and the government, caught in the struggles between the two military factions and the two labor groups, did little to stop them. According to the CGT leaders, at least fourteen unions had been seized by force. Therefore on October 26, Framini and Natalini, plus some 300 union officials, sought and obtained an interview with Cerrutti Costa and again pressed their demands.

Framini, speaking for the group, insisted that the CGT wanted to cooperate with the provisional government and was not, as some of the independents had charged, fulfilling political obligations. At the same time he warned the Minister of Labor that the workers would not permit their legitimate conquests to be taken away from them by force. The solution to the problem, Framini suggested, was to honor the agreement of October 6.

Framini then submitted a list of what he and his followers believed to be "violations" of the agreement and asked the government to restore all unions to their legitimate authorities until elections could be held; support the CGT interventors in their efforts to carry out their duties; restore the regional CGT's to their legitimate leaders; and release all workers detained for political reasons. The labor leaders accompanied the list with a warning that if the demands were not met within two days, they would call a general strike.[11]

The next day the government released the recently completed Prebisch Report on the state of the Argentine economy. Raúl Prebisch, the anti-Peronist director of the United Nations Economic Commission for Latin America and during the 1930's the general manager of the Argentine Central Bank, had coordinated the efforts of a group of prominent economists who immediately after the overthrow of Perón undertook to analyze the Argentine economy. They concluded that the country was in the worst economic crisis of its history, because the forces of production were no longer intact. Per capita production had risen only 3.5 per cent in the past ten years, and the Perón government had aggravated the situation by contracting bad loans and following a policy of decapitalization in order to meet the increases in

The Resurgence of Criollo Nationalism / 169

consumer demands. Perón's intervention in the economy, the report continued, was excessive and disorderly. In addition, state expenses were too high and were absorbing 22 per cent of the country's gross national product. Furthermore, the economists noted, the tremendous inflation of the past two years had been caused by rising wages without a corresponding increase in the productivity of the workers, and by expanding bank credit to cover deficits.[12]

The Prebisch Report went on to suggest means by which the economic crisis could be ended. Its author recommended increased foreign investment in Argentine oil production and in manufacturing, price increases to stimulate agricultural and livestock production, and the eventual establishment of a free exchange market.[13]

The criollo nationalists of the CGT were deeply disturbed by the Prebisch Report. In addition to its criticisms of Perón and the Perón era, the "solutions" of the economists suggested a desire by the government to return to a traditional laissez-faire export economy, which the workers feared would subordinate their interests to those of the rural landed oligarchy. "The only victim [of the Prebisch Plan]," the author of an article in the *CGT* pointed out, "will be the Argentine working class." This plan would devalue the peso, increase the cost of living, and "enrich the few at the expense of the misery of the many." [14]

Thus on October 28, when the Minister of Labor responded to the CGT demands of two days before, tensions were high. The government's answer came in the form of a decree providing for union elections. The decree suspended all officials of the CGT and its affiliates; permitted the Ministry of Labor to designate three overseers for each union to guarantee peace, to assure everyone free access to the organization, and to urge all to participate in the elections; established a central election committee of government officials to conduct the elections; permitted all men and women eighteen years or older who were members of the union to vote; provided that the vote would be direct, secret, and obligatory; permitted any group able to muster the signatures of 5 per cent of the union members to put up candidates; and insisted that the elections be held within 120 days.[15]

The CGT leaders were angered because the government had not consulted them about the decree and because they were relieved of their control over the CGT and the individual unions. Therefore Framini, Natalini, and the Secretary-Generals of the leading Peronist unions met and drew up three resolutions. The first provided for the appointment of a committee of six to meet with the CGT leaders to consider how they should respond to the government's new decree.[16] The second declared a general strike in principle. And the third declared the strike in effect if the labor leaders were unable to obtain adequate guarantees from the government.

For the next three days the special CGT committee met with Cerrutti Costa, but they reached no new agreement. Thus, on October 31, the labor leaders issued a general strike call. The Minister of Labor went on the radio the next day and appealed to the workers not to obey the strike order, but his appeal had little, if any, effect and the strike was considered very successful by many observers.[17]

At this point General Lonardi, fearful of the political consequences of continued labor agitation, took charge of the negotiations and on November 2 reached an agreement with the labor leaders. Framini and Natalini would remain at the head of the CGT and the CGT-designated interventors would remain in charge of the non-occupied unions until elections were held. Occupied unions would be placed under the intervention of the Ministry of Labor and would be run by a joint committee representing both Peronists and independents. And, finally, all workers detained for political reasons would be released.¹⁸

The settlement with the government delighted the majority of workers, but it further divided the two military factions of the Revolución Libertadora. Lonardi continued his effort to remain neutral in the struggle, but this proved impossible. The liberals, who were in the majority, believed that the President's neutrality, plus his labor policy, was an indication of his support for the anti-liberals. The crisis came to a head on November 12 when the government replaced the liberal Minister of the Interior, Eduardo Busso, with the ultra-right-wing, anti-liberal Luis María de Pablo Pardo. As a result, all but the extreme right-wing members resigned from the President's advisory council, the Junta Consultativa Nacional, and the next day the liberal General Pedro Aramburu led a bloodless coup and replaced Lonardi as Provisional President of Argentina.¹⁹

Lonardi had followed a policy of reconciliation with the moderate younger generation of Peronist labor leaders in the belief that this was the quickest way to return the country to civilian constitutional rule. His policy was successful in that he won the support of the CGT and the majority of the workers, but this failed to solve his problems as he had anticipated. The liberal military faction acted in part because the Peronists, after two months of the Revolución Libertadora, still controlled the CGT. Unlike Lonardi, Aramburu and his supporters saw no difference between the hard-line and moderate Peronists and therefore sought to purge the labor movement of all Peronist elements.

During his first two days in office, Aramburu manifested his attitude toward organized labor. He permitted the independents to take over any unions they could by force. He instituted government control over the editorial policy of the labor newspapers *El Lider* and *La Prensa*. And he replaced the Peronist Minister of Labor Cerrutti Costa with a staunch anti-Peronist, Raúl C. Migone.[20]

On November 15 the CGT leaders called a general strike to protest the new government's labor policy. There is some debate as to the effectiveness of the strike, but there is no doubt about the outcome. The government considered the strike an act of political subversion and forcefully suppressed it. Specifically, it declared the strike illegal, intervened in the CGT and all of its affiliates with military personnel, sent a detachment of marines to take over CGT headquarters, arrested Framini, Natalini, and many other labor leaders for ordering the "illegal" strike, and established a committee to investigate the CGT.[21]

The preamble to the intervention decree set forth the reasons for the government's actions. The Perón government, it claimed, had transformed the CGT into a political instrument with which to dominate the workers and to make them serve its "tyrannical and totalitarian goals." In addition, the CGT leaders had permitted a decline in real wages and savings, widespread corruption, and the suppression of strikes called for justified economic reasons. Furthermore, the law stated, the CGT was blind to the "heroic efforts" of the Revolución Libertadora to uproot tyranny and had initiated political strikes against the government for the purpose of reestablishing the former dictatorship.[22]

The intervention in the unions was followed during the next few weeks by the arrest of nearly all of the Peronist labor leaders. In addition to Framini and Natalini, the government arrested José Espejo, Eduardo Vuletich, Hugo Di Pietro, José Alonso, and many others. A reporter for the *New York Times* estimated that as many as 200 labor leaders were sent to the Ushuaía prison colony in Tierra del Fuego alone.[23]

At the same time that it arrested the Peronists, the government encouraged the independent minority to take over

The Resurgence of Criollo Nationalism / 173

positions of leadership in the labor movement. For example, it established a labor committee of independents, the Junta Asesora Gremial, to work with the government-appointed interventor of the CGT, Naval Captain Alberto Patrón Laplacette. This committee included the old-time syndicalist leader Sebastián Marotta, but it also included some of the most inflexible anti-Peronist labor leaders, such as Cándido Gregorio.[24]

In addition to its attacks on the Peronists, the government appeared to be reversing the social and economic revolution in many other ways. One way was carrying out a campaign to discredit Perón and Peronism. The government investigated the CGT as well as the entire Perón regime and published its findings in a book entitled *Libro negro de la segunda tiranía* (The Black Book of the Second Tyranny). The "first tyranny" was that of the nineteenth-century antiliberal caudillo Juan Manuel de Rosas and the "second" that of Perón.

According to its introduction, the purpose of the *Libro negro* was to find out how "the recent dictatorship . . . had achieved its destructive work, pointing out its aims, its accomplices and its collaborators, its methods of corruption and propaganda, and its totalitarian nature." The book devoted a substantial amount of attention to the corruption of the Perón regime, particularly in the labor movement, and then suggested that most important labor legislation had been passed before 1943.[25]

The defamation campaign was, unlike that of Lonardi, carried out in the labor newspapers under the control of the government-appointed interventors. The *CGT, El Obrero Ferroviario, La Fraternidad,* and other labor newspapers devoted considerable space to exposing the crimes of the Perón regime. For example, an article in the December 1955 edition of *El Obrero Ferroviario* entitled "Sabía Ud. Compañero . . ." pointed out that during the month of October 1948 the Executive Committee of the union had authorized the expenditure of $300 for a wedding gift for José Espejo, $4,500 for a lunch in honor of Evita Perón, and $1,000 for a birthday present for the President's wife. In addition, it had authorized $10,000 for Pablo López's trip to the United States for an operation and $50,000 for Perón's reelection campaign in 1951. The article ended, like many others of a similar nature, with the sentence: "Todos con fondos sociales." [26]

The government's economic policy also appeared to subordinate the interests of the workers to those of the *estancieros* and employers. An article in the *CGT* during the Lonardi period had made clear the Peronists' opposition to the economic development plan of economist Raúl Prebisch. Nevertheless, on January 28, 1956, the Aramburu government approved the plan and provided for its implementation. During the next few months the government invited foreign investors to return to Argentina, denationalized the central bank, lifted government controls on industry and agriculture, joined the World Bank and the International Monetary Fund, and initiated an austerity program.[27]

The immediate result of the government's new economic policy was a decline in real wages, particularly during the first half of 1956 before new contracts were signed, and a shift in the distribution of the gross national product in favor of the employers and property owners (see Table V).

In March and April 1956, the government further undermined the influence of the Peronists by restricting their participation in political and union activities. A decree of March 6 stated that those who after June 4, 1946, had held any national, provincial, or municipal elective office, any high appointive office, or any position in the Peronist Party would not now be able to hold public office of any kind.[28] On April 19 the government decreed that because it was

TABLE V

REAL WAGES OF INDUSTRIAL WORKERS:
DISTRIBUTION OF NATIONAL INCOME, 1954–1959
(IN PER CENT) *

Year	Real Wages	Workers' Percentage of GNP
1950	100	—
1954	—	58
1955	97	55.5
1956	96.7	53.8
1957	103.9	52.1
1958	110.2	53.1
1959	81.1	45.8

* CGT, *Boletín*, June 17, 24, 1963; Cafiero, *Cinco años*, pp. 127–128.

necessary to establish complete independence from the deposed dictatorship, the following persons would not be qualified to hold union office: those who held CGT posts from February 1, 1952, to September 16, 1955; those who held any union post for the same period; and those implicated in the investigation of the labor movement.[29]

In addition, on April 27 the Aramburu government decreed the Peronist Constitution of 1949 null and void and restored the liberal Constitution of 1853. Of great significance for the workers, Articles 37 through 40, those establishing the social function of private property and the rights of labor, were eliminated.

May 1, 1956, the traditional workers' holiday, was not a particularly enjoyable occasion for the Peronist workers. Aramburu, Migone, and Patrón spoke to a workers' gathering and reaffirmed their anti-Peronist and, in effect, anti-labor positions. Aramburu assured the workers that their rights and conquests had been and would continue to be protected. But, with obvious reference to the CGT, he warned that the government would not permit another state to exist with the Argentine state. The government would turn the unions over to the workers, he concluded, but it would not permit the Peronists to return to power.

In his speech Migone criticized the Perón regime and chided the workers for supporting it. The so-called benefits of the past regime, he insisted, were the result of the former President's desire to build a personalistic and dictatorial regime and not of a sincere desire for social justice. He went on to declare that the Revolución Libertadora, which had a genuine interest in the welfare of the workers, would end totalitarianism in the country and in the labor movement. It was only the anti-democratic influence in the movement that had provoked the revolutionary general strike of November 15 and had forced the government to intervene in the CGT and detain some of its leaders.

Interventor Patrón ended the session by assuring the workers that he and the government had no intention of replacing the union men as leaders of the labor organizations. Nevertheless, he pointed out that intervention was necessary as a temporary measure to end the totalitarian influence in the labor movement.[30]

On May 23 the government decreed a new Ley de Asociaciones Profesionales as Aramburu had promised. It provided for union elections to be held within 150 days, reaffirmed the proscription of Peronists who had been labor leaders during Perón's second administration, and explained in detail the electoral process. It also included a new provision for minority representation on the executive committee of every union, a provision that favored the independents, who were in the minority in most cases.[31]

Thus, during his first six months in office, Aramburu provided for the return of the unions to the workers, but he did so in such a way as to isolate the Peronist majority

The Resurgence of Criollo Nationalism / 177

of the labor movement and challenge its identity as a legitimate and influential sector of Argentine society. Aramburu treated the Peronist leaders and workers as subversives who represented a threat to his regime. He intervened in the CGT and all of its affiliates, arrested hundreds of Peronist labor leaders, initiated an economic policy that in the short run reduced real wages and redistributed wealth in favor of the employer and landowner classes, prohibited Peronists from competing for positions of leadership in the unions and in politics, and removed the "Rights of the Workers" from the Constitution.

Under these circumstances, it is not difficult to understand why the majority of workers felt that Aramburu had destroyed the social and economic revolution and had undermined the Argentine nation-state with which they had come to identify. Perón might have abandoned the workers' nation during his second term, but Aramburu's policies made the majority of workers forget this fact and caused them to begin to view the Perón period as a golden age.

The Peronist labor leaders describe the Aramburu period as *la revancha*—the revenge. José Alonso, an important labor leader during the Perón period and Secretary-General of the CGT from 1963 to early 1966, admitted that the leaders of every successful revolution had to imprison a certain number of the opposition. But the Aramburu regime did more than that; it arrested thousands of labor leaders and persecuted their families. He pointed out that he had been in jail eighteen months, his home had been ransacked several times and his property stolen while the police stood by, and his wife and young child had been forced to live in constant fear for their lives.[32]

Francisco Prado, Secretary-General of the light and power union, argued that the term "revancha" had a more general meaning. During the Perón period, he explained, the workers held many important government positions, exerted tremendous influence, and gained a new economic and social position in Argentina. However, Aramburu, by his arrests of workers, restrictive legislation, and economic policy, put an abrupt end to all of this. The revancha was the shock the workers felt at the abrupt change in their status.[33]

The independents by and large were less willing to use the term "revancha" to describe Aramburu's labor policy. Herminio Alonso, president of La Fraternidad, suggested that "revancha" was not entirely accurate, because Aramburu's actions were a response to the excesses of the Perón regime and should be viewed in this broader perspective.[34]

On the other hand Sebastián Marotta, the old-time syndicalist leader, freely used the term to describe Aramburu's labor activity. The revancha came about, he argued, because Aramburu permitted the businessmen and the estancieros to do what they wanted with regard to labor. Aramburu did not understand what was happening—that the workers were less than enthusiastic about the deposed regime in 1955, and that he might have weaned them away from Perón if he had tried. Instead he attempted to suppress all Peronist labor activity and thereby revived Perón's appeal for the worker.[35]

The important point is that the large majority of workers apparently believed this period was a revancha designed to obliterate the gains of the past twelve years. The next year and a half—from mid-1956 to the end of 1957—was a period of extreme frustration and bitterness for the Peronist workers and they protested in many ways the abrupt change in their status.

For example, on June 9, 1956, former General Juan José Valle and Raúl Tanco, joint commanders of the Movimiento de Recuperación Nacional, led a labor-supported revolt against the government.[36] These generals were revolting pri-

The Resurgence of Criollo Nationalism / 179

marily because Aramburu had purged them and other Peronist elements from the army. But they were supported by many Peronist workers because they opposed the revancha and promised to restore labor to its "rightful" position in society.

The Revolutionary Proclamation criticized the Aramburu government because, in addition to many other things, it had allegedly refused to recognize the legitimate conquests of labor, had persecuted and jailed many thousands of workers, had through restrictive legislation deprived some of the right to hold union office, and had by decree abolished a democratically enacted constitution that had guaranteed the rights of the people. The labor program of Valle and Tanco was to return the unions to the Peronist workers, to hold elections within forty-five days, to release all workers imprisoned for political reasons, and to repeal the decrees that limited Peronist participation in politics and union activity.[37]

The Valle Revolution, however, was not a success because the government acted quickly and the workers had little chance to support it actively. General Valle and at least twenty-seven other persons were summarily executed —a measure that had not been employed in Argentina for many years. In addition, hundreds of Peronist workers from all parts of the country were arrested.

After the Valle Revolution, labor continued to protest. The Peronist workers were accused of attacking government officials and sabotaging factories. More important, the unions initiated a number of strikes, which they claimed were called to support their demands for wage increases. The government rejected the unions' statements and insisted that the strikes were politically motivated and designed to overthrow the Revolución Libertadora. Actually, both political and economic motives were at work in varying degrees. Thus, the independent commercial employees, printers, and telephone workers went on strike for economic reasons, while the strikes of the Peronist textile and metallurgic workers were politically as well as economically motivated.[38]

Table VI, showing strikes in the federal capital during 1951–1960, suggests the extent of the protest, particularly if it is kept in mind that most of the strikes in 1956 took place during the second half of the year.

TABLE VI

Strikes in the Federal Capital, 1951–1960 *

Year	Strikes	Strikers
1951	23	16,356
1952	14	15,815
1953	40	5,506
1954	18	119,701
1955	21	11,990
1956	52	853,994
1957	56	304,209
1958	84	277,381
1959	45	1,411,062
1960	26	130,044

* República Argentina, Ministerio del Trabajo y Seguridad Social, *Conflictos del Trabajo*, p. 104.

As a result of these strikes, Minister of Labor Migone—unable to control the labor situation—resigned. The government arrested dozens more Peronist labor leaders, and the CGT—under the direction of interventor Patrón—carried on an intensive propaganda campaign designed to limit the use of the strike. In a radio speech Patrón argued that strikes, like war, were ultimate weapons to be used only

The Resurgence of Criollo Nationalism / 181

when all other means for solving the problem had been exhausted, and even then to be used only with the greatest restraint. An editorial in the *CGT* extended the argument. The right to strike was an important part of a democratic system, the editorial began, but the workers had a moral obligation to use the strike properly and not for political purposes. Some strikes, the editorial warned, were designed to serve political purposes even though they might appear legitimate on the surface.[39]

At the same time, the government also attempted to meet some of what it considered to be the legitimate demands of the workers. Most important, without abrogating the decrees restricting Peronist participation, it made an effort to normalize or turn back to the workers as many unions as possible. By April 1957, 59 out of the 119 CGT affiliates in the Buenos Aires area had been normalized, 36 were in the process, and 24 were not scheduled to achieve this status in the near future. Of the 159 unions in the interior, 113 had already been normalized.[40]

The culmination of this effort to return the unions to the non-Peronist workers was to normalize the CGT. On June 25, 1957, the government issued a decree which empowered the interventor to call a General Extraordinary Congress of the CGT affiliates with 1,000 members or more. The primary purpose of the Congress would be to sanction new statutes, elect leaders, and end the intervention.

The Congress, which met for five disorderly, stormy, and recriminating sessions between August 26 and September 4, failed to fulfill any of its goals. The issue that broke it up was the validity of the credentials of the delegates. In the fifth session of the Congress, the delegates voted 298 to 291 to protest the legal restrictions that prohibited Peronist leaders from becoming delegates, and then established a Comisión Verificadora to examine and validate the credentials of all the delegates. As a result, the leading independent unions—the Unión Ferroviaria, the commercial employees, the garment workers, the municipal employees, the state employees, the bank workers, and the printers—withdrew. There was no longer a quorum, the Congress was terminated, and the CGT was not normalized for another five and a half years.[41] The CGT affiliates then split into 62 Peronist unions and 32 independent unions. Later the 32 divided and a group of 19 mostly Communist-dominated unions emerged. But to date only the 62 Peronist unions have functioned as an effective organization.

The Peronists argue that the Congress failed because of the machinations of the government. José Alonso claimed that Aramburu—realizing that labor was the best-organized group in the country—was afraid to turn the government over to civilians with the CGT in the hands of the Peronists, and therefore called the Congress to deliver the organization to the independents. The government-appointed interventors padded the delegation of certain unions, such as the garment workers, and in this way hoped to include enough sympathetic delegates to control the Congress. The only problem with this scheme, concluded Alonso, was that some of the "government" delegates voted with the Peronists, giving them a majority, and thus the government was obliged to terminate the Congress.[42]

The independents, on the other hand, argued that the Congress failed because of the intransigence of the Peronists. Francisco Pérez Leirós claimed that the Peronists wanted to be absolute masters of the labor movement, without having to bother about the non-Peronists. Herminio Alonso stated that the Congress failed because the Peronists wanted the CGT at their disposal for political purposes. In Alonso's view, the issue was not a matter of credentials, as the Peronists claimed. It was a matter of whether or not the independents would be able to exist.[43]

Both the question of credentials and the "intransigence"

of the Peronists contributed to the failure of the Congress, and the chief results were that the CGT remained in the hands of the government, the Peronists remained proscribed, and the independents remained in control of a number of unions whose membership was Peronist in sympathy.

In retrospect, the Revolución Libertadora is particularly significant for the history of nationalism and organized labor in Argentina because it stimulated the revival of an apparently fading popular criollo nationalism, and indelibly associated this nationalism with Perón and a new, young generation of Peronist labor leaders. General Lonardi, hoping to exploit the confusion and resentment of the leaderless Peronist workers, left them in charge of their unions and sought to seduce them further away from Perón by continuing much of the social and economic revolution and by offering them a significant status in post-Perón Argentina. But General Aramburu, who took over from Lonardi after two months, had a different view of Peronism and organized labor. To him Peronism was an intolerable evil that had to be eradicated. The CGT was the main bastion of this evil and therefore had to be purged. It made no difference to him that the Peronists represented 70 per cent of the workers. In a manner reminiscent of the pre-World War I government leaders, Aramburu treated the Peronist workers as subversives who threatened the government and attempted to isolate and destroy them.

The problem was that Aramburu challenged the workers' identification with Perón and his workers' society without offering them a meaningful alternative with which to reidentify. He did not, as had Lonardi, attempt to provide them with significant status in post-Perón Argentina. In the process, Perón's abandonment of the workers' nation was forgotten and what resentment there had been toward him apparently disappeared. The Perón era became something of a mythical workers' paradise. Perón again became the symbol of the social and economic revolution and of the workers' nation. And a new generation of Peronist labor leaders developed influence and prestige of their own by fighting the Aramburu regime.

Aramburu's labor policy strengthened Peronism and criollo nationalism in the labor unions instead of weakening them as it was supposed to do, and it left a legacy with which all governments since that time have had to deal.

Conclusion

The most important stimulus to the organization and growth of the urban working class and to the development of popular nationalism in the Argentine labor movement was the rapid economic expansion of the late nineteenth and the twentieth centuries. Economic expansion brought about industrialization, urbanization, and immigration—both from Europe and from the interior of the country—and these in turn undermined the traditional associations of the workers and forced them to seek a new communal identity.

The primary means by which the uprooted worker in Argentina sought to reestablish communal identity and protect his interests were political. Over a period of time the worker came to understand that his economic and social problems were national problems which the local union was powerless to solve. He also recognized that his economic bargaining power—even in the case of skilled elements of the working force—was in itself insufficient to bring about the kind of reforms he wanted or the kind of society he envisioned. In this situation, the worker came to look to the state as the institution potentially most capable of protecting his interests and of solving his problems.

Popular nationalism was the articulation of the mobilized

workers' quest for status, security, and influence in his new physical and psychological environment. It developed as a political ideology when the workers began to associate their interests with those of the state, and it resulted logically in their efforts to take over the state. Labor began to associate its interests with those of the state during the first administration of Hipólito Yrigoyen, and this association has intensified ever since. Thus, since 1930 the leaders of the CGT have initially been favorably disposed toward all new governments with the exception of that of Pedro Aramburu, even though several of these governments were clearly dominated by groups hostile to the workers.

Popular nationalism was a political ideology for the workers. Its purpose was to legitimize the workers' aspirations, to bind together the diverse elements of society, and to justify a radical change in the social, political, and economic structures in order to create a new egalitarian community. The labor nationalists believed that they best represented the genuine interests of the Argentine people and sought political power to help them create and protect a national consensus around their ideals and programs.

Each group within the labor movement sought political power in a different way, and the way in which it sought this power tells us much about the specific meaning of its nationalism. The liberals and the laboristas sought political power through the Socialist Party and the Partido Laborista respectively. Although there were differences between them, both believed that democratic constitutional government provided the best means for changing society along the lines they desired and both worked through political parties to achieve their goals.

Liberal nationalism derived its meaning from the values and traditions of the European immigrant workers who were concentrated for the most part in Buenos Aires and Rosario, and who had absorbed much of Argentina's liberal tradition. It meant worker participation in the institutional structure of the country by means of civilian constitutional government and political parties. It also meant a belief in civil liberties, restrictions on the political activities of the Church and the military, and, without denying the principle of free trade, government control over foreign capital invested in Argentina. It was in general dynamic, internally directed, and cosmopolitan rather than nostalgic, xenophobic, and ethnically based. Its goal was the creation of an egalitarian society in accordance with Argentina's democratic liberal philosophy as modified by the immigrant working class.

In contrast to both the liberals and the laboristas, the criollo workers sought political power primarily through Perón. They were internal migrants familiar only with a personalistic form of government. Most of them were unskilled workers who had absolutely no economic bargaining power. For them political power was a more urgent need than it was for the liberals and the laboristas, and they willingly accepted the familiar type of rule of Perón rather than the abstract and unrealized promises of democratic constitutional government.

The meaning of criollo nationalism derived from the ethnocentric values and traditions of the migrant workers from the interior. It meant participation in the institutional structure of the country, but participation by means of a direct-personal relationship with a political leader. It had a nostalgic and xenophobic strain related to the nationalist tradition of the nineteenth-century rule of Juan Manuel de Rosas and to the cult of the gaucho. In the mid-twentieth century this strain was fused with another that emphasized the future over the past and the internal social revolution over the hatred of foreigners. The workers from the interior were influenced by their new environment and the longer they were in Buenos Aires, Rosario, and the other cities, the more they supported the latter strain. The goal of the criollo nationalists was the creation of an egalitarian society based on the Hispanic-Catholic traditions of the interior, but as modified by the lower-class migrants living in the cities.

Although the general purpose of both basic types of labor's nationalisms was to help the uprooted worker establish and protect an identity within his new environment, the popular nationalists in Argentina were unable to achieve their goal.

The liberal nationalists became an elitist group and did not create a unified democratic constitutional society. They were never an influential part of the institutional structure in pre-Perón Argentina, and after 1943 Perón and the increasingly powerful criollo nationalists continually challenged their status as part of the Argentine community. The laboristas also failed. For a brief period between 1943 and 1946 they seemed to have achieved their goal by cooperating with Perón. But Perón recognized their affinity with the liberals and their implicit challenge to his power, and after he had been elected President in 1946 he undermined their position.

During Perón's first administration the criollo nationalists established their identity as an influential part of society and appeared to have created the egalitarian nation they envisioned. But Perón's apparent abandonment of their interests during his second administration and Aramburu's open challenge of their claim to represent the Argentine nation denied them the fulfillment of their aspirations. Thus, all of labor's nationalisms were frustrated in one way or another.

One reason why the popular nationalists failed to achieve their goals was the vagueness of their ideology. Popular nationalism had at least two distinct meanings in the Argentine context and as a general ideology did not provide answers to a number of critical questions. In general it justified a redistribution of power in favor of the lower socioeconomic groups, but it did not explain which of these groups should rule, how power should be transferred from one person to another, or how to resolve conflicts within society. Popular nationalism legitimized broad changes within society, but it did not provide a legitimate, universally accepted procedure for governing society.

Another reason why the popular nationalists failed to achieve their goals was that they—like most other elements of society—were seriously divided. No labor nationalism—as distinct from the popular varieties of liberal and criollo nationalism—emerged and endured in Argentina. The workers' loyalty was never given exclusively to labor or even to the lower classes whose interests they identified with those of the nation-state. Instead, non-labor elements, many of which were identified with middle sector groups claiming to represent the interests of the workers, captured this loyalty. The liberals were loyal to the Socialist Party. The criollos were loyal to Perón. And the laboristas, who were loyal to labor and whose nationalism therefore might be called labor nationalism, were undermined by Perón. Perón recognized the challenge to his political position encompassed in the laborista appeal. If the workers were united, independent, and primarily loyal to labor, he could not count on their political support at all times. He therefore had to emasculate them to survive.

The development of organized labor and the emergence of popular nationalism within the labor movement have significant implications for Argentine society as a whole. For one, labor has become a major political force in Argentina and its aspirations—as articulated in its nationalisms—have by and large been frustrated. The popular nationalists have not succeeded in creating the united egalitarian society they envisioned and therefore constitute a potentially revolutionary force within the existing fragmented society.

Furthermore, although the workers are not united, the criollo nationalism so carefully nurtured by Perón has become and will very likely remain the dominant ideology of the labor movement. This means that those elements of Argentine society seeking to establish a unified community must make their peace not only with labor but with the criollo nationalists who are in control of a large part of the movement.

This does not mean that the present identification of the criollo nationalists with Perón and a by now mythical Perón era need be permanent, nor does it mean that the content of criollo nationalism must remain fixed. Perón used popular nationalism to advance his own interests, but there is no reason why others cannot use it for different purposes and modify its present content. For example, Arturo Frondizi, one of the important leaders of the Radical Party during and after the Perón period, professed a popular nationalism very similar to that of Perón and was supported by the criollo nationalists in the presidential election of 1958. Once in power, however, Frondizi abandoned this position and lost the support of the Peronists. This suggests that if some political group offered the workers new status and equal rights within society and maintained its position, Perón would cease to be the major symbol of their frustrated aspirations and would lose much of his influence within the labor movement.

Indeed, the process is already under way. Perón's influence within the Argentine labor movement is based on two things: his symbolic importance and his political power. Perón will always hold some symbolic importance for Argentine labor because he initiated a social revolution in behalf of the workers. But this importance could be minimized if a government were to fulfill some of labor's basic demands.

Perón's political power in Argentina has already been diminished by his absence from the country since 1955, and by the growing divisions within the Peronist movement. Furthermore, Perón is in his early seventies and cannot be expected to live very many more years. With his death his political power will cease, and in the meantime it is unlikely that he will be able to transfer it to anyone else.

Without Perón in Buenos Aires and without a charismatic leader to replace him, the criollo nationalists have relied increasingly on institutional means to achieve their goals. The CGT, returned to the Peronists in January 1963, has since become the focus of their political strength. In addition, a new and more professional generation of labor leaders (August Vandor, Francisco Prado, and others), most of whom were insignificant during the Perón period, has emerged. Many are anxious to assert their independence from Perón and, in a pragmatic spirit, wish to win support among the present leaders of the country. Furthermore, there is a new generation of workers whose parents migrated from the interior into Buenos Aires and other cities, but who themselves were born and raised in the cities. No one has adequately studied these people, but there is fragmentary evidence to indicate that the urban environment has modified their values and that they are considerably less devoted to the criollo tradition than were their fathers. All of these facts suggest that although criollo nationalism will endure, its identification with Perón and with the way of life of the interior need not. Criollo nationalists without Perón and with a more flexible ideology might more easily unite with other groups in Argentine society.

Argentina is deeply divided. It is difficult to predict how in the future the society will bind itself together, but one thing is clear. There can be no Argentine nation, no national consensus around which to construct a stable political system, that does not represent in some fundamental manner the ideals and aspirations of the popular nationalists and that does not also permit the workers to participate as equals in the institutional structure of the country.

Notes

INTRODUCTION

1. Karl Deutsch, "Social Mobilization and Political Development," *American Political Science Review*, LV, No. 3 (September 1961), 493–514.
2. The literature on nationalism and related subjects is extensive. Following is a list of those works that I have found most useful: E. H. Carr, *Nationalism and After* (London: Macmillan, 1945); D. Cosío Villegas, "Nacionalismo e desenvolvimento," *Revista Brasileira de Política Internacional*, v, No. 20 (December 1962), 673–690; Karl W. Deutsch, *Nationalism and Social Communication* (New York: Wiley & Sons, 1953); Rupert Emerson, *From Empire to Nation* (Boston: Beacon Press, 1962); Harvard University Center for International Affairs, *United States Foreign Policy: Ideology and Foreign Affairs* (Washington: United States Government Printing Office, 1960); Carlton J. H. Hayes, *Nationalism: A Religion* (New York: Macmillan, 1960); Carlton J. H. Hayes, *The Historical Evolution of Modern Nationalism* (New York: Macmillan, 1931); Helio Jaguaribe, *Burguesía y proletariado en el nacionalismo brasileño* (Buenos Aires: Editorial Coyoacán, 1961); John J. Johnson, "The New Latin American Nationalism," *Yale Review*, LIV (December 1964), 187–204; Clark Kerr and others, *Industrialism and Industrial Man* (Cambridge: Harvard University Press, 1960); Hans Kohn, *The Idea of Nationalism* (New York: Macmillan, 1960); Cândido Antônio Mendes de Almeida, *Nacionalismo e desenvolvimento* (Rio de Janeiro: Instituto Brasileiro de Estudos Afro-asiáticos, 1963); James O. Morris, "Consensus, Ideology and Labor Relations," *Journal of Inter-American Studies*, VII, No. 3 (July 1965), 301–315; Royal Institute of International Affairs, *Nationalism* (London: Oxford University Press, 1939); Robert E. Scott, "Nation Building in Latin America," in Karl W. Deutsch and William J. Foltz, eds., *Nation Building* (New York: Atherton Press, 1963), pp. 73–83; K. H. Silvert, ed., *Expectant Peoples* (New York: Random House, 1963); Arthur P. Whitaker, *Nationalism in Latin America* (Gainesville: University of Florida Press,

1962); Arthur P. Whitaker and David C. Jordan, *Nationalism in Contemporary Latin America* (New York: Free Press, 1966).
3. Emerson, *From Empire to Nation,* pp. 95–96.

CHAPTER 1

1. James R. Scobie, *Argentina* (New York: Oxford University Press, 1964), Ch. 5; H. S. Ferns, *Britain and Argentina in the Nineteenth Century* (London: Oxford University Press, 1960), Chs. 13, 14, 15.
2. As late as 1914 the immigrant represented 59 per cent of the organized workers, although only 47 per cent of the working-class population. See Alberto Belloni, *De anarquismo al Peronismo* (Buenos Aires: Editorial A. Peña Lillo, 1960), p. 29; José Luis Romero, *Las ideas políticas en la Argentina* (Buenos Aires: Fondo de Cultura Económica, 1946), pp. 178–179; Arthur P. Whitaker, *Argentina* (Englewood Cliffs, N.J.: Prentice-Hall, 1964), p. 55.
3. Gino Germani, *Estructura social de la Argentina* (Buenos Aires: Editorial Raigal, 1955), pp. 81–82. In addition to the permanent immigrants, there were thousands of *golondrinas* who came each year to harvest the crops and then return home. The golondrinas did not join labor unions and therefore are of little significance for this study.
4. Gino Germani, *Política y sociedad en una época de transición* (Buenos Aires: Editorial Paidos, 1962), p. 210. For discussions of the immigrant and his aspirations, see Juan A. Alsina, *El obrero* (Buenos Aires: Imprenta Calle de México, 1905); Tomás R. Fillol, *Social Factors in Economic Development: The Argentine Case* (Cambridge: Massachusetts Institute of Technology Press, 1961); Gastón Gori, *La pampa sin gaucho* (Buenos Aires: Editorial Raigal, 1952); José Ingenieros, *Sociología argentina* (Buenos Aires: Ediciones L. J. Rosso, 1925); Romero, *Las ideas políticas.*
5. Oscar Handlin, *The Uprooted* (New York: Grosset and Dunlap, 1951), p. 38.
6. Alsina, *El obrero,* pp. 88–89, 101–109; Germani, *Estructura,* pp. 202–203.
7. Sebastián Marotta, *El movimiento sindical argentino* (Buenos Aires: Ediciones Lacio, 1960), I, 19–23.
8. Lewis L. Lorwin, *Labor and Internationalism* (New York: Macmillan, 1929), p. 39.
9. Martín S. Casaretto, *Historia del movimiento obrero argentino* (Buenos Aires: Lorenzo, 1946), I, 6–7.
10. Jacinto Oddone, *Historia del socialismo* (Buenos Aires: La Vanguardia, 1934), I, 195.
11. Ferns, *Britain and Argentina,* pp. 445–446; Aldo Ferrer, *La economía argentina* (Buenos Aires: Fondo de Cultura Económica, 1963), p. 135.
12. Robert J. Alexander, "The Labor Movements of Latin America" (Unpublished manuscript, n.d.), p. 24; Jacinto Oddone, *Gremialismo proletario argentino* (Buenos Aires: La Vanguardia, 1949), p. 30.
13. Oddone, *Gremialismo,* pp. 42, 53–55.

14. The federation was known by a number of names. I am following Oddone when I refer to it as the FTRA.
15. Oddone, *Gremialismo*, pp. 66–68.
16. A total of 81,932 immigrants left Argentina in 1891 alone and net immigration for the year was minus 29,835. For the immigration statistics, see República Argentina, *Tercero Censo Nacional* (Buenos Aires: Rosso y Cía, 1917), x, 399.
17. The following biographical information on Justo is based on Dardo Cúneo, *Juan B. Justo* (Buenos Aires: Editorial Alpe, 1956), pp. 15–50.
18. *Ibid.*, p. 151.
19. Juan B. Justo, *La realización del socialismo* (Buenos Aires: La Vanguardia, 1947), pp. 29–31.
20. Quoted in Romero, *Las ideas políticas*, p. 193.
21. Justo, *Socialismo*, pp. 132–135; Romero, *Las ideas políticas*, pp. 193–194.
22. Jorge E. Spilimbergo, *Juan B. Justo o el socialismo cipayo* (Buenos Aires: Editorial Coyoacán, n.d.), p. 19.
23. Justo, *Socialismo*, pp. 21–25.
24. Oddone, *Socialismo*, I, 251, 258–260; H. H. Schultze, "The Socialist Movement in the Argentine Republic," *International Socialist Review*, v (July 1904), pp. 18–20.
25. Cúneo, *Justo*, p. 148; Ysabel F. Rennie, *The Argentine Republic* (New York: Macmillan, 1945), p. 200; Germani, *Política*, pp. 195, 203. Foreigners could vote in municipal elections in the city of Buenos Aires and a few other places.
26. Antonio Pellicer Paraire, *Análisis de la cuestión de la vida* (Barcelona: P. Cuesta, n.d.); Diego Abad de Santillán, *La FORA* (Buenos Aires: Ediciones Nervie, 1933), pp. 59–72.
27. Abad de Santillán, *La FORA*, p. 79; Oddone, *Gremialismo*, p. 95.
28. There are few reliable figures on union membership during this period. From those that exist it seems that the FORA and the UGT reached the peak of their strength in 1906 when the FORA had approximately 25,000 members, the UGT had about 10,000, and there were about 10,000 members of autonomous unions. The effective strength of organized labor was perhaps double the membership figures because many workers who did not actually join unions to avoid paying dues nevertheless supported them during strikes. After 1906 both the FORA and the UGT lost members and more unions became autonomous. See Buenos Aires, Departamento de Estadística Municipal, *Censo general de la ciudad de Buenos Aires*, 1906, pp. 212–235; República Argentina, *Tercero Censo Nacional*, VII, 402; República Argentina, Departamento Nacional del Trabajo, *Boletín*, Nos. 4, 5, 6, 9 (March 31, 1908; June 30, 1908; September 30, 1908; June 30, 1909); Casaretto, *Movimiento obrero*, I, 107; Oddone, *Gremialismo*, pp. 14, 187.
29. "Anarchist communism" refers to a communal form of anarchism, and not to a combination of the philosophies of anarchism and communism. See Abad de Santillán, *La FORA*, pp. 125–130.
30. *Ibid.*, p. 149.
31. *La Protesta*, May 3–8, 1909, and September 19, 1909; *La Nación*, May 2–8, 1909; Casaretto, *Movimiento obrero*, I, 90–93.

32. S. Fanny Simon, "Anarchismo and Anarcho-Syndicalismo in South America," *Hispanic American Historical Review*, xxvi, No. 1 (February 1946), 38–45.
33. James Bryce, *South America* (New York: Macmillan, 1913), p. 343.
34. For a comparison with the Spanish anarchists, see Gerald Brenan, *The Spanish Labyrinth* (Cambridge: Cambridge University Press, 1950).
35. República Argentina, Departamento Nacional del Trabajo, *Boletín*, No. 8 (March 31, 1909), pp. 16–30.
36. Abad de Santillán, *La FORA*, p. 104; Oddone, *Gremialismo*, pp. 108, 118.
37. *Anales de legislación argentina: 1889–1919* (Buenos Aires: Editorial La Ley, 1941), pp. 560–561.
38. Santos Primo Amadeo, *Argentine Constitutional Law* (New York: Columbia University Press, 1943), p. 167.
39. For a full discussion of this law, see Ingenieros, *Sociología argentina*, pp. 243–271.
40. Romero, *Las ideas políticas*, pp. 200–204; Rubens Iscaro, *Origen y desarrollo del movimiento sindical argentino* (Buenos Aires: Editorial Anteo, 1958), pp. 68–69.
41. Oddone, *Socialismo*, ii, 380.
42. For accounts of this period, see Abad de Santillán, *La FORA*, pp. 212–215, *La Nación*, May–June 1910.
43. Abad de Santillán, *La FORA*, p. 212.
44. Unión Industrial Argentina, *Boletín*, May 15, 1909; June 19, 1909; July 15, 1910.
45. *Anales de legislación argentina: 1889–1919*, pp. 788–789.

CHAPTER 2

1. The syndicalist faction of the FORA was led by Alberto Ghiraldo, writer and for a time editor of *La Protesta*. See Héctor Adolfo Cordero, *Alberto Ghiraldo* (Buenos Aires: Editorial Claridad, 1962).
2. Ferrer, *La economía argentina*, p. 108; Roberto M. Ortiz, *Historia económica de la Argentina* (Buenos Aires: Editorial Raigal, 1955), ii, 232, 290.
3. This is an estimate based on figures in Marotta, *Movimiento sindical*, ii, 182; Luis B. Cerrutti Costa, *El sindicalismo* (Buenos Aires: Editorial Trafac, 1957), p. 94; J. B. Chiti and F. Agnelli, *La Fraternidad* (Buenos Aires: Ravaschino Hnos., 1937), p. 371. The figures presented by these authors are somewhat exaggerated and I have reduced them about 25 per cent.
4. Germani, *Estructura*, p. 82.
5. Some of the jobs were filled by migrants from the interior, but before 1936 internal migration was insignificant and persons born in the provinces never constituted more than 12 per cent of the population of metropolitan Buenos Aires. See Germani, *Política*, p. 230.
6. Marotta, *Movimiento sindical*, ii, 257–259; Alfredo L. Palacios, *El*

Notes / 197

nuevo derecho (3rd ed., Buenos Aires: Editorial Claridad, 1934), p. 232.
7. Bryce, *South America*, p. 339. For further information on the assimilation of the immigrant in Argentina, see Germani, *Política*, pp. 197–210; Fillol, *Social Factors*, p. 35.
8. I use the term "middle sector," as does John J. Johnson, to designate the groups that ranged upward "from the poorly paid white-collar employee in government, with a limited education and often a lack of helpful family connections, to the wealthy proprietors of commercial and industrial enterprises on the one hand and to the educated professional men, teachers, and high-level government bureaucrats, usually from old established families, on the other" (p. ix). I am not suggesting that the middle sectors constituted a compact social stratum or class, or that its members necessarily had a common background or common values. My point is that the middle sectors were new elements in the government and that some of the middle-sector members —including Yrigoyen—held different attitudes toward organized labor than did the members of the traditional ruling class. See John J. Johnson, *Political Change in Latin America: The Emergence of the Middle Sectors* (Stanford: Stanford University Press, 1958); John P. Gillen, "Some Signposts for Policy," in Richard N. Adams and others, *Social Change in Latin America Today* (New York: Vintage, 1961), pp. 14–62; Ralph L. Beals, "Social Stratification in Latin America," *American Journal of Sociology*, LVIII, No. 4 (January 1953), 327–339; and Sugiyama Iutaka, "Social Stratification Research in Latin America," *Latin American Research Review*, I, No. 1 (October 1965), 7–34.
9. Gabriel del Mazo, ed., *El pensamiento escrito de Yrigoyen* (Buenos Aires: Editorial Raigal, 1945), p. 110.
10. Gabriel del Mazo, *El radicalismo* (Buenos Aires: Ediciones Gure, 1957), I, 209; Palacios, *Derecho*, pp. 194–203. For a detailed discussion of the maritime strike, see República Argentina, Departamento Nacional del Trabajo, *Boletín*, No. 37 (March 1918).
11. This account of the Semana Trágica is based on the following books, representing different points of view: Oddone, *Gremialismo*, pp. 286–295, presents the socialist view; Marotta, *Movimiento sindical*, II, 241–248, presents the syndicalist view; Rubens Iscaro, *Movimiento sindical*, pp. 105–107, presents the communist view; Nicolás Babini, *Enero de 1919* (Buenos Aires: Servicio Editorial y Periodístico Argentino, 1956), presents the Radical view; José R. Romariz, *La Semana Trágica* (Buenos Aires: Editorial Hemisferio, 1952), is the account of a police official involved in the events of the week; and Carlos Ibarguren, *La historia que he vivido* (Buenos Aires: Peuser, 1955), pp. 341–344, represents the Conservative point of view.
12. Marotta, *Movimiento sindical*, II, 186.
13. Alfredo Palacios discusses this dichotomy between doctrine and action. See Palacios, *Derecho*, p. 202.
14. Interview with Sebastián Marotta, Secretary-General of the FORA IX, June 20, 1963.
15. Germani, *Política*, p. 203.
16. Palacios, *Derecho*, p. 194.

17. *Ibid.*, p. 200; Marotta, *Movimiento sindical*, II, 188–192.
18. Enrico Ferri and Juan B. Justo, *El Partido Socialista en la República Argentina* (Buenos Aires: Lotito y Barberis, 1909).
19. Palacios, *Derecho*, p. 35.
20. Manuel Ugarte, *El provenir de América Latina* (Buenos Aires: Editorial Indoamérica, 1953), p. 44.
21. *Ibid.*, pp. 112–118.
22. *Ibid.*, p. xxi.
23. *Ibid.*
24. *Ibid.*, p. xxv.
25. Palacios, *Derecho*, p. 240.
26. Spilimbergo, *Justo*, p. 48.
27. *Ibid.*, pp. 48–49; Alberto Methol Ferre, *La izquierda nacional en la Argentina* (Buenos Aires: Editorial Coyoacán, 1963), pp. 56–57.
28. *Ibid.*, p. 54.
29. Juan B. Justo, *Internacionalismo y patria* (Buenos Aires: La Vanguardia, 1933), pp. 134–138; Adolfo Dickman, *Nacionalismo y socialismo* (Buenos Aires: Porter Hnos., 1933), p. 19.
30. The internationalists had a small temporary majority and won by a vote of 4,000 to 3,500. See Cúneo, *Justo*, pp. 366–369.
31. See Unión Sindical Argentina, *Carta Orgánica* (Buenos Aires: La Internacional, 1921), p. 2.
32. Interview with Francisco Pérez Leirós, Secretary-General of the Municipal Workers' Union, June 14, 1963.
33. Oddone, *Gremialismo*, p. 311; Iscaro, *Movimiento sindical*, p. 139; Casaretto, *Movimiento obrero*, I, 71.
34. By 1926 the Unión Ferroviaria had approximately 50,000 of the 90,000 organized workers. See note 3 above.
35. Unión Ferroviaria, *Memoria y balance: 1928* (Buenos Aires: La Vanguardia, 1929), p. 6.
36. See note 3 above.

CHAPTER 3

1. Oddone, *Gremialismo*, pp. 328–330.
2. Alberto E. Uriburu, ed., *La palabra del General Uriburu* (Buenos Aires: Roldán Editor, 1933), pp. 21–25.
3. Oddone, *Gremialismo*, p. 374; Alfredo Galletti, *La política y los partidos* (Buenos Aires: Fondo de Cultura Económica, 1961), p. 94.
4. *CGT*, January 15, 1932. This is the newspaper of the Confederación General del Trabajo.
5. *La Fraternidad*, August 20, 1930. This is the newspaper of the railroad engineers' and firemen's union of the same name.
6. Galletti, *La política*, p. 76.
7. *CGT*, January 25, 1934; December 14, 1934.
8. *CGT*, December 14, 1934; *La Fraternidad*, November 5, 1933.
9. *CGT*, February 28, 1934.
10. *CGT*, February 28, 1934; April 20, 1934.

Notes / 199

11. *CGT*, December 20, 1935.
12. *CGT*, April 10, 1936; Cerrutti Costa, *El sindicalismo*, p. 113.
13. *CGT*, April 10, 1936.
14. *CGT*, May 22, 1936.
15. Confederación General de Empleados de Comercio, *Memoria del Consejo Administrativo al II Congreso Ordinario* (Buenos Aires, 1936), p. 50.
16. *CGT*, August 21, 1936; May 31, 1937; and 1936–1939, *passim*.
17. *CGT*, December 2, 1938.
18. *La Fraternidad*, November 5, 1937.
19. *CGT*, December 31, 1937.
20. Nicolás Repetto, *Mi paso por la política: de Uriburu a Perón* (Buenos Aires: Santiago Rueda, 1957), pp. 150–153, 184–189, 212–216.
21. *CGT*, January 27, 1939; April 7, 1939.
22. Confederación General de Empleados de Comercio, *Memoria del Consejo Administrativo al III Congreso Ordinario* (Buenos Aires, 1939), p. 5.
23. Alfredo Palacios, *La justicia social* (Buenos Aires: Editorial Claridad, 1954).
24. Most of the unorganized workers were unskilled migrants from the interior. For a discussion of the internal migration and its significance for labor, see the following chapter.
25. Ferrer, *La economía argentina*, p. 190; Unión Industrial Argentina, *Anales* (January 1942), p. 20.
26. *CGT*, December 27, 1935; March 3, 1939. República Argentina, Departamento Nacional del Trabajo, División de Estadística, *Organización sindical: asociaciones obreras y patronales* (Buenos Aires, 1941), p. 6.
27. Confederación General del Trabajo, *Actas de las reuniones del Comité Central Confederal* (Buenos Aires: La Vanguardia, 1942), pp. 12, 13, 16.
28. *CGT*, October 11, 1940.
29. *CGT*, August 30, 1941.
30. *CGT*, December 27, 1940; April 18, 1941.
31. *CGT*, June 27, 1941.
32. *CGT*, *Actas del Comité Central* (1942), pp. 34, 230–233.
33. *Ibid.*, p. 111.
34. *Ibid.*, pp. 187–193.
35. Confederación General del Trabajo, *Acta del Segundo Congreso Ordinario* (Buenos Aires, 1943), p. 134.
36. Oddone, *Gremialismo*, pp. 376–378. Ángel Perelman, one of the first anti-liberal Peronist leaders, suggests that the Domenech group was also the more nationalist of the two. See Ángel Perelman, *Como hicimos el 17 de octubre* (Buenos Aires: Editorial Coyoacán, 1961), p. 43.
37. *CGT*, *Actas del Comité Central* (1942), p. 83.
38. Confederación General del Trabajo, *Actas de las reuniones del Comité Central Confederal* (Buenos Aires: La Vanguardia, 1943), p. 19.
39. Oddone, *Gremialismo*, pp. 398–400.

40. For a critical analysis of the figures on union membership and industrial and general employment, see Felix Weil, *Argentine Riddle* (New York: John Day, 1944), pp. 73–86, 225–226, 231–243, 268.

CHAPTER 4

1. *CGT*, June 11, 1943.
2. For the text of the law, see *Anales de legislación argentina: 1943*, pp. 227–230.
3. *CGT*, August 6, 1943.
4. *CGT*, August 7, 1943.
5. *CGT*, October 1, 1943.
6. *CGT*, October 16, 1943.
7. Interview with Francisco Pérez Leirós, head of the CGT Number Two, Socialist Deputy in the National Congress, June 14, 1963. "La historia del Peronismo, XI," *Primera Plana* (August 24, 1965), pp. 42–45.
8. *CGT*, November 1, 1943.
9. *CGT*, December 5, 1943.
10. Juan D. Perón, *El trabajo al través del pensamiento de Perón* (Buenos Aires: Secretaría de Prensa y Difusión, 1955), p. 12.
11. *Ibid.*, p. 20.
12. *La Fraternidad*, February 5, 1945.
13. Perón, *Pensamiento*, pp. 19, 20.
14. *CGT*, June 16, 1944.
15. *CGT*, August 1, 1944.
16. *CGT*, November 1, 1944.
17. *La Fraternidad*, June 5, 1944; October 5, 1944.
18. *El Obrero Ferroviario*, September and November 1944; December 1, 1944. This is the newspaper of the Unión Ferroviaria.
19. Germani, *Política*, p. 230; José Manuel Saravia, *Argentina 1959* (Buenos Aires: Ediciones del Atlántico, 1959), p. 28.
20. *CGT*, June 3, 1938; June 20, 1941.
21. For a discussion of the nature of the internal migrant, see Pedro R. David, "The Social Structure of Argentina" (Ph.D. Thesis, Indiana University, 1962); Vicente E. de Pablo and Marta Ezcurra, *Investigación social en agrupaciones de "Villas Miserias" de la ciudad de Buenos Aires* (Buenos Aires: Comisión Nacional de la Vivienda, 1958); Manuel Zymelman, "Cultural Patterns of Labor and Latin American Industrialization," *Journal of Inter-American Studies*, v, No. 3 (July 1963), 357–370; and James O. Morris, "Consensus, Ideology and Labor Relations," *Journal of Inter-American Studies*, vii, No. 3 (July 1965), 301–315.
22. The ideas of Perelman are set forth in his book *Como hicimos*.
23. Interview with Hilario Salvo, July 27, 1963.
24. I have used the term "laborista" to identify the liberals who supported Perón, because they were the most influential persons in the establishment of the Partido Laborista, to be discussed later in this chapter.
25. *La Fraternidad*, May 20, 1945.

26. Cerrutti Costa, *El sindicalismo,* p. 156.
27. *CGT,* September 1, 1945.
28. *El Obrero Ferroviario,* May 1, 1945.
29. *La Fraternidad,* September 6 and 20, 1945; *CGT,* September 16, 1945.
30. Arthur P. Whitaker, *The United States and Argentina* (Cambridge: Harvard University Press, 1954), pp. 132–134.
31. For the text of this law, see *Anales de legislación argentina: 1947,* pp. 143–168.
32. Interview with Luis Gay, first president of the Partido Laborista and for a brief period in late 1946 and early 1947 Secretary-General of the CGT, July 29, 1963. Colonel Domingo Mercante was with Perón during this period, and after Perón's imprisonment probably acted as a contact between labor and the ousted leader.
33. Belloni, *Peronismo,* pp. 50–53; Perelman, *Como hicimos,* pp. 71–79; Cipriano Reyes, *¿Que es el Laborismo?* (Buenos Aires: Ediciones RA, 1946), pp. 45–52. Interview with Luis Gay, July 29, 1963.
34. The role of Eva Duarte in the events of October 17 is debatable. It is my opinion that, compared with Luis Gay and Cipriano Reyes, Eva was not very important. She did not gain substantial influence in the labor movement until some time after Perón became President.
35. *Primera Plana* does not believe Gay was as important as I suggest, and instead gives more credit to Colonel Mercante. See "La historia del Peronismo, XVI–XX," *Primera Plana* (October 1965).
36. *El Obrero Ferroviario,* November 1, 1945.
37. *CGT,* November 1, 1945.
38. Interview with Luis Gay, July 29, 1963.
39. Reyes, *Laborismo,* p. 116.
40. Belloni, *Peronismo,* p. 56; Reyes, *Laborismo,* pp. 109–114.
41. The communist-dominated Comando Obrero Único staged a general strike on October 31, but it was easily suppressed by the government. In the beginning of December, the Conferencia Nacional de las Organizaciones Sindicales Independientes met under the leadership of the veteran communist labor leader Pedro Chiaranti and the old-time syndicalist leader Sebastián Marotta to condemn the state of seige, use of torture, corporate regulation of unions, and religious education in the schools, but it had little impact on the workers. See Iscaro, *Movimiento sindical,* pp. 229–232.
42. *CGT,* November 1, 1945; December 1, 1945.
43. *Argentine Fabril,* January 1946. This is the monthly magazine of the Unión Industrial Argentina.
44. *CGT,* January 16, 1946.
45. *CGT,* February 16, 1946.
46. United States Government Memorandum, *Consultation Among the American Republics with Respect to the Argentine Situation* (Washington, 1946), pp. 112–116.
47. *CGT,* March 1, 1946.
48. Whitaker, *The U.S. and Argentina,* p. 149.
49. Quoted in Robert J. Alexander, *The Perón Era* (New York: Columbia University Press, 1951), p. 52.

CHAPTER 5

1. CGE, *Informe*, pp. 181–192; Juan D. Perón, *Así cumple Perón* (Buenos Aires: Subsecretaría de Informaciones, 1951), p. 7.
2. For further information on Evita Perón, see the critical accounts of María Flores, *Woman with a Whip* (New York: Doubleday, 1953); Alexander, *The Perón Era*, pp. 103–114; and George I. Blanksten, *Perón's Argentina* (Chicago: University of Chicago Press, 1953), pp. 87–110. Also see the laudatory accounts of Roman J. Lombille, *Eva, la predestinada* (Buenos Aires: Ediciones Gure, 1955); Benigno Acossano, *Eva Perón, su verdadera vida* (Buenos Aires: Editorial Lamas, 1955); and Eva's ghost-written biography, *La razón de mi vida* (Buenos Aires: Peuser, n.d.).
3. Perón, *Pensamiento*, pp. 63–64.
4. Most published figures on the labor movement during this period are unreliable. The figures given here are estimated on the basis of information obtained in interviews with many of the leading labor leaders. In addition, the CGT today has approximately 2.5 million members and there is no reason to assume that its membership would have decreased substantially since the earlier period.
5. Faustino Legón and Samuel W. Madrano, *Las constituciones de la República Argentina* (Madrid: Ediciones Cultura Hispánica, 1953), pp. 478–484.
6. Juan D. Perón and Eva Perón, *Día de la Lealtad: Discursos del Gral. Juan Perón y de la Señora Eva Perón* (Buenos Aires: Subsecretaría de Informaciones, 1949), p. 6; Blanksten, *Perón*, pp. 252–256.
7. Quoted in Whitaker, *U.S. and Argentina*, p. 221.
8. Ferrer, *La economía argentina*, p. 108; Whitaker, *U.S. and Argentina*, p. 201; Ortiz, *Historia económica*, II, 232–237.
9. Palacios, *Derecho*, p. 201; Unión Ferroviaria, *Actas de la Asamblea General: 1938* (Buenos Aires, 1938), p. 245; La Fraternidad, *Actas del Congreso Nacional: 1942* (Buenos Aires, 1942), p. 162.
10. Blanksten, *Perón*, p. 241; Alexander, *Perón*, pp. 157–158.
11. Federación Empleados de Comercio, *Memoria de la Comisión Directiva: 1947–1949* (Buenos Aires: Imprenta Castromán, Ortiz y Cía., 1950), p. 35.
12. *La Fraternidad*, March 20, 1948.
13. *El Obrero Ferroviario*, February 27, 1948.
14. *La Fraternidad*, March 5, 1949.
15. Interview with Luis Gay, July 29, 1963. Walter Beveraggi Allende, *El fracaso de Perón y el problema argentino* (Buenos Aires: Rosso, 1956), p. 41.
16. *Ibid.*, pp. 41–45. Interview with Luis Gay, July 29, 1963; Luis Gay, letter to the author, May 4, 1964.
17. Interview with Luis Gay, July 29, 1963.
18. Beveraggi Allende, *El fracaso*, p. 47.
19. *CGT*, October 1, 1945; February 1, 1946.
20. Interview with Luis Gay, July 29, 1963.
21. *Ibid.*

22. *CGT*, November 16, 1946.
23. *CGT*, January 16, 1947.
24. Interview with Luis Gay, July 29, 1963.
25. *CGT*, February 16, 1947. The delegates claimed that the only reason they took off their coats was because they were hot. See American Federation of Labor, *American Labor Looks at the World* (Washington, 1947), pp. 20–27.
26. *Ibid.*, p. 26.
27. *Ibid.*, p. 25.
28. *CGT*, March 16, 1947.
29. CGT, *Labor realizada por el Secretariado Confederal* (Buenos Aires, 1947), pp. 15, 17.
30. As has been noted earlier, labor membership figures are not entirely reliable. These again are estimates based on interviews, plus information in *CGT*, October 1, 1946, and November 16, 1947; CGT, *Labor realizada*, p. 106; *El Obrero Ferroviario*, February 1, 1947; Cerrutti Costa, *El sindicalismo*, p. 184.
31. Alexander, *Perón*, p. 111.
32. AFL, *World*, p. 21. Interview with Cándido Gregorio, former Secretary-General of the textile workers' union, June 5, 1963.
33. CGT, *Labor realizada*, p. 23. Interview with Sebastián Marotta, July 11, 1963.
34. Federación Gráfica Argentina, *Memoria y balance: 1951* (Buenos Aires, 1951), p. 24.
35. *CGT*, February 16, 1947; November 1, 1947.
36. "Justicialism" is the label Perón gave to his ill-defined philosophy of government that lay between communism and capitalism. For a discussion of Justicialism, see Blanksten, *Perón*, pp. 276–305, 423–439; Alejandro Magnet, *Nuestros vecinos argentinos* (Santiago de Chile: Editorial del Pacífico, 1956).
37. Juan D. Perón, *La traición de los dirigentes de la FOTIA y la FEIA a los trabajadores del azúcar* (Buenos Aires: Subsecretaría de Informaciones, 1950), pp. 13–14.
38. Juan D. Perón, *Habla Perón a los ferroviarios* (Buenos Aires: Subsecretaría de Informaciones, 1951), pp. 7–13.
39. CGT, *Memoria y balance: 1950–1951* (Buenos Aires, 1952), pp. 25–29; *La Fraternidad*, April 20, 1951.
40. República Argentina, Dirección Nacional de Estadística y Censo, *Anuario estadística de la República Argentina* (Buenos Aires, 1957), p. 143.
41. *La Nación*, March 2, 1948.
42. *CGT*, September 16, 1949.
43. Blanksten, *Perón*, pp. 87–89.
44. Eva Perón, *La razón*, pp. 9–10. According to Bernardo Rabinovitz, the book was written by the Spanish journalist Manuel Penella de Silva. See Bernardo Rabinovitz, *Sucedió en la Argentina* (Buenos Aires: Ediciones Gure, 1956), p. 73.
45. Eva Perón, *La razón*, pp. 33, 88.
46. For example, see *CGT*, January 5, 1951.

47. *El Obrero Ferroviario*, November, 1950. For additional propaganda songs and poems, see A. Monti, *Antología poética de la revolución justicialista* (Buenos Aires: Librería Perlado, 1954).

CHAPTER 6

1. La Fraternidad later rejoined the CGT in an effort to reform it from within.
2. Interview with Cándido Gregorio, June 5, 1963. Interview with Sebastián Marotta, July 16, 1963. This was not the first success of the liberals in the international field. As a result of their efforts, the CGT representatives were excluded from the ILO Congress in 1945.
3. *La Fraternidad*, August 5, 1949.
4. La Fraternidad, *Actas: 1948*, pp. 27, 193.
5. La Fraternidad, *Actas: 1946*, p. 249; La Fraternidad, *Actas: 1950*, p. 252.
6. *La Fraternidad*, October 20, 1950.
7. Interview with Luis Gay, July 29, 1963. Although Gay was recalling events that had taken place more than fifteen years before, his story coincides with the facts and opinions he stated in an interview with Robert J. Alexander on November 22, 1946.
8. Reyes, *Laborismo*, pp. 22, 41. According to Luis Gay, this book was ghost-written. It is valuable nevertheless because it expresses the ideas of Reyes and his supporters.
9. *Ibid.*, pp. 103–104.
10. Interview with Hilario Salvo, July 27, 1963. Although Salvo was relaying opinions he had held from ten to fifteen years before, much of this interview can be corroborated in the *CGT* and in the Actas de la Comisión Administrativa, 1943–1951, Unión Obrera Metalúrgica, Buenos Aires (in the files of the union).
11. Statistics on strikes throughout the country are unavailable. The figures for the federal capital are significant because of the high concentration of workers and labor organizations in the area.
12. These figures were calculated on the basis of figures in República Argentina, Ministerio de Trabajo y Seguridad Social, Dirección General de Estudios e Investigaciones, *Conflictos del Trabajo* (Buenos Aires, 1961), p. 103. The results have been rounded off. For a comparison of Argentina with other countries, see International Labor Office, *Yearbook of Labor Statistics: 1951–1952* (Geneva, 1952), pp. 327–330.
13. Alexander, *Perón*, pp. 93–100; Iscaro, *Movimiento sindical*, pp. 242–251.
14. Unión Ferroviaria, *Actas: 1948*, p. 128.
15. *El Obrero Ferroviario*, June 1948.
16. Unión Ferroviaria, *Actas: 1946*, pp. 170–195.
17. Unión Ferroviaria, *Actas: 1947*, p. 198.
18. Unión Ferroviaria, *Actas: 1948*, pp. 274–275.
19. There was a group of anti-liberals that opposed Evita and her followers, but I have been unable to find reliable information on them. In

addition, the communists had some supporters in the union, but they are not particularly relevant to our discussion because during most of Perón's first administration they were not part of the opposition. During the war they worked with the liberals to oppose fascism and Perón, but in 1946—when Argentina reestablished diplomatic relations with Russia—they disbanded their own labor organizations and joined the Peronists. This alliance lasted only a few years because Perón closed down the communist newspaper *La Hora,* expelled communist leader Víctor Codovilla, and deported a number of communist workers involved in a strike. In response to these attacks, the communists did not appeal to liberal nationalism as they had in the late 1930's and early 1940's, but they did support some liberal ideas. They claimed, for example, that the government had destroyed union independence and had restricted the right to strike. In addition, they claimed that the government had organized the workers from above in order to serve its own interests, and that it had replaced the class struggle with a pernicious system of class cooperation. See Iscaro, *Movimiento sindical,* pp. 232–253.
20. Interview with Antonio Scipione, May 9, 1963. The fact that Perón and the CGT promised free union elections as part of the settlement of the conflict supports Scipione's contention that the elections were fraudulent.
21. The major sources of information for this account of the strikes are: (1) The following newspapers from November 1950 to February 1951—*El Obrero Ferroviario, La Fraternidad, Nuevas Bases, La Nación,* and the *CGT.* (2) Interviews with participants in the events: Antonio Scipione, leader of the liberal opposition during the Perón period and present Secretary-General of the Unión Ferroviaria, May 9, 1963; Víctor Vázquez, one of the leaders of the communist group within the Unión Ferroviaria both during and after the Perón period, May 7, 1963; and José Alonso, CGT interventor in the Unión Ferroviaria at the time of the strike and Secretary-General of the CGT from 1963 to 1966, July 19, 1963. I have also used the interview of Robert J. Alexander with Julio Falasco, the socialist leader of the strikes, August 4, 1952.
22. *El Obrero Ferroviario,* December 1950.
23. Alexander, *Perón,* p. 98.
24. Perón, *Ferroviarios,* p. 7; *CGT,* February 26, 1951.
25. Roberto Testa, interview with Robert J. Alexander, August 1, 1952.
26. Blanksten, *Perón,* p. 354.

CHAPTER 7

1. Antonio F. Cafiero, *Cinco años después* (Buenos Aires: El Gráfico, 1961), pp. 329–346; Ferrer, *La economía argentina,* pp. 212–213.
2. *CGT,* August 19, 1949.
3. U.S. Commerce, *Economic Review,* 1951, p. 15.
4. The Confederación General Económica represented the new man-

ufacturing industrialists, while the Unión Industrial Argentina represented groups related to the traditional export industries.
5. CGE, *Informe; La Nación*, March 25, 1952; *New York Times*, March 23, 1954.
6. For example, see *CGT*, May 23, 1952.
7. *CGT*, January 23, 1954.
8. *Congreso nacional de productividad y bienestar social: antecedentes, temario, conclusiones* (Buenos Aires, 1955), p. 20.
9. Ferrer, *La economía argentina*, p. 218.
10. *CGT*, May 1, 1954.
11. Cafiero, *Cinco años*, pp. 305–308.
12. Ferrer, *La economía argentina*, p. 218. United States Department of Labor, Bureau of Labor Statistics, *Foreign Labor Information: Labor in Argentina* (Washington, June 1959), p. 2.
13. For two estimates of the number of practicing Catholics in Argentina, see Peter M. Dunne, *A Padre Views South America* (Milwaukee: Bruce, 1945), p. 22; and José Luis de Ímaz, *Motivación electoral* (Buenos Aires: Instituto de Desarrollo Económico y Social, 1962), p. 26.
14. Although there are no statistics to support this statement, two influential anti-liberal labor leaders—Hilario Salvo of the metallurgic workers and Juan Carlos Loholaberry of the textile workers—believed that Perón's attack on the Church produced resentment among many workers. Interview with Hilario Salvo, July 27, 1963. Interview with Juan Carlos Loholaberry, July 23, 1963.
15. For differing accounts of the relationship between Perón and the Church, see Alexander, *Perón*, pp. 127ff.; John J. Kennedy, *Catholicism, Nationalism, and Democracy in Argentina* (Notre Dame: University of Notre Dame Press, 1958); Pablo S. Marsal, *Perón y la Iglesia* (Buenos Aires: Ediciones Rex, 1955); and Pedro Badanelli, *Perón, la Iglesia y un cura* (Buenos Aires: Editorial Tartessos, 1960).
16. Julio Meinvielle, *Política argentina: 1949–1956* (Buenos Aires: Editorial Trafac, 1956), pp. 171–178.
17. *Criterio*, May 24, 1951.
18. Alexander, *Perón*, p. 130.
19. Juan González, interview with Robert J. Alexander, July 3, 1956.
20. When Evita died in 1952, some elements of labor demanded that she be canonized as Saint Eva of America. The Church was unenthusiastic about the proposal and may have antagonized these workers. Perón did not take part in this effort, however, and did not attack the Church until late in 1954.
21. For the text of these speeches, see *Hechos e ideas* (October–November 1954), pp. 389ff. See also *CGT*, November 13 and 27, 1954.
22. República Argentina, *Libro negro de la segunda tiranía* (Buenos Aires, 1956), pp. 233–242; *CGT*, April 15, 1955; *New York Times*, June 16, 1955.
23. Magnet, *Vecinos*, pp. 181–212.
24. A small group of anti-liberals—which since that time has become known as the Izquierda Nacional—had some influence on Perón and supported his attacks on the Church. The Izquierda Nacional was a group of

radical Marxist intellectuals who, influenced by the writings of Leon Trotsky, rejected social democracy and Stalinist communism. These people believed that Argentina was an underdeveloped country in which the lower classes had to cooperate with the nationalist bourgeoisie in order to win economic independence. In their view, economic independence would provide the basis for genuine economic growth and the eventual socialization of society. They therefore supported Perón as an economic nationalist whose rule was an important step in the transition from the present society to the future socialist utopia.

There were two main factions within the Izquierda Nacional: first, those such as Rudolfo Puiggros and Eduardo Astesano who broke away from the Argentine Communist Party to form the Movimiento Obrero Comunista and support Perón; and second, those such as Jorge Abelardo Ramos, Jorge E. Spilimbergo, and Enrique Dickmann who formed the Partido Socialista de la Revolución Nacional. A few others such as Juan José Hernández Arregui, Ángel Perelman, and Juan Isaac Cooke did not belong to either group, but nevertheless shared many of the ideas of the adherents of both. Alberto Belloni, letter to the author, August 4, 1965; Juan José Hernández Arregui, *La formación de la conciencia nacional: 1930–1960* (Buenos Aires: Ediciones Hachea, 1960), pp. 485–494; Alberto Methol Ferre, *La Izquierda Nacional en la Argentina* (Buenos Aires: Editorial Coyoacán, 1963).

25. Quoted in Whitaker, *U.S. and Argentina*, p. 166.
26. *CGT*, July 28, 1952; August 1, 1952.
27. *La Nación*, October 18, 1952.
28. Alexander, *Perón*, pp. 188–193; *CGT*, February 22, 1952.
29. In 1948 the Confederación Interamericana de Trabajadores (CIT) replaced the communist-dominated Confederación de Trabajadores de América Latina (CTAL) as the major regional labor organization in the Western Hemisphere. The Argentine CGT did not join the CIT. In 1949, the free trade-unionists of the world, disturbed by the communist orientation of the World Federation of Trade Unions (WFTU), met in London and established the International Confederation of Free Trade Unions (ICFTU). To the annoyance of Perón, the ICFTU recognized the COASI instead of the CGT as its Argentine affiliate. In 1951 the hemispheric labor organizations got together, abolished the CIT, and formed the Organización Regional Interamericana de Trabajadores (ORIT) as the regional organization of the ICFTU. The CGT was excluded from ORIT.
30. *CGT*, February 29, 1952. For a discussion of the Third Position, see Blanksten, *Perón*, pp. 277–293, 423–439; and Magnet, *Vecinos*.
31. *CGT*, May 23, 1952.
32. *CGT*, November 28, 1952.
33. República Argentina, *Libro negro*, pp. 254ff.; Alexander, *Perón*, pp. 189ff.
34. *CGT*, February 27 and May 15, 1954; Magnet, *Vecinos*, p. 107.
35. Interview with William Thayer, former lawyer for the metal workers' union of Chile, August 6, 1963. Interview with Francisco Letelier,

public relations official for the Confederación de Viña del Mar, August 5, 1963.
36. Interview with William Thayer, August 6, 1963. United States Department of Labor, Bureau of Labor Statistics, *Foreign Labor Information: Labor in Chile* (Washington, July 1956), pp. 8–9.
37. Interview with Juan A. Acuña, Secretary-General of the Confederación de Sindicatos del Uruguay, July 8, 1963.
38. República Argentina, Vice-Presidencia de la Nación, Comisión Nacional de Investigaciones, *Documentación, autores y cómplices de las irregularidades cometidas durante la segunda tiranía* (Buenos Aires: 1958), v, 120.
39. Juan D. Perón, *Dijo Perón a los delegados al congreso extraordinario de la FONVIA* (Buenos Aires: Subsecretaría de Informaciones, 1953), pp. 11–12; República Argentina, *Libro negro*, pp. 227ff.
40. *La Vanguardia*, August 5, 1953; July 14, 1954. *COASI*, November 1952.
41. Unión Ferroviaria, *Actas: 1953*, p. 71.
42. *Ibid.*, pp. 19–20.
43. *Ibid.*, pp. 131–133.
44. Interview with Hilario Salvo, July 27, 1963. UOM, *Actas*, November 25, 1952.
45. *La Vanguardia*, May 26, 1954. Interview with August Vandor, Secretary-General of the metallurgic workers' union, July 30, 1963. In this interview Vandor suggested different figures, but the issue remains the same. Vandor said the union asked for a wage increase of 56 per cent, other unions were asking for increases of up to 45 per cent, and Baluch signed a wage agreement for a 25 per cent increase.
46. *Nuevas Bases*, June 1954; *La Vanguardia*, June 9, 1954.
47. *La Nación*, June 30, 1954.
48. *Nuevas Bases*, June 1954; *La Vanguardia*, June 9 and 16, 1954.
49. *CGT*, November 27, 1954; Unión Ferroviaria, *Actas: 1953*, pp. 35, 57, 239.
50. *CGT*, June 24, 1955; *La Nación*, June 30 and July 2, 1955; Arthur P. Whitaker, *Argentine Upheaval* (New York: Praeger, 1956), p. 25.
51. *La Nación*, July 16, 1955.
52. *Criterio*, July 28, 1955.
53. *La Nación*, August 14, 15, and 21, 1955.
54. *La Nación*, August 25, 1955; *Clarín*, August 25, 1955. The signers of this declaration included such labor leaders as Sebastián Marotta, former leader of the FORA IX, Jesús Fernández, former president of La Fraternidad, and Roberto Testa, former officer of the Unión Ferroviaria.
55. *CGT*, August 12 and 19, 1955.
56. *La Nación*, September 1, 1955.
57. *Ibid.*
58. *La Nación*, September 8, 1955; Franklin Lucero, *El precio de la lealtad* (Buenos Aires: Editorial Propulsión, 1959), p. 126.
59. *La Nación*, September 16–19, 1955; *New York Times*, September 19, 1955.
60. Interview with José Alonso, July 19, 1963. Interview with August Vandor, July 30, 1963.

61. Interview with Riego Ribas, Secretary-General of the printers' union, June 17, 1963.
62. Interviews with Daniel Vukasovich, July 15, 1963; Juan Carlos Loholaberry, July 23, 1963; Luis Gay, July 29, 1963; Hilario Salvo, July 27, 1963; and Sebastián Marotta, July 11, 1963.

CHAPTER 8

1. Bonifacio del Carril, *Crónica interna de la Revolución Libertadora* (Buenos Aires: Emece, 1959), p. 128. See also the account of Lonardi's son, Luis Ernesto Lonardi, *Dios es justo* (Buenos Aires: Editorial Itinerarium, 1958), pp. 192–200.
2. Division of the labor movement into these groups is based on information in *CGT*, November 11, 1955; Confederación General del Trabajo, "Congreso General Extraordinario de la CGT, 8/26/57–9/5/57" (Mimeographed copy in the files of the CGT, Buenos Aires). I use "independents" to designate all anti-Peronists, although the term was not generally employed in this sense until sometime later.
3. *La Prensa*, one of the oldest and most distinguished newspapers in Argentina, had been seized by Perón and given to the CGT in 1951.
4. *New York Times*, September 26 and 27, 1955. Interview with Luis B. Cerrutti Costa, May 30, 1963.
5. *New York Times*, September 29, 1955; October 1, 1955.
6. Most of this information on the Lonardi period comes from the only edition of the *CGT* published between early September 1955 and January 1956. See *CGT*, November 11, 1955.
7. Dante Viel of the state workers was originally designated, along with Framini and Natalini, as a leader of the CCT, but was dropped from this position the next day without explanation.
8. *CGT*, November 11, 1955; *El Obrero Ferroviario*, September 1955.
9. *CGT*, November 11, 1955; *New York Times*, October 14, 1955.
10. *COASI*, December 1955.
11. *CGT*, November 11, 1955.
12. Bank of Boston, *The Situation in Argentina*, October 31, 1955.
13. *Ibid*.
14. *CGT*, November 11, 1955.
15. *Anales de legislación argentina: 1955*, Vol. A, pp. 563–566.
16. The committee consisted of Rafael Colace, José F. Agarraberes, Humberto Mandrioni, Salvador A. Zucotti, Rafael Ginocchio, and Eustaquio Tolosa.
17. For example, see *New York Times*, November 3, 1955.
18. *CGT*, November 11, 1955.
19. David C. Jordan, "Argentina's Nationalist Movements and the Political Parties: 1930–1963" (Ph.D. Thesis, University of Pennsylvania, 1964), pp. 243–248.
20. *New York Times*, November 16, 1955.
21. *Anales de legislación argentina: 1955*, Vol. A, pp. 580–581.
22. *Ibid*.
23. *New York Times*, December 31, 1955.

24. *CGT*, January 1956. The *CGT* resumed publication in January 1956 under the supervision of the government and reflected the government's rather than labor's point of view.
25. República Argentina, *Libro negro*, pp. 21, 146.
26. *El Obrero Ferroviario*, December 1955. Like the *CGT*, the government controlled *El Obrero Ferroviario* and therefore it no longer reflected the views of labor.
27. Bank of Boston, *The Situation in Argentina*, August 27, 1956; September 24, 1956.
28. *Anales de legislación argentina: 1956*, pp. 243–244.
29. *Ibid.*, pp. 294–295.
30. República Argentina, Ministerio de Trabajo y Previsión, *Política social y libertad sindical* (Buenos Aires: Departamento de Publicaciones y Biblioteca, 1956).
31. *Anales de legislación argentina: 1956*, pp. 476–479.
32. Interview with José Alonso, July 19, 1963.
33. Interview with Francisco Prado, July 23, 1963.
34. Interview with Herminio Alonso, July 22, 1963.
35. Interview with Sebastián Marotta, July 11, 1963.
36. Interview with Daniel Vukasovich, July 15, 1963. Interviews with José Alonso and Marotta cited above.
37. Comisión Popular Permanente de Homenaje a los Héroes y Mártires del 9 de Junio, *Documentos de la Revolución de 9 de Junio* (Buenos Aires, 1962).
38. Interview with August Vandor, July 30, 1963. Interview with Juan Carlos Loholaberry, July 23, 1963. Also interviews with Herminio Alonso and Marotta cited above.
39. *CGT*, October–November 1956.
40. *CGT*, April 1957.
41. *CGT*, "Congreso 1957," pp. 365ff.
42. Interview with José Alonso, July 25, 1963.
43. Interview with Francisco Pérez Leirós, June 14, 1963. Interview with Herminio Alonso, July 22, 1963.

Bibliography

The most important books on organized labor in Argentina are the histories written by some of the leading participants in the movement. Diego Abad de Santillán presents the anarchist point of view. Jacinto Oddone and Martín S. Casaretto have written two socialist accounts. Sebastián Marotta, the most impartial of all the labor historians, generally follows the syndicalist line. Rubens Iscaro is a Stalinist, and Cipriano Reyes represents the laborista position. The Peronist point of view is best expressed by Alberto Belloni, Ángel Perelman, and Luis B. Cerrutti Costa.

These labor histories have several characteristics in common. First, they are partisan works attempting to justify a certain position. Second, they contain many factual errors. And third, they are poorly written, often bogging down in meaningless detail. Nevertheless, these books are extremely valuable because they do present different points of view and because they often include many documents that cannot be obtained anywhere else.

Comprehensive and reliable statistical information on the labor movement and other related subjects does not exist. However, the best of what is available can be found in the Industrial Censuses of 1950 and 1954 and in *Organización sindical: asociaciones obreros y patronales,* all three published by the Argentine government.

Labor newspapers and reports were by far the most important source material used in this study. The wealth of information and opinion they provided cannot be found anywhere else. The newspapers *CGT, La Fraternidad, El Obrero Ferroviario,* and *COASI* proved most useful. These were supplemented by the *Actas* of the National Congresses and Executive Committee meetings of the CGT, the Confederación General de Empleados de Comercio, La Fraternidad, and the Unión Ferroviaria. The unpublished Actas de la Comisión Administrativa of the Unión Obrera Metalúrgica were an invaluable source of information on the Peronist movement during the Perón years.

Lastly, mention should be made of interviews with the major participants in the events discussed. These interviews were helpful primarily in guiding the author to an understanding of the complex issues involved. They have been used to supplement printed sources or to substantiate a particular point of view.

Books and Pamphlets

Abad de Santillán, Diego: *La FORA.* Buenos Aires: Ediciones Nervie, 1933.

Acossano, Benigno: *Eva Perón, su verdadera vida.* Buenos Aires: Editorial Lamas, 1955.

Alexander, Robert J.: *The Perón Era.* New York: Columbia University Press, 1951.

Alsina, Juan A.: *El obrero.* 2 vols. Buenos Aires: Imprenta Calle de México, 1905.

Amadeo, Mario: *Ayer, hoy, mañana.* Buenos Aires: Ediciones Gure, 1956.

Amadeo, Santos Primo: *Argentine Constitutional Law.* New York: Columbia University Press, 1943.

Astesano, Eduardo B.: *Ensayo sobre el Justicialismo a la*

Bibliography / 213

luz del Materialismo histórico. Rosario: Edición del Autor, 1953.
Astesano, Eduardo B.: *Rosas: bases del nationalismo popular.* Buenos Aires: Editorial A. Peña Lillo, 1960.
Babini, Nicolás: *Enero de 1919.* Buenos Aires: Servicio Editorial y Periodístico Argentino, 1956.
Badanelli, Pedro: *Perón, la Iglesia y un cura.* Buenos Aires: Editorial Tartessos, 1960.
Belloni, Alberto: *Del anarquismo al Peronismo.* Buenos Aires: Editorial A. Peña Lillo, 1960.
——: *Peronismo y socialismo nacional.* Buenos Aires: Editorial Coyoacán, 1962.
Beveraggi Allendi, Walter: *El fracaso de Perón y el problema argentino.* Buenos Aires: Rosso, 1956.
Blanksten, George I.: *Perón's Argentina.* Chicago: Chicago University Press, 1953.
Bravo, Mario: *La revolución de ellos.* Buenos Aires: La Vanguardia, 1932.
Brenan, Gerald: *The Spanish Labyrinth.* Cambridge: Cambridge University Press, 1950.
Bryce, James: *South America.* New York: Macmillan, 1913.
Cafiero, Antonio F.: *Cinco años después.* Buenos Aires: El Gráfico, 1961.
Carr, E. H.: *Nationalism and After.* London: Macmillan, 1945.
Carril, Bonifacio del: *Crónica interna de la Revolución Libertadora.* Buenos Aires: Emecc, 1959.
Casaretto, Martín S.: *Historia del movimiento obrero argentino.* 2 vols. Buenos Aires: Lorenzo, 1946, 1947.
Cerrutti Costa, Luis B.: *El sindicalismo.* Buenos Aires: Editorial Trafac, 1957.
Chiti, J. B., and Agnelli, F.: *La Fraternidad.* Buenos Aires: Ravaschino Hnos., 1937.
Coca, J.: *El contubernio.* Buenos Aires: Editorial Coyoacán, 1961.

Cochran, Thomas C., and Reina, R. E.: *Entrepreneurship in Argentine Culture: Torcuato Di Tella and S.I.A.M.* Philadelphia: University of Pennsylvania Press, 1962.

Comisión Popular Permanente de Homenaje a los Héroes y Mártires del 9 de Junio: *Documentos de la Revolución de 9 de Junio.* Buenos Aires: 1962.

Cordero, Héctor Adolfo: *Alberto Ghiraldo.* Buenos Aires: Editorial Claridad, 1962.

Cuello, Nicolás: *El Partido Socialista y la nacionalidad.* Buenos Aires: Talleres Gráficos Orientación, 1958.

Cúneo, Dardo: *Juan B. Justo.* Buenos Aires: Editorial Alpe, 1956.

Deutsch, Karl W.: *Nationalism and Social Communication.* New York: Wiley & Sons, 1953.

Dickman, Adolfo: *Nacionalismo y socialismo.* Buenos Aires: Porter Hnos., 1933.

Dunne, Peter M.: *A Padre Views South America.* Milwaukee: Bruce, 1945.

Emerson, Rupert: *From Empire to Nation.* Boston: Beacon Press, 1962.

Esbozo de historia del Partido Comunista de la Argentina. Buenos Aires: Editorial Anteo, 1948.

Ferns, H. S.: *Britain and Argentina in the Nineteenth Century.* London: Oxford University Press, 1960.

Ferrer, Aldo: *La economía argentina.* Buenos Aires: Fondo de Cultura Económica, 1963.

Ferri, Enrico, and Juan B. Justo: *El Partido Socialista en la República Argentina.* Buenos Aires: Lotito y Barberis, 1909.

Figuerola, José: *La colaboración social en Hispanoamérica.* Buenos Aires: Editorial Sudamericana, 1943.

Fillol, Tomás R.: *Social Factors in Economic Development: The Argentine Case.* Cambridge: Massachusetts Institute of Technology Press, 1961.

Flores, María: *Woman with a Whip*. New York: Doubleday, 1953.
Galenson, Walter, ed.: *Labor in Developing Economies*. Berkeley: University of California Press, 1962.
Galletti, Alfredo: *La política y los partidos*. Buenos Aires: Fondo de Cultura Económica, 1961.
Germani, Gino: *Estructura social de la Argentina*. Buenos Aires: Editorial Raigal, 1955.
———: *Política y sociedad en una época de transición*. Buenos Aires: Editorial Paidos, 1962.
Gori, Gastón: *La pampa sin gaucho*. Buenos Aires: Editorial Raigal, 1952.
Guardo, R. C.: *Horas difíciles*. Buenos Aires: Ediciones A. Peña Lillo, 1963.
Handlin, Oscar: *The Uprooted*. New York: Grosset and Dunlap, 1951.
Harvard University Center for International Affairs: *United States Foreign Policy: Ideology and Foreign Affairs*. Washington: United States Government Printing Office, 1960.
Hayes, Carlton J. H.: *The Historical Evolution of Modern Nationalism*. New York: Macmillan, 1931.
———: *Nationalism: A Religion*. New York: Macmillan, 1960.
Hernández Arregui, Juan José: *La formación de la conciencia nacional: 1930–1960*. Buenos Aires: Ediciones Hachea, 1960.
Ibarguren, Carlos: *La historia que he vivido*. Buenos Aires: Peuser, 1955.
Ímaz, José Luis de: *La clase alta de Buenos Aires*. Buenos Aires: Universidad de Buenos Aires, 1962.
———: *Motivación electoral*. Buenos Aires: Instituto de Desarrollo Económico y Social, 1962.
Ingenieros, José: *Sociología argentina*. Buenos Aires: Ediciones L. J. Rosso, 1925.

Iscaro, Rubens: *Origen y desarrollo del movimiento sindical argentino.* Buenos Aires: Editorial Anteo, 1958.
Jaguaribe, Helio: *Burguesía y proletariado en el nacionalismo brasileño.* Buenos Aires: Editorial Coyoacán, 1961.
Johnson, John J.: *Political Change in Latin America: The Emergence of the Middle Sectors.* Stanford: Stanford University Press, 1958.
Juárez, Juan C.: *Los trabajadores en función social.* Buenos Aires, 1947.
Justo, Juan B.: *Internacionalismo y patria.* Buenos Aires: La Vanguardia, 1933.
———: *La realización del socialismo.* Buenos Aires: La Vanguardia, 1947.
Kennedy, John J.: *Catholicism, Nationalism, and Democracy in Argentina.* Notre Dame: University of Notre Dame Press, 1958.
Kerr, Clark, and others: *Industrialism and Industrial Man.* Cambridge: Harvard University Press, 1960.
Kohn, Hans: *The Idea of Nationalism.* New York: Macmillan, 1960.
Legón, Faustino, and Madrano, Samuel W.: *Las constituciones de la República Argentina.* Madrid: Ediciones Cultura Hispánica, 1953.
Liberal, J. R.: *Culminación del sindicalismo argentino.* Buenos Aires: D. Francisco A. Colombo, 1952.
Lombille, Roman J.: *Eva, la predestinada.* Buenos Aires: Ediciones Gure, 1955.
Lonardi, Luis Ernesto: *Dios es justo.* Buenos Aires: Editorial Itinerarium, 1958.
López, Alfredo: *La clase obrera y la revolución del 4 de junio.* Buenos Aires, 1945.
Lorwin, Lewis L.: *The International Labor Movement.* New York: Harper, 1953.
———: *Labor and Internationalism.* New York: Macmillan, 1929.

Lucero, Franklin: *El precio de la lealtad.* Buenos Aires: Editorial Propulsión, 1959.
Mafud, J.: *El desarraigo argentino.* Buenos Aires: Editorial Américalee, 1959.
Magnet, Alejandro: *Nuestros vecinos argentinos.* Santiago de Chile: Editorial del Pacífico, 1956.
Marotta, Sebastián: *El movimiento sindical argentino.* 2 vols. Buenos Aires: Ediciones Lacio, 1960, 1961.
Marsal, Pablo S.: *Perón y la Iglesia.* Buenos Aires: Ediciones Rex, 1955.
Martínez Estrada, Ezequiel: *Radiografía de la pampa.* 5th ed. Buenos Aires: Editorial Losada, 1961.
Mazo, Gabriel del: *El radicalismo.* 2 vols. Buenos Aires: Ediciones Gure, 1957.
———, ed.: *El pensamiento escrito de Yrigoyen.* Buenos Aires: Editorial Raigal, 1945.
Meinvielle, Julio: *Política argentina: 1949–1956.* Buenos Aires: Editorial Trafac, 1956.
Mendes de Almeida, Cándido Antônio: *Nacionalismo e desenvolvimento.* Rio de Janeiro: Instituto Brasileiro de Estudos Afro-asiáticos, 1963.
Methol Ferre, Alberto: *La Izquierda Nacional en la Argentina.* Buenos Aires: Editorial Coyoacán, 1963.
Millen, Bruce H.: *The Political Role of Labor in Developing Countries.* Washington: The Brookings Institute, 1963.
Monti, A.: *Antología poética de la revolución justicialista.* Buenos Aires: Librería Perlado, 1954.
Oddone, Jacinto: *Gremialismo proletario argentino.* Buenos Aires: La Vanguardia, 1949.
———: *Historia del socialismo.* 2 vols. Buenos Aires: La Vanguardia, 1934.
Ortiz, Roberto M.: *Historia económica de la Argentina.* 2 vols. Buenos Aires: Editorial Raigal, 1955.
Pablo, Vicente E. de, and Ezcurra, Marta: *Investigación social en agrupaciones de "Villas Miserias" de la ciudad*

de Buenos Aires. Buenos Aires: Comisión Nacional de la Vivienda, 1958.

Padroni, Adrian: *Los trabajadores en la Argentina.* Buenos Aires, 1896.

Palacios, Alfredo L.: *El nuevo derecho.* 3rd ed. Buenos Aires: Editorial Claridad, 1934.

⸺: *En defensa de las instituciones libres.* Santiago de Chile: Ediciones Ercilla, 1936.

⸺: *La justicia social.* Buenos Aires: Editorial Claridad, 1954.

Pan, Luis: *La agonía del régimen de junio a septiembre.* Buenos Aires: La Vanguardia, 1956.

Pellicer Paraire, Antonio: *Análisis de la cuestión de la vida.* Barcelona: P. Cuesta, n.d.

Perelman, Ángel: *Como hicimos el 17 de octubre.* Buenos Aires: Editorial Coyoacán, 1961.

Perón, Eva: *La razón de mi vida.* Buenos Aires: Peuser, n.d.

Perón, Juan D.: *Así cumple Perón.* Buenos Aires: Subsecretaría de Informaciones, 1951.

⸺: *Del poder al exilio.* Buenos Aires, n.d.

⸺: *Dijo Perón a los delegados al 3er Congreso Extraordinario de la FONVIA.* Buenos Aires: Subsecretaría de Informaciones, 1953.

⸺: *La fuerza es el derecho de las bestias.* Montevideo: Ediciones Cicerón, 1958.

⸺: *Habla Perón a los Ferroviarios.* Bueno Aires: Subsecretaría de Informaciones, 1951.

⸺: *El trabajo a través del pensamiento de Perón.* Buenos Aires: Secretaría de Prensa y Difusión, 1955.

⸺: *La traición de los dirigentes de la FOTIA y la FEIA a los trabajadores del azúcar.* Buenos Aires: Subsecretaría de Informaciones, 1950.

Perón, Juan D., and Perón, Eva: *Día de la Lealtad: Discursos del Gral. Juan Perón y de la Señora Eva Perón.* Buenos Aires: Subsecretaría de Informaciones, 1949.

Ponce, Ángel L.: *Historia del movimiento obrero argentino.* Santa Fe, Argentina: Universidad Nacional de Litoral, 1947.
Portnoy, L.: *Análisis crítico de la economía.* Buenos Aires: Fondo de Cultura Económica, 1961.
Rabinovitz, Bernardo: *Sucedió en la Argentina.* Buenos Aires: Ediciones Gure, 1956.
Ramicone, L.: *La organización gremial obrera en la actualidad.* Buenos Aires: Editorial Bases, 1963.
Ramos, J. Abelardo: *Revolución y contrarevolución en la Argentina.* Buenos Aires: Ediciones La Roja, 1961.
Ramos Mejía, J. M.: *Las multitudes argentinas.* Buenos Aires: Editorial Tor, 1956.
Real, J. J.: *Treinte años de historia argentina.* Buenos Aires: Ediciones Actualidad, 1962.
Rennie, Ysabel F.: *The Argentine Republic.* New York: Macmillan, 1945.
Repetto, Nicolás: *Mi paso por la política: de Uriburu a Perón.* Buenos Aires: Santiago Rueda, 1957.
Reyes, Cipriano: *¿Qué es el Laborismo?* Buenos Aires: Ediciones RA, 1946.
Romariz, José R.: *La Semana Trágica.* Buenos Aires: Editorial Hemisferio, 1952.
Romero, José Luis: *Las ideas políticas en la Argentina.* Buenos Aires: Fondo de Cultura Económica, 1946.
Royal Institute of International Affairs: *Nationalism.* London: Oxford University Press, 1939.
Saravia, José Manuel: *Argentina 1959.* Buenos Aires: Ediciones del Atlántico, 1959.
Sarobe, J. M.: *Memorias sobre la revolución del 6 de septiembre de 1930.* Buenos Aires: Ediciones Gure, 1957.
Scobie, James R.: *Argentina.* New York: Oxford University Press, 1964.
Silvert, Kalman H., ed.: *Expectant Peoples.* New York: Random House, 1963.

Solari, J. A.: *Trabajadores del Norte Argentino.* Buenos Aires, 1937.
Spilimbergo, Jorge E.: *Juan B. Justo o el socialismo cipayo.* Buenos Aires: Editorial Coyoacán, n.d.
Strasser, C.: *La izquierdas en el proceso político argentino.* Buenos Aires: Editorial Palestra, 1959.
Tieffenberg, D.: *Exigencias proletarias a la revolución.* Buenos Aires: Ediciones Populares Argentinas, 1956.
Ugarte, Manuel: *El porvenir de América Latina.* Buenos Aires: Editorial Indoamérica, 1953.
Uriburu, Alberto E., ed.: *La palabra del General Uriburu.* Buenos Aires: Roldán Editor, 1933.
Varela, A. H.: *El nacionalismo argentino y los obreros socialistas.* Buenos Aires: Imprenta López, 1935.
Weil, Felix: *Argentine Riddle.* New York: John Day, 1944.
Whitaker, Arthur P.: *Argentina.* Englewood Cliffs, N.J.: Prentice-Hall, 1964.
———: *Argentine Upheaval.* New York: Praeger, 1956.
———: *Nationalism in Latin America.* Gainesville: University of Florida Press, 1962.
———: *The United States and Argentina.* Cambridge: Harvard University Press, 1954.
———, and David Jordan: *Nationalism in Contemporary Latin America.* New York: Free Press, 1966.

Articles

Agosti, Héctor P.: "La expresión de los argentinos: la conciencia nacional," *Cuadernos Americanos,* VIII, No. 1 (January–February 1949), 117–130.
Beals, Ralph L.: "Social Stratification in Latin America," *American Journal of Sociology,* LVIII, No. 4 (January 1953), 327–339.
Cosío Villegas, Daniel: "Nacionalismo e desenvolvimento,"

Revista Brasileira de Política Internacional, v, No. 20 (December 1962), 673–690.

Deutsch, Karl: "Social Mobilization and Political Development," *American Political Science Review*, LV, No. 3 (September 1961), 493–514.

Gillen, John P.: "Some Signposts for Policy," in Richard N. Adams and others, *Social Change in Latin America Today*. New York: Vintage Books, 1961.

Iutaka, Sugiyama: "Social Stratification Research in Latin America," *Latin American Research Review*, I, No. 1 (October 1965), 7–34.

Johnson, John J.: "The New Latin American Nationalism," *Yale Review*, LIV (December 1964), 187–204.

Morris, James O.: "Consensus, Ideology and Labor Relations," *Journal of Inter-American Studies*, VII, No. 3 (July 1965), 301–315.

Schultze, H. H.: "The Socialist Movement in the Argentine Republic," *International Socialist Review*, v (July 1904), 18–20.

Scott, Robert E.: "Nation Building in Latin America," in Karl W. Deutsch and William J. Foltz, eds., *Nation Building*. New York: Atherton Press, 1963.

Simon, S. Fanny: "Anarchism and Anarcho-Syndicalism in South America," *Hispanic American Historical Review*, XXVI, No. 1 (February 1946), 38–59.

Zymelman, Manuel: "Cultural Patterns of Labor and Latin American Industrialization," *Journal of Inter-American Studies*, v, No. 3 (July 1963), 357–370.

Periodicals

Bank of Boston: *The Situation in Argentina*. 1955–1966.
CGT (Buenos Aires), 1932–1957.
Clarín (Buenos Aires), 1955.
COASI (Montevideo), 1952–1956.

Confederación General del Trabajo: *Boletín Informativo Semanal*. Buenos Aires, 1963–1966.
Criterio (Buenos Aires), 1946–1955.
Documentación e Información Laboral, *Informe 34*, December 1962.
La Fraternidad (Buenos Aires), 1920–1955.
Hechos e Ideas (Buenos Aires), 1946–1955.
La Nación (Buenos Aires), 1951–1955.
New York Times, 1930–1957.
Nuevas Bases (Buenos Aires), 1950–1955.
El Obrero Ferroviario (Buenos Aires), 1930–1957.
La Prensa (Buenos Aires), 1943–1951.
Primera Plana (Buenos Aires), 1965.
La Protesta (Buenos Aires), 1904–1910.
Unión Industrial Argentina: *Anales*. 1930–1945.
———: *Boletín*. 1909–1929.
———: *Argentine Fabril*. 1946.
La Vanguardia (Montevideo), 1952–1955.

Public Documents

Anales de legislación argentina. Buenos Aires: Editorial La Ley, 1889–1957.
Buenos Aires, Departamento de Estadística Municipal: *Censo general de la ciudad de Buenos Aires*. Buenos Aires, 1906.
República Argentina: *Libro negro de la segunda tiranía*. Buenos Aires, 1956.
———: *Cuatro Censo Nacional*. Buenos Aires, 1949.
———: *Tercero Censo Nacional*. Buenos Aires: Rosso y Cía, 1917.
———, Departamento Nacional del Trabajo: *Boletín*. Buenos Aires, 1907–1921.
———, Departamento Nacional del Trabajo, División de Estadística: *Estadística de las huelgas*. Buenos Aires, 1940.

República Argentina, Departamento Nacional del Trabajo, División de Estadística: *Estadística de las huelgas.* Serie B, No. 10. Buenos Aires, 1941.

———, Departamento Nacional del Trabajo, División de Estadística: *Organización sindical: asociaciones obreros y patronales.* Buenos Aires, 1941.

———, Dirección Nacional de Estadística y Censo: *Anuario estadístico de la República Argentina.* Buenos Aires, 1957.

———, Ministerio de Hacienda de la Nación, Dirección Nacional de Estadística y Censos: *Censo Industrial 1950.* Buenos Aires, 1957.

———, Ministerio de Trabajo y Previsión: *Política social y libertad sindical.* Buenos Aires: Departamento de Publicaciones y Biblioteca, 1956.

———, Ministerio de Trabajo y Seguridad Social, Dirección General de Estudios e Investigaciones: *Conflictos del Trabajo.* Buenos Aires, 1961.

———, Secretaría de Estado de Hacienda, Dirección Nacional de Estadística y Censos: *Censo Industrial 1954.* Buenos Aires, 1960.

United States Department of Commerce, Bureau of Foreign and Domestic Commerce, Foreign Service Report Series: *Economic Review of Argentina.* Washington, 1951, 1953.

United States Department of Commerce, Business Information Service, World Trade Series: *Economic Review of Argentina.* Washington, 1951.

United States Department of Labor, Bureau of Labor Statistics: *Foreign Labor Information: Labor in Argentina.* June 1959.

United States Department of Labor, Bureau of Labor Statistics: *Foreign Labor Information: Labor in Chile.* July 1956.

United States Department of Labor, Bureau of Labor Statistics: *Foreign Labor Information: Latin American Labor*

Legislation—Comparative Summaries of Selected Provisions. August 1956.
United States Government Memorandum: Consultation Among the American Republics with Respect to the Argentine Situation. Washington, 1946.

Reports of Labor and Business Organizations

American Federation of Labor: *American Labor Looks at the World.* Washington, 1947.
Confederación General de Empleados de Comercio: *Memoria del Consejo Administrativo al II Congreso Ordinario.* Buenos Aires, 1936.
Confederación General de Empleados de Comercio: *Memoria del Consejo Administrativo al III Congreso Ordinario.* Buenos Aires, 1939.
Confederación General del Trabajo: *Acta del Primer Congreso Ordinario Confederal.* Buenos Aires, 1940.
———: *Acta del Segundo Congreso Ordinario Confederal.* Buenos Aires, 1943.
———: *Actas de las reuniones del Comité Central Confederal.* Buenos Aires, 1942.
———: *Actas de las reuniones del Comité Central Confederal.* Buenos Aires, 1943.
———: *Anteproyecto de estatutos de la Confederación General del Trabajo.* Buenos Aires, 1934.
———: *Labor realizada por el Secretariado Confederal.* Buenos Aires, 1947.
———: *Memoria y balance.* Buenos Aires, 1948–1954.
Confederación General Económica de la República Argentina: *Informe económico.* Buenos Aires, 1955.
Confederación General Económica de la República Argentina con la colaboración del Instituto Argentino de Relaciones Industriales: *Primer congreso de organización y relaciones del trabajo, 23 al 28 de agosto de 1954.* Buenos Aires, 1954.

Congreso nacional de productividad y bienestar social: antecedentes, temario, conclusiones. Buenos Aires, 1955.

Federación de Obreros y Empleados Ferroviarios: *Motivos de su creación.* Buenos Aires, 1939.

———: *La verdad sobre la administración de la Unión Ferroviaria.* Buenos Aires: La Argentina, 1939.

Federación Empleados de Comercio: *Memoria de la Comisión Directiva: 1947–1949.* Buenos Aires: Imprenta Castromán, Ortiz y Cía., 1950.

Federación Gráfica Argentina: *Memoria y balance: 1951.* Buenos Aires, 1951.

Federación Obrera Regional Argentina: *Memoria y balance del Consejo Federal al Undécimo Congreso.* Buenos Aires: 1920.

La Fraternidad: *Actas del Congreso Nacional.* Buenos Aires: 1930–1950, 1955–1963.

International Labor Office: *Yearbook of Labor Statistics.* Geneva, 1936–1955.

Unión Ferroviaria: *Actas de la Asamblea General.* Buenos Aires, 1930–1963.

———: *Memoria y balance.* Buenos Aires, 1928–1963.

Unión Sindical Argentina: *Carta Orgánica.* Buenos Aires, 1921.

———: *Memoria y balance.* Buenos Aires, 1922–1926.

Unión Tranviarios: *Memoria y balance.* Buenos Aires, 1930–1946.

Unpublished Material

Abad de Santillán, Diego: "El movimiento obrero y el socialismo: 1900–1910." Unpublished manuscript, n.d. (In the files of the author.)

Alexander, Robert J.: "The Labor Movements of Latin America." Unpublished manuscript, n.d. (In the files of Robert J. Alexander.)

Calello, H., Marín, J. C., and Murmis, M.: "Formas de lucha e ideología del sindicato y el medio social e industrial." Instituto de Sociología de la Facultad de Filosofía y Letras de la Universidad Nacional de Buenos Aires, Publicación Interna No. 10, Buenos Aires, 1962. (Mimeographed.)

Confederación General del Trabajo: "Congreso General Extraordinario de la CGT 8/26/57–9/5/57." (Mimeographed copy in the files of the CGT, Buenos Aires.)

David, Pedro R.: "The Social Structure of Argentina." (Ph. D. Thesis, Indiana University, 1962.)

Di Tella, T. B., et al.: "Planteo de una investigación sobre estructura sindical." Instituto de Sociología de la Facultad de Filosofía y Letras de la Universidad Nacional de Buenos Aires, Publicación Interna No. 29. Buenos Aires, n.d. (Mimeographed.)

Germani, Gino: "El proceso de urbanización en la Argentina." Instituto de Sociología de la Facultad de Filosofía y Letras de la Universidad Nacional de Buenos Aires, Publicación Interna No. 4. Buenos Aires, 1962. (Mimeographed.)

Jordan, David C.: "Argentina's Nationalist Movements and the Political Parties: 1930–1963." (Ph.D. Thesis, University of Pennsylvania, 1964.)

Unión Obrera Metalúrgica: Actas de la Comisión Administrativa. 1943–1955, 1959–1962. (In the files of the union.)

Other Sources

INTERVIEWS

Acuña, Juan A. Secretary-General of the Confederación de Sindicatos del Uruguay. Montevideo. July 8, 1963.

Alonso, Herminio. President of La Fraternidad. Buenos Aires. April 10 and July 22, 1963.

Alonso, José. Secretary-General of the CGT. Buenos Aires. July 19 and 25, 1963.

Borges, Jorge Luis. Author. Buenos Aires. March 18, 1963.

Cafiero, Antonio F. Minister of Commerce, 1952–1955; member of the Coordinating Council of the Peronist Movement. Buenos Aires. July 31, 1963.

Carbone, Oscar. Industrial Relations Manager, Monsanto Argentino. Buenos Aires. July 3, 1963.

Casanova, Enrique. Member of the National Committee of the Partido Laborista. Buenos Aires. May 26, 1963.

Cerrutti Costa, Luis B. Minister of Labor under Lonardi; labor lawyer. Buenos Aires. May 30, 1963.

Del Mestre, Mario Luis. Press Secretary of La Fraternidad. Buenos Aires. April 11, 16, 17, and 24, 1963.

Falasco, Julio. Socialist leader of the railroad strikes, 1950–1951. Interview with Robert J. Alexander. Buenos Aires. August 4, 1952. (Typewritten notes.)

Gay, Luis. Former Secretary-General of the Unión Sindical Argentina; former Secretary-General of the CGT; former President of the Partido Laborista. Buenos Aires. July 29, 1963.

———. Interview with Robert J. Alexander. Buenos Aires. November 1946. (Typewritten notes.)

Ghioldi, Américo. Long-time leader of the Socialist Party and present leader of the Partido Socialista Democrático. Buenos Aires. May 31, 1963.

González, Juan. Catholic labor leader. Interview with Robert J. Alexander. Buenos Aires. July 3, 1956. (Typewritten notes.)

Goyeneche, Juan Carlos. A leader of the right-wing Catholic nationalist group headed by Marcelo Sánchez Sorondo. Buenos Aires. April 17, 1963.

Gregorio, Cándido. Pre-Perón leader of the Unión Obrera Textil; leader of COASI in Argentina and in exile. Buenos Aires. June 5, 1963.

Letelier, Francisco. Public relations official for the Confederación de Viña del Mar. Santiago. August 5, 1963.
Loholaberry, Juan Carlos. Acting Secretary-General of the Asociación Obrera Textil. Buenos Aires. July 23, 1963.
Marcovecchio, Salvador. Secretary-General of the Confederación de Empleados de Comercio. Buenos Aires. August 1, 1963.
Marotta, Sebastián. Secretary-General of the FORA IX (1917–1920) and long-time syndicalist leader of the printers who was active in the movement until 1957. Buenos Aires. June 20, July 11 and 16, 1963.
Moreno, Carlos Ernesto. Secretary-General of the Empleados de Comercio of Tucumán. Tucumán. May 20, 1963.
Oneto Gaona, Juan Martín. President of the Unión Industrial Argentina. Buenos Aires. July 15, 1963.
Palacios, Alfredo L. Old-time socialist leader. Buenos Aires. July 24, 1963.
Palacios, Alfredo L. Interview with Robert J. Alexander. Buenos Aires. November 1946. (Typewritten notes.)
Pepe, Lorenzo A. Vice-President of the Unión Ferroviaria and leader of the union's Peronist faction. Buenos Aires. May 10, 1963.
Pérez Leirós, Francisco. Former Socialist Deputy in the National Congress; Secretary-General of the CGT No. 2 in 1943; and long-time Secretary-General of the Unión Empleados y Obreros Municipales. Buenos Aires. June 14, 1963.
Pozo, Luis del. Manager of the traditional business association ACIEL. Buenos Aires. July 12, 1963.
Prado, Francisco, Secretary-General of Luz y Fuerza. Buenos Aires. July 23, 1963.
Pueyrredón, Gustavo A. Vice-President of the Sociedad Rural. Buenos Aires. July 18, 1963.
Recalde, Ildefonso. President of the Confederación General Económica. Buenos Aires. July 12, 1963.

Ribas, Riego. Assistant Secretary-General of the CGT; Secretary-General of the printers. Buenos Aires. June 17, 1963.

Rodríquez, José. Secretary-General of the Unión Obrera Metalúrgica, Rosario. Rosario. July 1, 1963.

Rodríquez, Victorino. Secretary-General of the Asociación Empleados de Comercio of Rosario. Rosario. July 1, 1963.

Ruberto, Pedro Pascual. Catholic priest of the Barrio Obrero of Berisso. Berisso. June 18, 1963.

Salvo, Hilario. Secretary-General of the Unión Obrera Metalúrgica, 1945–1951. Peronist Deputy in the National Congress, 1951–1954. Luján. July 27, 1963.

Sapag, Elías. Argentine Senator. Member of the Movimiento Popular Neuguén. Leader of provincial Peronist parties in the National Senate. Philadelphia. April 21, 1964.

Scipione, Antonio. President of the Unión Ferroviaria and leader of the liberals in the union during the Perón period. Buenos Aires. May 9, 1963.

Simo, Alejo. Secretary-General of the Unión Obrera Metalúrgica, Córdoba. Córdoba. May 18, 1963.

Testa, Roberto. Former official of the Unión Ferroviaria. Interview with Robert J. Alexander. Buenos Aires. August 1, 1952. (Typewritten notes.)

Thayer, William. Former lawyer for the metal workers' union of Chile. Santiago. August 6, 1963.

Torres, Elpidio. Secretary-General of the Regional CGT of Córdoba. Córdoba. May 17, 1963.

Vandor, August. Secretary-General of the Unión Obrera Metalúrgica; member of the Coordinating Council of the Peronist movement. Buenos Aires. July 30, 1963.

Vázquez, Víctor. Leader of the communist faction in the Unión Ferroviaria. Buenos Aires. May 7, 1963.

Vincelli, Ricardo E. Secretary-General of the chemical workers. Buenos Aires. July 30, 1963.

Vukasovich, Daniel. Member of the Executive Commission of SUPE (State Petroleum Workers). Buenos Aires. July 15 and 29, 1963.

LETTERS

Gay, Luis. Buenos Aires: September 12, 1963; October 10, 1963; January 12, 1964; March 30, 1964; May 4, 1964. (In the files of the author.)

Belloni, Alberto. Buenos Aires: August 4, 1965. (In the files of the author.)

Index

Abad de Santillán, Diego, 26
Abelardo Ramos, Jorge, 207n
Acción Argentina, 66
Acción Católica, 146
ADES (Asociación Democrática de Estudiantes Secundarios), 146
Agarraberes, José F., 209n
Agrupación de Trabajadores Latino Americanos Sindicalizados, 150–152
Alberdi, Juan Bautista, 124
Alonso, Herminio, 178, 182
Alonso, José, 160, 172, 178, 182
Álvarez, Néstor, 88
Alvear, Marcelo T. de, 36, 47
Anarchist communism, 21, 30, 195n
Anarchists: in early labor movement, 12–15; take over movement, 19–23; government opposes, 24–26; Uriburu suppresses, 53. *See also* FORA
Andrea, Miguel de, 144, 146
Antarctica, 122
Anti-liberals: and criollo nationalism, 7–8, 82–84; on October 17, 1945, 89–91; Perón sympathetic to, 97–98; organized by Perón, 111–112; Perón appeals to, 116–120; oppose Perón, 126–128; in Unión Ferroviaria, 131; group opposed to Evita, 204n. *See also* Criollos, Internal migrants, Peronists
Aramburu, General Pedro: replaces Lonardi as Provisional President, 171; antagonizes labor, 171–177; labor protests policies of, 178–181; attempts to normalize CGT, 181–183; policies strengthen Peronism, 183–184; mentioned, 188
Arbenz, Jacobo, 150
Argaña, José, 69, 74
Argentine Libre, 66
Argentine Socialist Party. *See* Socialist Party of Argentina
Argentine Socialist Workers' Party. *See* Socialist Party of Argentina

232 / Index

Armed forces, 56, 85, 90, 157, 161, 163, 171
Asociación Democrática de Estudiantes Secundarios, 146
Asociación de Trabajo, 37, 38
Astesano, Eduardo, 207n
ATLAS (Agrupación de Trabajadores Latino Americanos Sindicalizados), 150–152
Ávalos, General Eduardo, 87, 88

Balino, Pedro, 45
Baluch, Abdula, 155, 156, 208n
Bank of Industrial Credit, 79
Belgrano, Manuel, 124
Beveraggi Allende, Walter, 107
"Blue Book," 94, 95
Borlenghi, Ángel, 65, 68, 69, 74, 88, 101, 106, 108, 146, 157
Braden, Spruille, 87, 95, 117, 155
Bramuglia, Juan, 74, 78, 101, 133, 134
Bravo, Mario, 59
British Labour Party, 90, 106
Bryce, James, Viscount Bryce, 22, 23
Buenos Aires, 7, 9, 11, 81
Busso, Eduardo, 171

Capozzi, Francisco Pablo, 74
Castillo, Vice-President Ramón S., 65, 67, 72, 124
Castro, Juan F., 132–134 *passim*
Catholic Church in Argentina, 56, 82, 143–147, 158, 206n
Celman, Miguel Júarez, 14
Centennial of Argentine Independence, 10, 25, 26
Central Única de Trabajadores de Chile, 151
Cereijo, Ramón, 101

Cerrutti Costa, Luis B., 165–170, 172
CGE (Confederación General Económica), 139, 140
CGT (Confederación General del Trabajo): established, 49, 51; and Uriburu, 52–54; Minimum Program, 53; socialists and syndicalists struggle to control, 55–57; Constituent Congress, 58; anti-fascist campaign, 58–61; and new industrial unions, 62–63; First Ordinary Congress, 63; and communist-socialist conflict, 64–67; Second Ordinary Congress, 67; divides, 68–70; and Ramírez, 72–74; and Perón's rise to power, 76, 78–80; ignores internal migrants, 81–82; liberals withdraw from, 86, 121; and October 17, 1945, 88–90; attacks Socialists and Communists, 93; Perón destroys independence of, 108–112; intervenes in printers' union, 113; on right to strike, 114; intervenes in La Fraternidad, 124, 133; and anti-inflation campaign, 138–140; and CUSL, 149; and ATLAS, 150; and metal workers' strike, 155–156; and Church, 156–157; and overthrow of Perón, 159–160; and Lonardi, 163–171; and Aramburu, 171–184; General Extraordinary Congress, 181–183; and response to new governments, 186; and Pe-

ronists, 191; and 1948 election in Unión Ferroviaria, 204n; and international labor organizations, 207n. *See also* Labor movement, Strikes, Unions
CGT (Buenos Aires), 111, 173, 210n
Chiaranti, Pedro, 64, 201n
Chile, 150, 151
Christian Democratic Party of Argentina, 146
CIT (Confederación Interamericana de Trabajadores), 149, 207n
CNT (Confederación Nacional de Trabajadores), 151
COA (Confederación Obrera Argentina), 49, 51–53 *passim*, 55
COASI (Comité Obrero Argentino de Sindicatos Independientes), 122, 207n
Codovilla, Víctor, 205n
Colace, Rafael, 209n
Colombia, 44, 45, 150, 151
Comando Obrero Único, 201n
Comité de Unidad Clasista, 63
Comité de Unidad Sindical Latinoamericana, 149, 150
Comité Internacional Obrero, 14, 15
Comité Obrero Argentino de Sindicatos Independientes, 122, 207n
Commercial employees' union. *See* Unions, trade
Communist Party of Argentina: formation of, 46; Perón attacks, 71, 78, 105; and Perelman, 82; joins Unión Democrática, 93; and 1946 election, 95; Perón limits activities, 141; and independents, 164. *See also* Communists
Communists: and USA, 46–47; Uriburu suppresses, 53; organize industrial unions, 62–63; and socialists, 63–70; oppose Perón, 84; blamed for strikes, 114–115, 133–135; stage strike, 201n; and antiliberals, 205n. *See also* Communist Party of Argentina
Confederación de Trabajadores de América Latina, 149, 207n
Confederación General del Trabajo. *See* CGT
Confederación General Economica, 139, 140
Confederación Interamericana de Trabajadores, 149, 207n
Confederación Nacional de Trabajadores, 151
Confederación Nacional de Sindicatos Obreros de Viña del Mar, 151
Confederación Obrera Argentina, 49, 51–53 *passim*, 55
Confederación Obrera de la Región Argentina, 25, 30
Conferencia Nacional de las Organizaciones Sindicales Independientes, 201n
Congress of Argentina, National, 24, 26
Conservative Party of Argentina, 93, 115
Constitution of 1949, 101, 102, 175. *See also* Rights of the Workers

234 / Index

Cooke, Juan Isaac, 146, 207n
CORA (Confederación Obrera de la Región Argentina), 25, 30
Costa Rica, 150
Costas, Patrón, 72
Criollos: nationalism of, 7, 8, 187–188; and Ugarte and Palacios, 41–46; and Perelman and Salvo, 82–84; and October 17, 1945, 90; Perón appeals to, 116–120; oppose Perón, 126–128; in Unión Ferroviaria, 131; and future of Argentina, 189–192. *See also* Anti-liberals, Internal migrants, Nationalism, Peronists
Criterio (Buenos Aires), 144
Cruz, María de la, 151
CTAL (Confederación de Trabajadores de América Latina), 149, 207n
Cuba, 150
CUSL (Comité de Unidad Sindical Latinoamericana), 149, 150
CUTCH (Central Única de Trabajadores de Chile), 151

Declaration of Economic Independence (1947), 119
Descamisados, 90, 117, 118, 119
Deutsch, Karl, 4, 5
Díaz, Omar, 152
Dickmann, Enrique, 207n
Di Pietro, Hugo, 160, 165, 166, 172
Domenech, José, 59, 63, 64, 66–69 *passim*, 73, 199n
Duarte, Eva. *See* Perón, Eva

Echeverría, Esteban, 42, 86, 124
Economic Council, National, 102, 139
Eisenhower, President Dwight D., 141
Eisenhower, Milton, 141
Emerson, Rupert, 5
Episcopal Declaration Denouncing the Religious Persecution in Argentina, The (Argentine Catholic hierarchy), 158
La Escoba (Montevideo), 152
Espejo, José, 112, 117, 148, 150, 172, 174
European labor movement, 12

Falcón, Colonel Ramón L., 22
Falkland Islands. *See* Islas Malvinas
Farrell, Edelmiro, 77, 86, 89, 94
Fascism, 52, 55, 56, 57–70, 84, 93
Federación de Trabajo de la República Argentina, 15
Federación Gráfica Bonaerense, 69, 113
Federación Obrera Argentina, 20
Federación Obrera Marítima, 40
Federación Obrera Nacional de la Construcción. *See* Unions, trade: construction
Federación Obrera Regional Argentina. *See* FORA
Federation of Catholic Workers' Associations, 144
Fernández, Jesús, 86, 104, 208n
Ferri, Enrico, 41
Fiat Company, 140
Fidanza, Alfredo, 121
Five Year Plan: first, 102
FOA (Federación Obrera Argentina), 20

FONC (Federación Obrera Nacional de la Construcción). See Unions, trade: construction
FORA (Federación Obrera Regional Argentina), 20, 23, 25, 26, 30, 31, 158, 199n. See also Anarchists
FORA V, 30
FORA IX, 30, 35, 39–40, 41, 47, 48, 50, 93
Framini, Andrés, 166, 168, 170, 172, 209n
Franceschi, Monsignor Gustavo J., 144
Franco, General Francisco, 59
La Fraternidad. See Unions, trade: railroad
La Fraternidad (Buenos Aires), 60, 103, 122, 123, 173
Freire, José María, 101
Frondizi, Arturo, 59, 190
FTRA (Federación de Trabajo de la República Argentina), 15

Gay, Luis, 65, 88, 89, 91, 106, 107, 108–110, 111, 124, 125, 127, 160, 201n, 204n
Germani, Gino, 11
Ginocchio, Rafael, 209n
Gómez, Laureano, 150
González, Joaquín V., 23
Gori, Pedro, 20
Gregorio, Cándido, 121, 173
Griffiths, John, 107

Handlin, Oscar, 11
Hernández, Aurelio, 111–112
Hernández Arregui, Juan José, 207n
Hitler, Adolf, 63, 66

Hitler-Stalin Pact (1939), 66
La Hora (Buenos Aires), 67, 205n
Hurtado, Rubén, 151

Ibáñez del Campo, Carlos, 150, 151
ICFTU (International Confederation of Free Trade Unions), 122, 207n
ILO (International Labor Organization), 93, 204n
IMF (International Monetary Fund), 174
Immigrants, European: came to Argentina, 4; liberal nationalism of, 7–8; in early labor movement, 10–11; Justo's attitude toward, 17–18; and anarchists, 22; and Ley de Residencia, 24; second generation, 32–33; and internal migrants, 81–83; and popular nationalism, 185–186; leave Argentina in 1891, 195n. See also Anarchists, Liberals, Socialists, Syndicalists
Import-Export Bank, United States, 140
"Independents," 164, 172–173, 178, 182, 209n
Instituto Argentino de Producción e Intercambio, 102
Instituto Cultural Gremial, 144
Internal migrants: nationalism of, 7–8, 187–189; and organized labor, 80–84; and Perón, 98, 116–120; before 1936, 196n. See also Anti-liberals, Criollos, Peronists
International Confederation of

Free Trade Unions, 122, 207n
International Labor Organization, 93, 204n
International Monetary Fund, 174
International Socialist Workers' Party. *See* Socialist Party of Argentina
International Workingmen's Association, First, 12, 13; Second, 14
Iscaro, Rubens, 93
Islas Malvinas, 122, 124
Izquierda Nacional, 201n

Jockey Club (Buenos Aires), 152
Junta Asesora Gremial, 173
Justicialismo, 115, 149, 203n
Justo, Augustín P., 54, 61, 124
Justo, Juan B., 15–18, 41, 45, 46, 57, 82

Kaiser Industries, 140

Laborismo, 92
Laboristas, 84, 85–86, 88–92, 124–126, 130, 186, 188, 200n. *See also* Partido Laborista Argentino
Labor movement: popular nationalism in, 6–8, 186–188; influence of European immigrants in, 10; Vorwärts in, 14; and Justo, 17; and socialists, 15–19; anarchists in, 19–23; government hostile to, 23–27; and syndicalists, 29–30; changes in, 31–34; under Yrigoyen, 34–41; fragments, 46–50; reunites, 51–53; anti-fascist campaign, 53–61; and communists, 62–63; divides, 63–70; and Ramírez, 72–74; courted by Perón, 74–80; internal migrants in, 80–84; opposition to Perón in, 84–87; and October 17, 1945, 88–90; and election of 1946, 90–96; independence destroyed by Perón, 105–116; and the Church, 146, 147, 156–157; and overthrow of Perón, 158–161; and Lonardi, 163–171; and Aramburu, 171–184; as force in Argentina, 189–192; size of, 202n, 203n. *See also* CGT, Strikes, Unions
Latin American Union, 43
Legión Cívica, 54
Lestelle, Marcos D., 69
Ley de Asociaciones Profesionales, 72, 73, 75, 87, 176
Ley de Defensa Social, 26, 36
Ley de Residencia, 24, 25, 36, 60, 122, 123, 130
Ley González, 24
Liberalism, 7, 8, 16, 17, 42, 44
Liberals: nineteenth century, 9; in the labor movement: 6–8, 78–80, 84–85, 86, 90, 91–92, 121–124, 131, 153, 186, 188, 189, 204n. *See also* Immigrants, Laboristas, Nationalism, Socialist Party, Socialists
Libro negro de la segunda tiranía (Aramburu government), 173
El Líder (Buenos Aires), 164, 171
Liga Patriótica, 37, 38

Loholaberry, Juan Carlos, 160, 206n
Lombardo Toledano, Vicente, 93
Lonardi, General Eduardo, 160, 163–171, 173, 183
López, Pablo, 131–134 *passim*, 174
Loyalty Day (Peronist), 118, 148

Magloire, Paul, 150, 180
Mandrioni, Humberto, 209n
March of the Constitution and Liberty (1945), 87
Marotta, Sebastián, 39, 160, 173, 178, 201n, 208n
Marx, Karl, 113
Meat packers' union. See Unions, trade
Meinvielle, Julio, 144
Mende, Raúl, 119
Mercante, Domingo, 74, 75, 89, 91, 106, 133, 134, 201n
Metal workers' union. See Unions, trade
Mexico, 150
"Middle sector," 34, 197n
Migone, Raúl C., 172, 175, 176
Military, Argentine. See Armed forces
Mitre, Bartolomé, 9, 16, 41, 42
Modernization, 3, 4, 31–32
Montiel, Alcides, 87, 88
Moreno, Mariano, 86, 104, 124
Moscow International, 47
Movimiento Nacional Comunista, 207n
Movimiento Nacional Revolucionario La Escoba, 152
Movimiento Recuperación Nacional, 179

Municipal workers' union. See Unions, trade
Mussolini, Benito, 52, 66
Mutual aid societies, 11–13

Natalini, Luis, 166, 168, 170, 172, 209n
Nation, concept of, 5, 6, 21
National Commission of Unemployment, 54
National Congress of Productivity and Social Well-Being, 140
Nationalism
  Criollo: defined, 7–8; of Palacios and Ugarte, 42–45; of Perelman, 82–83; of Salvo, 83–84; Perón appeals to, 92, 95, 97–98, 116–120; of CGT, 169; stimulated by Revolución Libertadora, 183–184; content, 185–188; success, 188–192
  Liberal: defined, 6–8; Justo's, 17, 18; in Socialist Party, 41–46; in Unión Ferroviaria, 48–50; emerges in labor movement, 61–70; becomes elitist, 82; used to attack Perón, 86; in Partido Laborista, 91; used by railroad workers, 122; ineffective against Perón, 128; significance of, 185–188
  Popular: defined, 4–6; Perón embodies, 135; content, 185–188; success of, 188–192
Nazis, 94

Obregón, Juan de Dios, 154
El Obrero Ferroviario (Buenos Aires), 90, 104, 119, 131, 173, 210n

Odría, Manuel, 150
La organización obrera (Pellicer Paraire), 19
Organización Regional Interamericana de Trabajadores, 149, 150, 152, 207n
ORIT (Organización Regional Interamericana de Trabajadores), 149, 150, 152, 207n
Ortiz, Roberto M., 60, 61, 65

Pablo Pardo, Luis María de, 171
Padroni, Adrian, 20
Palacios, Alfredo, 41–45, 57, 83
Paris Commune, 12
Partido Concentración Obrera, 158
Partido Laborista Argentino, 91–92, 105–108, 116, 124, 125, 127, 186. See also Laboristas
Partido Socialista de la Revolución Nacional, 207n
Partido Socialista Internacional, 46
Partido Único, 106
Patrón Laplacette, Naval Captain Alberto, 173, 175
Pellicer Paraire, Antonio, 19, 20, 22
Pelligrini, Carlos, 23
Perelman, Ángel, 82, 83, 89, 199n, 207n
Pérez Leirós, Francisco, 47, 65, 68, 69, 93, 182
Perón, Eva: on October 17, 1945, 89, 201n; role in labor movement, 99–100; and Perón, 103, 104, 111, 152; and Aurelio Hernández, 112; denounces La Fraternidad, 116; as symbol of the nation, 117–119; and anti-liberal supporters, 131; death, 147–148; mentioned, 133, 150, 167, 174, 204n, 206n
Perón, Juan Domingo: role in June 4, 1943 coup, 71–72; courts organized labor, 74–80; becomes Secretary of Labor, 75; on virtue of work, 76; becomes Minister of War and Provisional Vice-President, 77; intensifies appeal to workers, 77–78; attacks Communists and Socialists, 78; helps internal migrants, 80–82; attacked by liberal nationalists, 84–88, 121–124; on October 17, 1945, 88–90; campaign for President, 92–96; on revolutions, 95; continues social and economic revolution, 98–105; proclaims Argentine economic independence, 102; nationalizes railroads, 103–104; destroys Partido Laborista, 105–108; destroys independence of CGT, 108–112; attacks independent unions, 112–116; limits right to strike, 113–115; appeals to internal migrants, 115–120; and Year of San Martín, 119; intervenes in La Fraternidad, 124; and railroad strikes, 130–134; new economic policy, 138–143; attacks Catholic Church, 143–147; excommunicated, 145, 158; and Evita's death, 147–148; and ATLAS, 148–152; provokes worker discon-

tent, 153–157; and overthrow, 157–161; Revolución Libertadora discredits, 165; Prebisch Report criticizes, 169; Aramburu attacks, 172–173; compared to Aramburu, 177, 178; and criollo nationalism, 187–191; and the Izquierda Nacional, 206n–207n
Peronist Party, 159
Peronists, 134, 153, 157, 159–161, Chapter 8 *passim*, 205n. See also Anti-liberals, Criollos, Internal migrants
Peronist Women's Party, 148
Personería gremial, 87
Pontieri, Silverio, 87, 88, 93
Prado, Francisco, 178, 191
Prebisch, Raúl, 168
Prebisch Report, 168, 169, 174
La Prensa (Buenos Aires), 164, 165, 171
Printers' union. See Unions, trade
Puerto Rico, 150
Puiggros, Rudolfo, 207n

¿*Qué es el laborismo?* (Reyes), 125
Quijano, J. Hortensio, 91, 106
Quintana, Manuel, 21

Radical Party, 21, 93, 115, 133, 134, 164, 190
Railroad unions. See Unions, trade
Ramírez, Pedro P., 72–74, 77, 80
La razón de mi vida (Eva Perón), 118, 147, 203n
"La revancha," 178
Revolución Libertadora, 160, 163–184 *passim*

Reyes, Cipriano, 75, 88–89, 91, 106, 107, 124, 125
Ribas, Riego, 160
Rights of the Workers (Constitution of 1949), 101, 114, 122, 177
Rivadavia, Bernardino, 42, 124
Rivas, "Nellie," 165
Roca, General Julio, 9, 17
Rodríguez, Juan, 69
Rojas Pinilla, General Gustavo, 150
Rosas, Juan Manuel de, 79, 123, 130, 163, 173, 187
Russian Revolution, 36, 46

Saenz Peña, Roque, 23, 60, 86
Salvo, Hilario, 83, 89, 126, 127, 155, 160, 204n, 206n
San Martín, José de, 113, 118, 119
San Martín, Méndez, 146
Sarmiento, Domingo F., 9, 16, 41, 42, 57, 82, 124, 130
Scipione, Antonio, 131, 205n
Secretary of Industry and Commerce, 79
Semana Trágica, 36–38
Shoemakers' union. See Unions, trade
Social Democrats of Germany, 13, 14
Social Welfare Foundation, Eva Perón, 100, 147
Socialism, 13, 16–18
Socialist Party of Argentina: liberal nationalism in, 7–8, 45–46; and Justo, 15–18; and early labor movement, 19; and Palacios and Ugarte, 41–45; and Unión Ferroviaria, 48, 50; opposed by USA, 65;

and CGT split, 68–70; Perón attacks, 71, 78, 105, 115; Perelman opposes, 82–83; and Partido Laborista, 91; and Unión Democrática, 93; and 1946 election, 95; and 1950 railroad strike, 133, 134, 135; opposes Perón, 158; and independents, 164; and liberals, 186, 189. *See also* Socialists

Socialists: in First International, 12, 13; in FTRA, 15; and Justo, 15–18; in 1896 election, 18; and FOA, 20; and Palacios and Ugarte, 41–45; and syndicalists, 55–57; and communists, 61–67; and split in CGT, 68–70; ignore internal migrants, 81–82; and Perón, 84. *See also* Immigrants, Liberals

Social mobilization, 4, 5

Sociedad Tipográfica Bonaerense, 12

Somoza, Anastasio, 150

Spillembergo, Jorge E., 207n

Stalin, Joseph, 63, 113

Standard Oil Company of California, 140

Strikes: printers', 12, 115, 129, 180; shoemakers', carpenters', 13; bricklayers', 13, 60; railroad, 13, 35, 40, 48, 115, 124, 129, 130–134; general, 21, 23, 172; threatened, 25; increase in, 30; maritime, 35, 40, 129; metal workers', 37–38, 155–156, 180; construction, 62; meat packers', 75, 129; sugar workers', 115, 129; to oppose Perón, 128–130; bank employees', 129; telephone, textile, 180

Sugar workers' union. *See* Unions, trade

Supreme Court, 87, 94, 98

Syndicalism, 29–30

Syndicalists: join FORA, 30; a-political unionism of, 39–40; control USA, 47; and socialists in CGT, 55–57, 65; and Perón, 84. *See also* Unión Sindical Argentina

Tanco, General Raúl, 178, 179

Testa, Roberto, 133, 208n

Textile union. *See* Unions, trade

"Third Position," 149

Tolosa, Eustaquio, 209n

Torre, Lisandro de la, 59

Transportation unions. *See* Unions, trade

Trotsky, Leon, 207n

Ugarte, Manuel, 41–46, 48, 83

UGT (Unión General de Trabajo), 20, 25, 30, 195n

Unión Cívica, 16

Unión Democrática, 93, 95, 143, 155

Unión de Estudiantes Secundarios, 146

Unión de Trabajadores de Colombia, 150

Unión Ferroviaria. *See* Unions, trade: railroad

Unión General de Trabajo, 20, 25, 30, 195n

Unión Industrial Argentina, 94

Unión Obrera Metalúrgica. *See* Unions, trade: metal workers'

Unión Sindical Argentina, 47, 49, 51, 52, 53, 55–57, 65. *See also* Syndicalists
Unions, trade: bank workers', 32, 182; beer workers', 70; commercial employees', 32, 56, 59, 61, 62, 64, 65, 70, 77, 84, 86, 103, 179, 182; construction, 62, 63, 64, 70; journalists', 32; maritime, 32, 33, 35, 167; meat packers', 35, 75, 88, 89, 166; membership, 195n; metal workers', 35, 64, 84, 89, 155, 156; municipal employees, 47, 49, 56, 64, 65, 70, 84, 182; post office, 32; printers, 12, 47, 56, 70, 88, 182; railroad: 47, 56, 77, 88, 103–104, 166, La Fraternidad, 48, 49, 56, 62, 64, 70, 73, 79, 84, 85, 86, 103, 116, 121–124 *passim*, Unión Ferroviaria, 48–50, 56, 62, 64, 68, 70, 73, 80, 86, 103, 130–134, 154, 165, 182; shoemakers, 31, 84, 86, 121; state employees, 56, 70, 182; sugar workers, 35, 77; telegraph, 32; telephone, 167; textile, 35, 62, 64, 84, 86, 121, 139; transportation, 62, 64; trolley car workers, 56, 62, 64, 70, 73, 84, 86; wine workers of Mendoza, 77; wood workers, 77
Unión Tipográfica. *See* Unions, trade: printers'
Unión Tranviaria. *See* Unions, trade: trolley car workers'
United States: 43, 141; labor delegation, 109–110
UOM (Unión Obrera Metalúrgica). *See* Unions, metal workers'
Uriburu, José E., 51, 52, 53–61, 73, 124
Urquiza, Justo José, 163
Uruguay, 150, 151
USA (Unión Sindical Argentina), 47, 49, 51, 52, 53, 55–57, 65. *See also* Syndicalists

Valle, General Juan José, 178, 179
Vandor, August, 160, 191, 208n
La Vanguardia (Buenos Aires), 16, 18, 44
Viel, Dante, 209n
Vorwärts, 13, 14
Vukasovich, Daniel, 160
Vuletich, Eduardo, 156, 157, 172

WFTU (World Federation of Trade Unions), 207n
World Bank, 174
World Federation of Trade Unions, 207n
World War I, 10, 32, 44, 46
World War II, 80, 84, 138

Year of San Martín (1950), 119
Yrigoyen, Hipólito, 34–39, 53, 72, 82, 91, 93, 186

Zucotti, Salvador A., 209n